DUE DATE

CONSUMPTION VALUES AND MARKET CHOICES

THEORY AND APPLICATIONS

JAGDISH N. SHETH
Robert E. Brooker Professor of Marketing
Graduate School of Business
University of Southern California

BRUCE I. NEWMAN
Department of Marketing
DePaul University

BARBARA L. GROSS
Department of Marketing
University of Southern California

COLLEGE DIVISION South-Western Publishing Co.

CINCINNATI   DALLAS   LIVERMORE

Sponsoring Editor: David L. Shaut
Editorial Production Manager: Christine O. Sofranko
Production House: Julia Chitwood
Cover Designer: Hulefeld Associates Inc.
Interior Designer: Jim DeSollar
Marketing Manager: Tania Hindersman

ST61AA

Copyright © 1991

by SOUTH-WESTERN PUBLISHING CO.
Cincinnati, Ohio

1 2 3 4 5 6 7 8 9   MT   7 6 5 4 3 2 1 0

Printed in the United States of America

Library of Congress Cataloging-in-Publication Data

Sheth, Jagdish N.
    Consumption values and market choices : theory and applications /
    Jagdish N. Sheth, Bruce I. Newman, Barbara L. Gross.
        p.   cm.
    Includes bibliographical references and index.
    ISBN 0-538-80563-3
    1. Consumer behavior. 2. Consumers' preferences. I. Newman,
Bruce I. II. Gross, Barbara L.   III. Title.
HF5415.2.S473 1991   90-19943
658.8′342—dc20   CIP

PREFACE

This book is about understanding how people make choices in the marketplace. It is founded on the axiom that all voluntary choices made by individuals are based on their perceptions of consumption values associated with market choices.

We have classified all consumption values into five categories: functional, social, emotional, epistemic, and conditional. Of course not all choices are driven by all five consumption values, nor do they all contribute equally in a given choice situation. Which values determine a specific choice and to what extent is an empirical question.

We divide market choices into three categories: to use or not to use a product or service (for example, smoking vs. nonsmoking or flying vs. not flying); the type of product or service to use (filtered or nonfiltered cigarettes, flying first class or coach class); and the brand name to use (Marlboro vs. Virginia Slims or American Airlines vs. Southwest Airlines).

The theory of market choice behavior described in this book has been tested over a hundred different market choices with consistently good predictive validity. Although it has evolved from the Howard-Sheth theory of buying behavior (Howard and Sheth 1969), it is both conceptually and structurally unique in several respects. First, it is more a predictive model than a process-oriented model. Second, the determinants of choice are *consumption values* and not purchase criteria. Third, the theory provides operational measures and procedures so that it can be applied in marketing practice. Fourth, it is more managerial and less descriptive than the Howard-Sheth theory. Finally, it is a theory of *market* choice behavior, although the unit of measurement is the individual choice maker.

Consumption Values and Market Choices can be easily used as a supplement in an advanced undergraduate or graduate class in consumer behavior. The best way to use the book in the classroom is to organize students into teams and conduct empirical research on market choices of interest with the use of operational procedures described in the book. Over the years our students have participated in research projects on a wide variety of market choices including playing pinball machines, eating pizza, buying automobiles, cigarette smoking, attending church, and using birth control pills. This book is also an excellent resource for an extensive bibliography related to underlying constructs of market choice behavior.

Jagdish N. Sheth
Bruce I. Newman
Barbara L. Gross

CONTENTS

PART 1
EXPLAINING
MARKET CHOICES

1

UNDERSTANDING
CHOICE BEHAVIOR

This book presents and operationalizes a theory of consumption values to explain and predict market choices. A market is defined as a collection of users (consumers) who make choices among alternatives. These include the choice to buy or not to buy; the choice of one type over the other; and, finally, the choice of one brand over others. The theory explains why a collection of consumers choose to buy or not to buy a specific product, why they choose one product type over another, and why they choose one brand over another. Part One of the book explains the theory; Part Two provides guidance for applying the theory; and Part Three demonstrates the theory in use and its application to a wide range of market choice situations. With the information and step-by-step guidance provided in this book, readers will be able to actually *apply* this theory to learn what is driving the decisions users make regarding *any* product or service. Given this insight, readers may more effectively appeal to user wants and needs and influence market choice.

The theory of consumption values is applicable to choices involving a full range of products and services. Products can be categorized into three general types: consumer nondurables, consumer durables, and industrial goods. Consumer nondurables are short-lived products that wear out or are quickly consumed. Grocery items and personal care products are examples of nondurables. In contrast, consumer durables are longer-lasting products such as appliances, automobiles, and homes. While consumer products are used primarily in household settings, industrial goods are used in organizational settings by businesses and other institutions. Products included in this category range from small, nondurable office and industrial supplies such as paper and nails to large, durable capital items such as mainframe computers and robots. Finally, services include both profit- and nonprofit-oriented activities and facilities utilized by individuals, households, or organizations. Examples of profit-oriented services include banking, dry cleaning, airline transportation, repair and maintenance companies, and telephone service. Nonprofit services include governmental agencies that offer free assistance and information, charities, and legal aid societies as well as public facilities such as parks, highways, and museums.

THE IMPORTANCE OF UNDERSTANDING MARKET CHOICE BEHAVIOR

An understanding of market choice behavior is useful for influencing a wide range of human behavior and is therefore relevant to readers in numerous and diverse professions. Most notably, an understanding of market choice behavior is helpful in affecting behavior in the marketplace and for designing and implementing public policy—as examples, the choice to vote and whom to vote for or the choice to conserve energy by carpooling. The following paragraphs outline some key motivations for pursuing knowledge about market choice behavior.

Universality of Market Choice Behavior

Market choice behavior is universal in that most individuals living in most cultures make choices regarding their consumption of goods and services. Central to consumer decision making is the allocation of three precious resources: money, time, and effort. Thus, anyone concerned with influencing another's allocation of money, time, or effort will benefit from an understanding of market choice behavior.

Observers of market choice behavior have traditionally focused on decisions regarding the allocation of money. Indeed, in situations where money is the primary resource constraint, monetary allocations are paramount. Perhaps the most basic market choice is whether to spend or save. Then, given the decision to spend, the consumer must decide on what. Because practically all consumers have a limited supply of money, most purchases require some consideration of monetary tradeoffs. It is clear that a consumer choosing between a new car and a new stereo system must consider the tradeoffs. Likewise, even shopping for groceries usually calls for some deliberation between competing items. Needless to say, most users are regularly confronted with choice situations involving money.

Time is another critical—and usually scarce—resource. Consumers today are faced with a seemingly infinite array of alternative activities that "compete" for their finite time. Further, the growing number of dual-earner and single-parent households has resulted in heightened time pressures. While some products are specifically designed to help consumers save time, most products are associated with the use of time. Even the act of choosing and purchasing a product can be very time-consuming. Then, once purchased, products require time for their use, maintenance, repair, and so on. As a result, many consumption choices are primarily time allocation decisions, with alternative activities and products vying for consumers' limited time. Often, the ability of a product to facilitate time savings is a key attribute motivating its purchase, and the choice between one product and another may be largely determined by "time price."

Finally, consumers must make choices involving the allocation of effort. A very common situation involves the choice between doing something oneself, often realizing a monetary savings but expending more effort, versus paying someone else to do it. Examples include the choice between preparing dinner at home versus eating out in a restaurant, the choice between delivering one's own furniture (cash and carry) versus paying for delivery, and the choice between repairing one's own car versus taking it to a mechanic. It should be noted that some products are more amenable to the "do-it-yourself" option than others. To illustrate, for most consumers the choice of assembling a bicycle rather than paying for assembly is more practical than the choice of building a house rather than buying one, even though the latter would involve much greater monetary savings. Decisions regarding the allocation of effort confront consumers on a regular basis and have provided an impetus for the creation of numerous personal services and labor-saving products.

Diagnostic Value

An understanding of the processes underlying market choice is critical to efforts aimed at shaping that behavior. It is perhaps obvious that an understanding of market choice is vital for marketers attempting to influence consumers to purchase their products. Indeed, anyone with a product to sell can benefit from an understanding of what motivates consumers to use that particular product as well as an understanding of what motivates consumers to choose one brand over another. Further, such information is as useful to nonprofit organizations (e.g., churches, hospitals, schools, charities) as it is to for-profit businesses because they both compete for consumers' resources.

In addition to organizational situations, circumstances exist in which individuals try to influence the consumer behavior of others. To illustrate, parents regularly try to influence their children's consumption choices. For example, they may hope to influence their teenagers to stay away from illegal drugs. If it were determined that teenagers use drugs because of peer pressure rather than because they enjoy getting high, parents would have a very valuable piece of information. Their efforts would probably focus on watching the types of people with whom their teenagers associate.

Many other situations exist in which individuals attempt to influence the choices made by others. To cite a few examples, political candidates aim to influence voters to support their campaigns, managers encourage their employees to adopt new procedures, teachers endeavor to inspire their students to study, and coaches try to motivate their teams to train outside of regular practice. By diagnosing the motivations underlying alternative choices, such individuals have a greater chance of favorably influencing the behavior of the groups they are appealing to.

Public Policy

An understanding of market choice behavior may be particularly useful to public policy makers. Any number of social problems and concerns may be addressed more efficiently if the motivations underlying consumer choices are understood.

To illustrate, if it is known that excessive alcohol consumption is a response to emotional problems rather than to social pressure or some other cause, an appropriate public policy (perhaps preventive counseling) may be enacted. As another example, if it is found that people refuse to use condoms because of negative social imagery rather than because they are not aware of the danger of AIDS, public policy directed at changing this imagery (perhaps by using celebrity spokespersons) may be indicated.

By zeroing in on the driving forces underlying market choices, public resources allocated for influencing such choices can be used most effectively. The antismoking campaign in this country originally focused on smoking as a health hazard. However, as a result of market research showing that the choice to smoke or not to smoke is largely a function of social norms, the campaign was altered to also evoke the perception of smoking as an unattractive and socially undesirable habit.

Marketing Efficiency

A final reason for studying market choice behavior is to enhance marketing efficiency. Marketing resources—particularly as applied to product design, personal selling, distribution, and advertising—are often wasted because marketers do not know what motivates consumer choice. Marketing resources can be used more efficiently if it is understood why consumers desire a particular product, product type, or brand.

For example, consumers buy home computers for a diversity of reasons. Some want a computer for entertainment, others for school work, still others for financial budgeting and recordkeeping, and so on. Consumers who want a computer for financial budgeting and recordkeeping, for example, are unlikely to be persuaded by the same selling appeals as consumers who want a computer for entertainment. By first determining what motivates purchase choices and then segmenting the market accordingly, marketers may use their limited resources to appeal specifically to the most salient motives operating in each group.

A BRIEF DESCRIPTION OF THE THEORY

The theory of market choice behavior presented in this book rests on three fundamental propositions or axioms:

1. Market choice is a function of multiple values.

2. These values make differential contributions in any given choice situation.

3. The values are independent.

Multiple Values

Our theory is based on the fundamental premise that market choice is a multidimensional phenomenon involving *multiple values*. As shown in Figure 1-1, we have identified five values as impacting market choice behavior. These are *functional* value, *social* value, *emotional* value, *epistemic* value, and *conditional* value. While some choices may be influenced by only one value, most are influenced by two or more, and some are influenced by all five.

Figure 1-1   The five values influencing market choice behavior

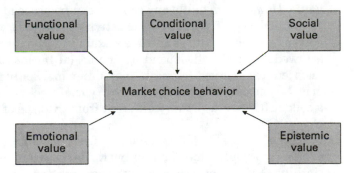

As documented in Chapters 3 and 4, various disciplines (including economics, sociology, anthropology, several branches of psychology, and marketing and consumer behavior) have contributed theory and research relevant to these values. The following is a brief description of each of the five values.

Functional Value.   Some market choices depend on the degree of functional or utilitarian value associated with the alternatives. This is the position advanced by utility theory in economics and popularly expressed in terms of "rational economic man." Functional value pertains to the ability of a product to perform its functional, utilitarian, or physical purposes.

Functional value may be based on any salient physical attribute. For example, for a significant segment of the automobile market, the decision to purchase a particular model may be based primarily on fuel economy (gas mileage). Similarly, the selection of a set of stereo speakers may be based on the quality of sound, and the selection of a pair of athletic shoes may be based on comfort. In these examples, fuel economy, sound quality, and comfort are all aspects of functional value.

Sometimes price is the most salient functional value. Most notably, industrial commodities often possess equivalent product quality regardless of source, so price is the most influential functional value. Similarly, choices involving consumer commodities such as gasoline may be based primarily on price. In general, where products are regarded as equivalent with respect to other salient values, price determines the final decision.

Social Value.   Other market choices may be determined primarily by social value. Users driven by social value choose products that convey an image congruent with the norms of their friends or associates or that convey the social image they wish to project. Social value exists when products come to be associated with positively perceived social groups. Similarly, a product associated with a negatively perceived social group has negative social value. Highly visible products and products that are easily differentiated by sight often acquire positive or negative social value. However, virtually any product can be associated with social value.

The choice of products and activities to share with others is often driven by social value. To cite a few examples, the selection of an appropriate wedding gift will depend on the social norms of the couple getting married, food served to guests may differ markedly from food consumed privately or just with family, and the type of weekend activity shared with a college friend may be very different from the type of activity shared with parents.

Even choices involving products for individual consumption may be driven by social value. This is particularly common in the selection of clothing and other items where consumption, however individual, is highly visible. For example, in buying blue jeans, the Levi Strauss & Co. or Guess patch on the back pocket may be more important than the physical characteristics of the jeans. In general, the choice of almost any visibly identifiable product, from beer and soft drinks to automobiles and neighborhoods, is likely to be influenced partially, if not primarily, by social value.

Emotional Value.   Still other market choices are made primarily because of their potential to arouse emotion. Many products and activities suggest desired emotions. While such emotions are often positive and therefore enjoyable (e.g., the feelings of sexuality and romance aroused by spraying on a special perfume or the enhanced feeling of confidence from wearing attractive clothing), others are enjoyable even though they may be generally described as negative (e.g., the feelings of fear aroused by viewing a horror movie or the feelings of anger aroused by reading about a villainous historical figure).

Emotional value is often associated with aesthetic alternatives such as music and art and with various forms of entertainment. For example, an individual may choose to listen to jazz, classical, or rock music in order to arouse different types of feelings. Sports fans often purchase shirts, caps, and other items bearing their team's name and colors, thereby enhancing their feelings of competition, team loyalty, and excitement.

Choices of ideology and religion are also frequently influenced by emotional values. An individual may attend a church or temple in order to express or enhance feelings of faith, to assuage feelings of guilt, or to maintain feelings of peace. Zealous support for a social or political cause (for example, nuclear disarmament or animal rights) may stem from feelings of fear, anger, or frustration; it may evoke positive feelings of involvement, responsibility, and comradeship.

Epistemic Value.   A significant share of market choice behavior is driven by curiosity, novelty-seeking, and knowledge-seeking motivations. Consumers often choose alternatives to satisfy curiosity, to provide novel experiences, or to enhance their general knowledge. Thus, alternatives are chosen for their epistemic value.

Many entertainment choices are based on epistemic value. Entertainment often satisfies the desire to get away from the everyday routine (novelty), or it satisfies the desire to learn about or experience something new (knowledge and curiosity). Seeing the "hottest" new rock band in concert can provide a novel experience, reading the latest issue of *People* magazine can satisfy curiosity about the rich and famous, and traveling to another culture can enhance knowledge.

Quite often, curiosity about a new product is the primary reason for its purchase. This can even be true when the product class is familiar and purchase is usually motivated by functional, social, or emotional values. For example, a consumer may be completely satisfied with her current brand of shampoo, associating it with superior functional value (it makes her hair shiny and manageable and is sold at a reasonable price). However, just noticing an interesting shampoo ad or seeing a new brand in the store may provide sufficient impetus for the consumer to try the new brand. The new brand can provide epistemic value, in the form of novelty, as well as functional value. The existing brand provides only functional value.

Conditional Value.   Finally, some market choices are contingent on the situation or set of circumstances faced by the consumer. In choosing between alternatives, the value associated with each may vary greatly depending on the situation. A consumer driven by conditional value may alter his/her plan or typical pattern of choice because of the situation.

Some products have only seasonal value. For example, Christmas cards have little value except in the celebration of Christmas. While the cards have significant social value during the Christmas season, they have virtually no value in July. Indeed, to send a Christmas card in July would communicate negative social value.

Similarly, products associated with "once in a lifetime" events, such as weddings, have little value except as the events are anticipated, celebrated, and remembered. A white wedding gown is simply inappropriate attire for any occasion other than one's wedding. Once that day is past, the gown and veil may take on nostalgic (emotional) value but will no longer have functional or social value.

Social, physical, and economic situations may all influence choice, creating temporary or conditional social and functional value. A particular gourmet coffee may provide no social value to a user except as he entertains a friend who particularly likes it. A consumer caught in the physical situation of a downpour may be willing to buy even the most unattractive or expensive umbrella, and the consumer whose car runs out of gas will be willing to pay a higher than normal price for gasoline. The umbrella and gasoline acquire heightened functional value in these "emergency" situations. Regarding economic situations, monetary constraints often severely limit choices. The amount of money spent on personal entertainment may be much greater just after payday than at the end of the pay period. On a macro level, expenditures for luxury items may vary significantly depending on whether the overall state of the economy is in recession or prosperity. Finally, the political situation can have a major impact on consumption. For example, priorities may differ greatly in wartime as opposed to peacetime.

Differential Contributions

The second axiom upon which our theory of consumption values is based is that the five values make *differential contributions* to specific choices. Thus, while multiple values drive market choice making, their contributions are usually unequal. In any specific choice situation, some values contribute more than others. This point is evident from examples cited in previous paragraphs, and the following examples clarify it.

The purchase of gold coins may be motivated primarily by functional and emotional value. Purchase may be motivated by the investment value of the coins (functional value) and by the feelings of security derived from having a sound investment (emotional value). However, the purchase may be associated with little or no social, epistemic, or conditional value. On the other hand, the purchase of gold jewelry may be driven almost entirely by social value. To illustrate, a consumer buying a gold bracelet may believe that the bracelet will be noticed and admired by others whose taste she respects. However, she may associate little functional, emotional, epistemic, or conditional value with the bracelet.

Similarly, the purchase of a textbook might be driven almost entirely by functional value. A student knows he must read and master the material in the assigned text in order to pass a class. In contrast, he may purchase another type of book, such as a detective novel, for its emotional value. He expects that the story will arouse feelings of excitement and suspense.

Finally, consumers often purchase a variety of products within the same product class because each provides a different type of value. Using beverages as an example, a consumer may purchase orange juice for its nutritional content (functional value), beer to serve to friends (social value), milk because it provides a sense of comfort associated with childhood (emotional value), a new soft drink just because he is curious about it (epistemic value), and champagne because he has been asked to bring it to a New Year's Eve party (conditional value).

Knowledge of the differential contributions of the five values can greatly enhance marketing efficiency. Not only can appeals be designed to specifically address the values that are most salient to target consumers, but the mode of promotion may be varied to match the type of learning associated with each value.

Specifically, marketers promoting products generally associated with emotional and/or social value will benefit from using persuasive advertising appeals that promote *associative learning*. In contrast, marketers promoting products associated with functional and/or epistemic value will benefit from using promotional techniques that facilitate *reinforcement learning*.

Through persuasive advertising appeals, consumers may learn to associate products with desirable emotions and with positively regarded social groups. Thus, through associative learning, they come to attribute emotional and social value to products. Advertising that arouses salient emotions and that associates a product with an attractive social group can greatly increase the emotional and social appeal of an advertised product. A good example is the association of sex appeal with Ultrabrite toothpaste.

In contrast, promotional tools oriented to reinforcement learning, such as product samples, coupons, rebate offers, and price appeals, encourage product trial and allow consumers to experience firsthand the functional and/or epistemic value provided by the products. Regarding epistemic value, these promotional techniques call attention to the products in question, thereby arousing curiosity. Further, they reduce barriers that might discourage users from satisfying their curiosity. It is much easier to "justify" the satisfaction of one's curiosity if the product is free or available at a reduced price. Regarding functional value, reinforcement-oriented promotional techniques encourage users to experience for themselves how well a product can perform its functional purposes. In the case of functional products, personal experience is generally more persuasive than even the most professionally executed advertising.

Part Two of this book provides operational guidance, assisting the reader in measuring the contributions of the five values in any choice situation of interest. Once the relative contributions are known, this information may be used in designing effective and efficient marketing strategies.

Independence Among Values

The third axiom underlying our theory of consumption values is that the five values are independent. They relate additively and contribute incrementally to choice. Therefore, in statistical terms, their intercorrelations are very low and, in practical terms, a change in a user's perception of one value will not affect his or her perception of the other values. Although it is desirable to maximize all five values, users are often willing to accept less of one value in order to obtain more of another. That is, consumers are willing to trade off less salient values in order to maximize those that are most salient.

To illustrate, suppose that a consumer shopping for a new car is very interested in social value and only moderately interested in functional value. The consumer may be willing to accept a suboptimal level of functional value in order to maximize social value. However, because she places such a high priority on social value, if she perceives a car as having negative social value, it is unlikely that any amount of functional value could make up for that. She may recognize that the car offers more functional value, but that recognition will not influence the perceived social value.

Of course, choice may be influenced positively by all five values. For example, to a first-time home buyer it is conceivable that the purchase of a new home could provide functional value (because the home contains more space than his present apartment), social value (because the buyer's friends are also buying houses), emotional value (because he derives a secure feeling from owning a home), epistemic value (because he enjoys the novelty of purchasing and decorating the home), and conditional value (because he would not have considered buying a home had he not been planning to start a family).

LIMITATIONS OF THE THEORY

Although pertinent to all types of products, the theory's application is limited to a particular, although sizable, subset of consumer choice dynamics. Specifically, the theory is applicable to choices that are made by an individual on a systematic and voluntary basis. The theory is not applicable to choices that are group or dyadic based, that are made randomly, or that are made involuntarily or by mandate.

Choices by Individual

The theory presented in this book has been developed to explain and predict market choices made by individuals as users. To illustrate, the theory may be used to examine factors influencing an individual to choose a particular make of automobile. However, the theory does not address factors contributing to the relative influences of a husband and a wife as they jointly decide which car to buy. In this case, the buying process involves dyadic behavior. Similarly, the theory cannot be used to examine the persuasiveness of various members of a corporation—say, the chief executive officer, the chief operating officer, several functional managers, and the purchasing manager—as they jointly decide to purchase a computer system. In this case, the choice process involves group behavior. However, the theory is applicable to the analysis of factors driving a sole proprietor to purchase a computer system for his or her retail store.

Systematic Choices

The theory is further limited to *systematic choices*, as opposed to random, or stochastic, selections. For example, the choice of a winning lottery ticket is stochastic, based on a probability distribution. Although the probability of choosing a winning lottery ticket may be determined, it is impossible to predict which ticket will be a winner.

Random choices are not uncommon in market choice settings. A consumer may perceive a choice situation as not important enough to warrant deliberation, or a consumer may perceive that the various alternatives are equivalent, making deliberation unnecessary. In both cases, a random or stochastic decision is likely. To illustrate, a consumer may regard the choice of light bulb as so unimportant that she or he does not want to take the time to compare brands. In fact, the consumer may not even be aware of the various brands and may simply pull one off the shelf at random. Another consumer may be aware of the brands but feels that no real difference exists. Thus, since any brand will do, the consumer is likely to make a random choice.

Random choice also occurs when consumers do not know how to make the "correct" choice and do not have the time to learn. For example, in selecting a bottle of wine, a restaurant patron may lack knowledge of the varieties available, and therefore be unable to choose the one to best complement the entrée. Without this knowledge, and perhaps being embarrassed to ask for help, the diner may simply make a random selection and hope for the best.

As contrasted with these random choice situations, the theory is applicable to situations involving systematic choice. Such choice situations require a nominal degree of deliberation. Systematic choice implies that the decision is at least somewhat important; that the alternatives are differentiated; and that the consumer knows how to choose among alternatives, either as a function of experience or of product knowledge.

Voluntary Choices

Finally, the market situations addressed by the theory are limited to those involving *voluntary choice*. The theory is not applicable to "choices" that are mandatory or made involuntarily. A number of situations lead to involuntary "choices."

Sometimes choices are made by others rather than by the user. As examples, professors choose the textbooks that their students must read, doctors prescribe the medications that their patients must use, and employers sometimes select uniforms that their employees must wear on the job. The theory cannot be used to analyze such purchase situations because the purchases do not reflect voluntary choice. The users are required to comply with choices made by others.

Situations also exist in which market choices are severely limited by the monopoly power of sellers. Common examples include utilities and public schools. Consumers generally purchase utilities from those companies servicing their neighborhoods, and parents usually send their children to the nearest public schools. Although these choices may not be completely limited (some utilities are available through private companies and many parents choose to send their children to private schools), the market structure generally limits the alternatives.

Finally, situations exist in which public policy makers offer strong incentives or sanctions to encourage or discourage acceptance of a product. In these situations, users frequently adopt or reject a particular product because of the incentive or sanction rather than because they deliberately choose to use or not use the product. Many consumers have adopted seat belts, child safety seats in automobiles, unleaded gasoline, and insulation in homes because of mandates or incentives rather than because of their own desires or preferences.

SUMMARY

Chapter 1 has introduced our theory of consumption values. As discussed, consumption behavior is universal. Thus, anyone concerned with influencing others' allocations of money, time, and/or effort can benefit from an understanding of consumer choices. Our theory provides diagnostic value, and it can aid in the design of effective and efficient marketing programs and public policy.

Specifically, the theory presented and operationalized in this book is applicable to market choices involving a full range of services and products. Further, it is applicable to consumption choices that are individual (as opposed to dyadic or group), systematic (as opposed to random or stochastic), and voluntary (as opposed to mandatory or involuntary). It is axiomatic to the theory that: 1) consumer choice is driven by multiple consumption values, 2) these consumption values make differential contributions to choice, and 3) these consumption values operate independently. Finally, as defined by the theory, the multiple values driving market choice are functional, social, emotional, epistemic, and conditional.

Next, Chapter 2 discusses three levels of market choice—buy versus no-buy, product type, and brand—to which the theory may be applied. The chapter also more formally defines each of the five values, clarifying with additional examples. The latter half of Chapter 2 compares our theory with others whose constructs have influenced its development, and we briefly overview the theory's operationalization.

2
CONSUMPTION VALUES
AND MARKET CHOICES

This chapter further describes our theory of consumption values and compares it with other theories and models that include similar constructs. These other theories and models have been contributed by a variety of disciplines, including economics, sociology, various branches of psychology, and marketing and consumer behavior.

CLASSIFICATION OF MARKET CHOICE BEHAVIOR

The broad topic of market choices behavior involves three levels or types of choices:

1. The choice to buy or not to buy
2. The choice of product type
3. The choice of brand

We regard these three types of choices as levels because they generally do not operate simultaneously. Rather, they usually occur in progression. It is important to recognize, however, that not every choice involves the decision sequence listed above. For example, sometimes a consumer will become sold on a particular brand prior to even deciding that he or she wants to buy the product. However, for convenience, we will discuss the levels in the sequence listed above.

Our theory of consumption values behavior is applicable to all three levels of market choice. Chapter 7 presents a detailed example for each type of application. The following paragraphs present examples illustrating each of the three types of choices.

Buy Versus No-Buy Choice

The initial level of choice involves the decision to buy or not to buy a particular class of product. For example, a retailer might consider buying a microcomputer to assist in keeping track of inventory, and a college student might be interested in buying a microcomputer for doing papers. Before actually purchasing, both consumers must decide if the values they expect to receive warrant the required expenditure. That is, both must answer "Is it worth it?"

The retailer might decide not to buy a computer, opting to continue with his present system of tracking inventory. On the other hand, he might feel that his present system is too cumbersome and time-consuming and that buying a computer would be ultimately more cost effective. Likewise, the student might decide not to buy a computer, opting to continue writing papers at her typewriter or at her university's computer center. On the other hand, she might feel that she needs both the increased efficiency of a computer and the convenience of being able to work at home.

Product Type Choice

Once a consumer has determined to buy a particular class of product, the decision-making process will often progress to the choice of product type. Various product types contain features that may or may not be preferred by a consumer. When many options are available, the choice can be difficult. Thus, consumers will often seek additional information before making the product type decision.

Continuing the microcomputer example, both the retailer and the student, having decided to purchase computers, will need to determine the options they want. For example, they need to decide whether to purchase a portable or standard computer, whether a hard drive is needed, what amount of memory is required, and whether a color monitor is desired.

The retailer may prefer a standard desktop computer because the computer will stay in his store. Further, he may decide that the color monitor is not worth the additional expenditure, but that a hard-disk drive and additional memory will give him the speed of operation and capacity for expansion that he wants. The student, on the other hand, wants to take her computer to school for work on group projects and may decide that a portable computer is ideal for her needs. She may also decide that the color monitor is not important and that, although she would like them, hard drive and extra memory are not worth the extra expenditure.

Brand Choice

The third level of choice concerns the selection of a specific brand and/or model. Consumers often find that several makes and models offer the features they want. In the microcomputer example, the brands being considered might include IBM, Apple, Compaq, and Tandy, as well as a number of IBM-compatible brands.

The retailer, somewhat confused by the many brands, may decide to purchase an IBM because he knows others who are satisfied with it. Although he may consider a less expensive IBM-compatible brand, he trusts the IBM name. Further, he knows that, because IBM is a leader in the field, new software is always available. Finally, he may decide to purchase the IBM Personal Computer AT model because he places a high priority on speed of operation and on having state-of-the-art technology. The student, on the other hand, placing a high degree of value on portability, may decide to purchase a portable Compaq.

FIVE VALUES DRIVING CHOICE

Market choice behavior may be driven by any or all of the five values identified in our theory. The five values are inherent in choice behavior, but not all need be relevant in the context of a specific choice. Since we do not know *a priori* which values are pertinent to a specific market choice, subsequent chapters will demonstrate how to conduct research to determine their relative salience. The following discussion defines and illustrates the five values.

Functional Value

Market choice has traditionally been regarded as influenced primarily by functional value. The functional value of an alternative is defined as follows:

Functional Value: The perceived utility acquired by an alternative as the result of its ability to perform its functional, utilitarian, or physical purposes. Alternatives acquire functional value through the possession of salient functional, utilitarian, or physical attributes.

Functional value generally relates to such attributes as performance, reliability, durability, and price. The assumption that choice is based on functional value underlies economic utility theory, popularly expressed in terms of "rational economic man." Utility theory posits that the alternative chosen will be the one that maximizes utility.

A consumer basing a buy versus no-buy decision on functional value would consider whether the functional or physical attributes inherent in the product are needed, and if the product possesses desired functional attributes. For example, a consumer without dependents will probably not perceive functional value in term life insurance designed to provide financial protection for survivors. However, the consumer may perceive functional value in a long-term annuity contributing to financial security at the time of retirement.

Functional value is equally operable in product type and brand choices. In consumer durables, the choice of a particular type of refrigerator, for example, may be dependent on such physical attributes as energy efficiency and size. A specific brand of toothpaste, a consumer nondurable, may be selected because of its demonstrated ability to prevent tooth decay or because it promises to remove tobacco stains. In the service sector, a consumer may choose a particular physician because that doctor specializes in treating a specific type of illness, or because the physician's office is located near the consumer's home. Finally, in an industrial buying situation, a purchasing agent may choose a supplier on the basis of price or because the supplier can meet the company's engineering standards.

Social Value

Many choices are also influenced by social value. The social value of an alternative is defined as follows:

Social Value: The perceived utility acquired by an alternative as a result of its association with one or more specific social groups. Alternatives acquire social value through association with positively or negatively stereotyped demographic, socioeconomic, and cultural-ethnic groups.

The attribution of social value occurs most frequently for very visible items of consumption.

Again, a wide range of examples is applicable. Certainly, choices of products, activities, and locations to be shared with others may be influenced by social value. To illustrate, choices involving gifts and recreational alternatives are often influenced by social norms. However, products generally thought to be functional or utilitarian and products acquired for personal use may also be selected on the basis of social value. Examples include automobiles and kitchen appliances.

Buy versus no-buy decisions are influenced by social value in that consumers perceive various product classes as either congruent or incongruent with the norms of the reference groups to which they belong or aspire. To cite some very common examples, men traditionally use "men's products" but not "women's products" such as dresses and colored nail polish; women traditionally use "women's products" but not "men's products" like cigars and after-shave lotion; and teenagers may seek out "adult" products such as alcohol and cigarettes in an effort to feel more grown up, but they rarely want to use childish toys or other "children's products." Similarly, a "yuppie" white-collar male might refuse to go bowling because he regards the activity as too "blue collar," and a teenager may refuse to attend an opera because he sees it as "stuffy" and for "old people."

Product type and brand choices are similarly influenced by social value. With regard to consumer durables, a consumer residing in an affluent suburb will probably furnish her home to appeal to her neighbors and the upper classes in general. Looking at a consumer nondurable, a young man who prides himself on being "macho" would almost certainly not smoke Virginia Slims or other "women's" cigarettes. In the service category, a prospective college student may choose a state university over an Ivy League school because she thinks that Ivy League students are overly competitive and snobbish. In an organizational buying situation, a law firm catering to corporate and wealthy clients will probably choose a location and furnishings appealing to refined, sophisticated tastes, while a law firm catering to working-class clients may choose less expensive real estate and furnishings to avoid the perception that the firm's fees are inflated to cover costly overhead.

Emotional Value

Choice may also be based on emotional values relating to the alternative's ability to arouse desired emotions. The emotional value of an alternative is defined as follows:

Emotional Value: The perceived utility acquired by an alternative as a result of its ability to arouse feelings or affective states. Alternatives acquire emotional value when associated with specific feelings or when they facilitate or perpetuate feelings.

Many products are associated with or facilitate the arousal of specific emotions or feelings—for example, comfort, security, excitement, romance, passion, anger, fear, and guilt. Music, art, religion, and products that affect self-image (e.g., clothing and cosmetics) are often associated with emotional value. However, seemingly utilitarian products are also associated with emotional value. Many foods arouse feelings of comfort and security through their association with pleasant childhood experiences, and many consumers are said to have "love affairs" with their cars. Emotions are presumed to have no underlying cognitive structure or "rationale" because they are difficult to describe or explain to others.

Again, all three levels of choice—buy versus no-buy, product type, and brand—may be influenced by emotional value. In the category of consumer durables, a consumer may desire to purchase a house because the idea of home ownership arouses feelings of independence, security, and success. Among consumer nondurables, a consumer may select Sure deodorant because he or she believes that it will contribute to confidence in social situations. In the service area, the act of signing up for an aerobics class may be motivated as much by the desire to experience feelings of optimism and self-worth as by the desire to shape up. Finally, emotional value can even dominate in an organizational buying situation. A specific supplier may be favored because rapport has been established with the supplier's sales representative, and this has been translated into feelings of friendship, loyalty, and trust.

Epistemic Value

Choices are also sometimes based on the ability of alternatives to satisfy curiosity, knowledge, and novelty needs. The epistemic value of an alternative is defined as follows:

> **Epistemic Value:** The perceived utility acquired by an alternative as a result of its ability to arouse curiosity, provide novelty, and/or satisfy a desire for knowledge. Alternatives acquire epistemic value through the capacity to provide something new or different.

Epistemic value is certainly provided by alternatives associated with entirely new experiences. However, an alternative representing a simple change of pace can also provide epistemic value. An alternative selected due its epistemic value may be anything perceived by the consumer as new or different. It may be chosen because the consumer is bored or satiated with her or his current brand (buys a new brand of coffee), is curious about a potential experience (visits a new night club), or desires to learn more about the alternative (experiences another culture).

Again, epistemic value influences all three levels of choice—buy versus no-buy, product type, and brand. In terms of consumer durables, the purchase of a personal computer may be triggered by the desire to enhance one's knowledge about the new technology. Many consumers without a clear functional need have purchased computers, learned to use them, and then rarely touched them once the novelty wore off. In consumer nondurables, many consumers try new grocery and drugstore items (e.g., soft drinks, frozen dinners, or cosmetics) as they are introduced into the market. Although they may become loyal users, they just as often return to their regular brands, having satisfied the desire for a change of pace.

In the service sector, package vacation options like Club Med or Princess Cruises appeal to consumers as a source of novelty and reprieve from the regular routine; guided tours have epistemic value in that they enhance knowledge and satisfy curiosity. Many leisure activities, such as movies, concerts, and sporting events, are pursued for the sake of curiosity and novelty. Finally, even an organizational buying decision may be motivated by epistemic value. The universal need for novelty enhances the attractiveness of new products and new suppliers.

Conditional Value

Finally, the value of an alternative is contingent on the specific situation faced by the choice maker. This is conditional value. The conditional value of an alternative is defined as follows:

> **Conditional Value:** The perceived utility acquired by an alternative as a result of the specific situation or the context faced by the choice maker. Alternatives acquire conditional value in the presence of antecedent physical or social contingencies that enhance their functional or social value, but do not otherwise possess this value.

Thus, conditional value often influences the choice maker to deviate from his or her typical or planned pattern of behavior.

As with the other four values, conditional value influences all three levels of choice, and it may be involved in decisions pertaining to all product classes. Further, conditional value is likely to dominate in several specific choice situations. For example, conditional *functional* value often dominates in emergency situations, in situations where an alternative is available at a special sale price, and in situations characterized by unusual resource constraints or abundances. Conditional *social* value often dominates in situations where cultural norms dictate behavior. The saying "when in Rome, do as the Romans do" reflects such a situation.

As an example from consumer nondurables, a consumer who enters a convenience store expecting to buy a six-pack of Pepsi but finds that Coca-Cola is on sale is likely to perceive Coke as having temporarily enhanced functional value. Thus, the consumer may decide to buy Coke. A consumer who usually purchases a new car, a consumer durable, every three years but has also recently taken on another major financial obligation (e.g., sending a child to college, buying a new home, or paying for a "dream" vacation) may decide to forego the new car (a buy versus no-buy decision) or acquire a used car instead (a product type decision). Given his resource constraints, the functional and social value associated with the new car is temporarily decreased.

In the service category, ambulance service acquires immense functional value during an emergency involving an injury or illness, but it is not an appropriate mode of transportation at any other time. Even a small "emergency" can provide a situation where conditional value is enhanced. To illustrate, a sudden rainstorm can greatly enhance the functional value of a taxi. Organizational buying decisions may be influenced by conditional value as well. A company finding itself with excess cash reserves, a resource abundance, might make an investment that would otherwise not have been considered. The functional value of the investment is enhanced by the surplus cash situation. In terms of conditional social value, a company may willingly expend a great deal for employee

Christmas or year-end bonuses (a culturally conditioned norm) but would not consider giving such bonuses at any other time of year.

A Comprehensive Yet Parsimonious Theory

The five values discussed above were selected as the basis for our theory because, when integrated, they provide a framework that is both comprehensive (rich) and economical or parsimonious (simple). The framework is comprehensive in that it facilitates an understanding of a wide range of market choice behaviors: all individual, voluntary, and systematic choices across product types. Further, it integrates the constructs used in theories contributed from several other disciplines. For example, functional value represents the primary focus of utility theory in economics, social value is a significant focus in sociology, and emotional value is discussed in several branches of psychology. The framework is economical or parsimonious in that its impressive latitude is accomplished with only five constructs.

COMPARISON WITH OTHER MODELS AND THEORIES

Many models and theories contributed by diverse disciplines contain constructs analogous to the values in our theory, and they have greatly influenced its development. However, none is as comprehensive as our theory. Seminal work relevant to these models and theories is summarized in the following pages,* and a comparison of this work with our theory is presented in Table 2-1.

Social Psychology

Social psychologists have relied primarily on three constructs in their models of choice behavior. These are *attitude*, *social norms*, and *beliefs*. Attitude refers to the affect, either positive or negative, associated with an alternative, and it is subsumed within the domain of our emotional value construct. Social norms refer to behavior perceived as desirable and encouraged by referent others; it is subsumed within our social value construct. Finally, beliefs refer to perceptions of how alternatives will perform

---

*A few individuals have contributed impressively comprehensive frameworks, identifying multiple forces that influence human behavior. These authors are Daniel Katz in social psychology, Abraham H. Maslow in humanistic psychology, and George C. Katona in consumption economics. Because their work has so greatly influenced our theory, we have chosen to discuss their contributions separately as exceptions (see Some Exceptions, page 28).

Table 2-1   Comparison of the theory of consumption values with other theories from various disciplines

Discipline	Constructs similar to:				
	Functional value	Social value	Emotional value	Epis-temic value	Condi-tional value
Economics (utility theory)	x				
Sociology/social stratification		x			
Consumption economics/ economic psychology	x		x		
Clinical psychology (Freudian)	x	x	x		
Marketing/ consumer behavior (comprehensive models)	x	x		x	
Social psychology (attitude models)	x	x	x		x[a]
Experimental psychology (learning theory)	x		x	x	x

[a]Triandis's model only.

and is similar in scope to our functional value construct. Several models of choice have been developed in social psychology, using some or all of the three constructs listed above.

As a pioneer in this area, Rosenberg (1956) developed a model relating attitude toward an object to the perceived potential of the object for bringing about a desired state. The model posits that an individual's attitude toward an alternative depends on his or her perception of its *instrumentality* for attaining or blocking a specific value and on the *importance* placed on that value. Both are concepts subsumed by our functional value construct, and the concept of attitude is subsumed by our emotional value construct. However, the Rosenberg model does not acknowledge the influence of social, epistemic, or conditional values.

Fishbein developed a model to predict behavioral intention as a function of *attitude* (defined similarly to Rosenberg's model) and *subjective norms* (Fishbein 1967, Fishbein and Ajzen 1975). He posited that an individual's behavioral intention depends on beliefs about the alternative and on beliefs about the opinions of referent others. Further, behavioral intention is dependent on the individual's motivation to comply with these subjective social norms. Thus, the Fishbein model includes concepts relevant to our functional, emotional, and social value constructs, but it does not include concepts analogous to our epistemic and conditional values.

Finally, Triandis (1971) advanced a model with components similar to both Rosenberg's and Fishbein's, and he added a fourth component termed *facilitating conditions*. The facilitating conditions construct refers to situational factors and is similar in domain to our conditional value construct. The Triandis model is clearly the richest of these choice models, containing constructs similar to four of the five constructs in our theory. However, even it does not account for the effects of epistemic value.

Clinical Psychology

Explanations for choice provided by clinical psychology are primarily derived from psychoanalytic theory as posited by Sigmund Freud and his followers, most notably Carl Jung and Alfred Adler. These explanations represent an elaboration of Freud's idea of anxiety and his segmentation of the personality into the *id*, the *ego*, and the *superego* (Freud 1966).

According to Freud, the id is the source of psychic energy and seeks the unrestrained gratification of basic needs. This concept bears resemblance to our concept of emotional value. In contrast to the id, the superego represents societal and personal norms that serve to constrain behavior; it is subsumed by our social value construct. Finally, the ego mediates the demands of the id and the prohibitions of the superego. Representing the requirements of physical reality, it is similar to our concept of functional value.

Psychoanalytic theory was applied to marketing through motivation research, founded on the premise that consumer choice behavior is largely driven by subconscious motives. Led by the pioneering efforts of Ernest Dichter (Dichter 1964), motivation researchers applied the theories and methods of clinical psychology to develop some interesting, although controversial, explanations for consumer choice behavior.

As applied to consumer choice behavior, psychoanalytic theory is limited in that it does not contain concepts analogous to our epistemic value and conditional value constructs. In regard to epistemic value, Freudian theory is limited in that it conceives of behavior as a tension-reducing system, motivated by the interplay of the id, ego, and superego. In contrast, our conceptualization of epistemic value also suggests that consumers may seek out situations that *produce* tension.

Experimental Psychology

Experimental psychologists studying the phenomenon of learning have developed models with a range of constructs most similar to our theory of choice. Most notably, Hull (1943) constructed a theory of learning focusing on the role of habit and on the human tendency to form expectations about the future. Hull's theory posits that learning is a function of *drive*, *goal object*, *habit*, and *stimulus dynamism*. Drive captures some of the domain of our epistemic value construct; goal object is pertinent to functional value; habit falls within the domain of emotional value; and stimulus dynamism focuses on situational factors, resembling our conditional value construct.

Although learning theory comes closest to our theory in its range of constructs, it does not account for the separate influence of social value and conditional value. While Hull's stimulus dynamism may pertain to conditional social value, we also recognize that social value influences behavior independently.

Economics

Economists, as proponents of utility theory, have generally argued that consumer choice behavior is, or should be, motivated by the desire to *maximize utility* (Marshall 1890, Stigler 1950). It has been postulated that people prefer more utility to less, and they will allocate scarce resources so as to maximize utility. Given that individuals seek to maximize utility, the economic law of demand posits that preference in a given choice situation will be constrained by price and income.

In general, the assessment of choice behavior presented by economists accounts only for "rational" behavior, expressed in terms of "rational economic man." Although utility maximization principles can be applied to any of the five values in our theory, the "economically rational" behavior discussed by economists is generally analogous to behavior motivated by functional value. Thus our theory is much broader in scope than economic utility theory, incorporating behavior that is not "economically rational," that is, behavior driven by noneconomic considerations based on emotional, social, and epistemic values. Further, we suggest that consumers are not always motivated to optimize utility. Given that choice is driven by multiple values and that tradeoffs occur among them, consumers are often only interested in satisficing on even highly salient values.

Consumption Economics and Economic Psychology

Researchers in the fields of consumption economics and economic psychology have modified classical economic utility theory, adopting a descriptive focus that contrasts with the normative focus characterizing classical economics. Central to these disciplines is the fundamental question of how consumers make economic choices.

At least two concepts relevant to our theory have been contributed by these fields. First, it has been suggested that *sentiments* and *subjective expectations* are important determinants of economic choices. In fact, it has been argued that psychological reality is often a more important determinant of choice than economic reality (Katona 1951, 1953, 1963, 1975). Second, it has been suggested that *satisficing* behavior, with an emphasis on minimizing downside risk, is more prevalent in decision making than behavior aimed at maximizing utility (Simon 1963).

Despite this enhancement of classical economic theory, the disciplines of economic psychology and consumption economics have not generated concepts to explain choices driven by social, epistemic, or conditional values. Most of the focus has been on functional value, with some attention to emotional value.

Sociology and Social Stratification

In contrast to the focus on individual behavior found in psychology and economics, sociology focuses on the group as the fundamental unit of analysis. Individual behavior is seen as resulting from the influences of the social structure. Sociological theory relevant to choice has largely centered on such concepts as *reference groups*, *social class*, and *social norms*.

Reference group theory was originated by Hyman (1942), who defined a reference group as one that influences the attitudes of individuals who use it as a reference point. Later, Sherif (1953) clarified that a group may serve as a referent even though the individual is not a member. Whether a membership or aspired-to group, a reference group influences the individual's behavior by promoting conformity or compliance with group norms (Bourne 1957). It has been demonstrated that such compliance usually represents the path of least resistance for the individual, and compliance also facilitates the achievement of personal goals (Thibaut and Kelley 1959, Asch 1960, Williams 1970, Hechter 1978).

In the area of choice behavior, researchers taking a sociological perspective have provided concepts relevant to our social value construct and have contributed greatly to its development. However, the other values proposed in our theory receive far less attention. The numerous choices motivated by functional, emotional, epistemic, and conditional values clearly support the need to look beyond the sociological theories of choice.

Marketing and Consumer Behavior

The disciplines of marketing and consumer behavior have provided numerous theoretical contributions relevant to choice behavior. Recent contributions represent "middle-range theories" focusing on one or a few aspects of choice behavior. For example, research on variety seeking has focused on a domain of behavior subsumed by our epistemic value construct, research on opinion leadership has examined a domain of behavior subsumed by our social value construct, and research on situational factors has investigated a domain of behavior subsumed by our conditional value construct. Earlier contributions, however, include some "comprehensive theories" that attempt to provide a broader perspective on buying behavior.

The comprehensive theories of buying behavior are "process theories," attempting to describe and explain the process by which consumers reach purchase decisions. For example, Howard and Sheth (1969) used a learning framework to model the buying process; Engel, Kollat, and Blackwell (1968) modeled the buying process with a decision-making framework. These theories differ from ours in that they do not include an integrative typology to explain just why consumers make the choices they do. Further, although they do use concepts consistent with those in our theory—particularly its functional, social, and epistemic values—the models do not specifically explain how these concepts influence choices among alternatives, and they cannot predict the choices that will be made. As such, our theory represents an advance within the fields of consumer behavior and marketing.

Some Exceptions

There have been a few individual thinkers, exceptions to the norm, who have developed conceptual frameworks identifying multiple forces that work independently to influence human behavior. Maslow's (1943, 1954, 1970) famous hierarchy of needs—physiological, safety, belongingness and love, esteem, and self-actualization: Katz's (1960) classification of utilitarian, value expressive, ego defensive, and knowledge needs; and Katona's classification of necessities, fun and comfort, and spiritual and artistic needs (Katona 1953, Katona et al. 1971) are examples of conceptual frameworks that overlap significantly with our theory.

Comparing these theories with our own, our concept of functional value subsumes Maslow's physiological and safety needs, Katz's utilitarian need, and Katona's survival need. Our social value and emotional value constructs correspond with Maslow's belongingness and love needs, Katona's fun and comfort needs, and Katz's value expressive need. Further, our concept of social value subsumes Maslow's esteem need, and our concept of emotional value subsumes Katz's ego defensive need. Finally, our epistemic value construct is similar to Maslow's self-actualization need, Katona's spiritual and artistic needs, and Katz's knowledge need.

Despite the overlap between the theories, there are at least three important distinctions between our theory and the theories cited above. First, none includes concepts that tap the domain of our conditional value construct. Second, in addition to defining the five values that comprise our theory, we have operationalized our constructs, attempting to provide predictive value as well as descriptive and explanatory value. In contrast, the theories cited above have remained primarily descriptive, with little attempt at operationalization. Third, our theory has been specifically developed to explain market choice behavior. We have started with the questions of why and how people make specific consumption or purchase decisions and have worked back to develop a classification of values relevant to consumer choice. The theories cited above represent generic typologies of needs and values; they do not focus specifically on either market behavior or choice behavior.

OPERATIONALIZATION OF THE THEORY

The following paragraphs briefly describe the operationalization of our theory. Chapters 5 and 6 provide detailed guidelines and instructions with examples; Chapter 7 demonstrates the theory's application to three specific choice situations.

Application-Specific.   Although a generic procedure is provided, operationalization is necessarily *application-* or *choice-specific*. Data specific to choice situations of interest are collected to determine which values drive decisions. The user may hypothesize the values that will be important and then test his or her hypotheses. To this extent, the theory is more empirical than deductive. The procedure provided allows the researcher to simultaneously determine the relative influence of all five values.

Choice Domains.   To use the theory, the relevant domain or level of choice must be identified. In addition to specifying the product category, it must be specified whether the decision of interest is at the "buy versus no-buy" level, at the product type level, or at the brand level. Of course, not every market choice involves a purchase or product decision. Thus, the levels of choice may be translated into more general decisions pertaining to whether to engage or not to engage in a particular behavior, and decisions as to the type of behavior in which to engage.

Perceptual Base.   Operationalization of the theory requires that consumer perceptions be identified. Thus, subjects are required to verbalize their thoughts and perceptions. Information relevant to consumer perceptions is most conveniently gathered via verbal self-report instruments.

The perceptual base of the theory implies a number of benefits. First, it affords substantial *explanatory power*. The researcher can go beyond simple observations about choice behavior to acquire a deeper understanding of the values driving choice. In other words, the researcher can learn about the "whys" as well as the "whats" of consumer choice behavior. Second, the perceptual base facilitates the *control power* of the theory. Findings can be readily translated into marketing strategy, with consumers' perceptions providing direct input for product development, promotional strategy, market segmentation, and the like. Third, the perceptual base enhances the *predictive power* of the theory. Given that behavior is anchored in perceptual beliefs, respondents' own thoughts are used as the basis for predicting their future choices. Finally, measurement theory is more advanced for verbal measures than for nonverbal measures, resulting in greater *measurement sophistication*. A wealth of information exists on proper wording, scaling, and reliability and validity testing for verbal measures.

Of course, the perceptual base necessitates that the researcher be on guard against the potential biases and threats to validity that commonly plague verbal measures. These include interviewer bias, problems with wording and scaling, demand bias, and the like. However, all measurement methods are associated with their own inherent limitations. After numerous iterations, we feel satisfied that the wording and scaling suggested in our measurement instruments (see Chapter 5) contain minimal bias. Guidance for minimizing bias and maximizing reliability and validity may be obtained from any of a number of excellent resources (Carmines and Zeller 1979, Cook and Campbell 1979, Sudman and Bradburn 1982, Converse and Presser 1986, Kerlinger 1986).

Analytical Technique.   The fundamental analytical technique used in operationalizing the theory is *discriminant analysis*. It is recommended that independent variables be developed through *factor analysis*. However, if preferred, individual questionnaire items may be used as independent variables.

SUMMARY

Chapter 2 has provided a description of our theory of market choice behavior, including formal definitions and illustrative examples. As discussed, the theory is applicable to three levels of choice: the choice to buy or not to buy, the choice of product type, and brand choice. In developing the theory, we have started with questions of how and why people make specific market choices, and have worked back to develop a classification of values relevant to market choice.

The theory is based on five constructs representing five kinds of value possessed by choice alternatives. Each value pertains to the perceived utility of an alternative. Functional value is acquired through functional, utilitarian, or physical attributes; social value through association with social groups; emotional value through association with feelings; epistemic value through the arousal of curiosity and/or contribution to novelty and knowledge; and conditional value through situations that enhance functional or social value. When integrated, the five values provide a framework that is both comprehensive and parsimonious in explaining market choice behavior.

A number of models and theories from economics, sociology, psychology, and marketing/consumer behavior have been contributed that contain constructs analogous to the values in our theory. While all have greatly influenced the development of our constructs, none is as comprehensive as our theory. Even the most comprehensive works (by Maslow, Katona, and Katz) do not include concepts that tap the domain of all five of our constructs.

In addition to descriptive and explanatory value, our theory provides predictive value through its operationalization. As discussed, operationalization relies on a perceptual base, is application-specific, and requires that the level of choice be identified. The recommended analytical technique is discriminant analysis.

In Chapter 3 we review interdisciplinary theory and research relevant to functional and social values. Influences subsumed within the functional value and social value domains have traditionally been regarded as primary determinants of market choice behavior. In contrast, Chapter 4 will review literature pertaining to those values—emotional, epistemic, and conditional—that have received less attention as drivers of market choice.

3

FUNCTIONAL AND
SOCIAL VALUES

The next two chapters briefly review literature pertaining to the five values identified by our theory as drivers of market choice behavior. Chapter 3 reviews literature relating to those values that have traditionally been regarded as primary influences on market choice: functional and social values. Chapter 4 reviews literature relevant to values that have received lesser recognition: emotional, epistemic, and conditional values.

Many of the topics relevant to these five values have been researched extensively, with pertinent books and papers numbering in the thousands. Thus, it is not practical to provide an exhaustive review of the literature. Rather, these chapters attempt, by allotting a few pages to each value, to provide a flavor for the origins of our concepts and for the types of theory and research that have been advanced relevant to each. In general, the references cited are limited to those that we consider to be seminal, highly influential, or representative of the wider base of research.

FUNCTIONAL VALUE

The *functional value* of an alternative represents the utility it is perceived to possess on criteria salient to its physical or functional purposes. Our definition is based on the concept of intrinsic, as opposed to extrinsic, value. To illustrate, an automobile's functional value might be based on the intrinsic values of its safety specifications or ease of handling but not, for example, on the status or prestige associated with its ownership, an extrinsic value.

A consumer driven by functional value will choose the alternative that performs best on salient physical and utilitarian attributes, or the alternative that possesses the most of those attributes. Our concept of functional value has been influenced by theory and research from such varied disciplines as economics (including consumption economics), psychology (including social psychology), political science, and marketing and consumer behavior. The majority of work has focused on the concepts of utility, attributes, and needs. Table 3-1 provides an overview of work cited by discipline.

Table 3-1 Functional value: traditions, disciplines, authors

	Economics	Consumption economics	Political science	Psychology and social psychology	Marketing and consumer behavior
Utility	Marshall 1890 Stigler 1950 Alchian 1953 Strotz 1953 Ellsberg 1954 Arrow 1963	Burk 1968 Katona 1951, 1953, 1963, 1975 Morgan 1980	Downs 1957 Frohlich et al. 1978 Chapman/ Palda 1983	Simon 1963	Engel et al. 1968 Howard/Sheth 1969 Ferber 1973 Haines 1973 Monroe 1975 Hauser/Urban 1979 Silberg 1982 Rao/Gautschi 1982 Srinivasan 1982 Archibald et al. 1983 Rao 1984 Erickson/Johansson 1985
Attributes	Lancaster 1971 Rosen 1974			Rosenberg 1956 Fishbein 1967 Fishbein/Ajzen 1975 Triandis 1971	Bass/Talarzyk 1972 Ferber 1973 Wilkie/Pessemier 1973 Sheth 1974a Bettman et al. 1975 Lutz 1975, 1977 Mazis et al. 1975 Ratchford 1975, 1977 Ryan/Bonfield 1975 Holbrook 1977 Lutz/Bettman 1977 Agarwal/Ratchford 1980 Green et al. 1981 Myers/Shocker 1981 Holbrook/Havlena 1988
Needs	Galbraith 1958 Scitovsky 1976	Katona 1953 Katona et al. 1971		Murray 1938 Maslow 1943, 1954, 1970 Katz 1960 Alderfer 1969, 1972	Howard/Sheth 1969 Dichter 1971 Fennell 1975 Hanna 1980

Utility

The concept of functional value is similar in domain to the economic concept of *utility* advanced by such influential theorists as Marshall (1890) and Stigler (1950). Utility refers to the satisfaction derived from using a product or service. It is implied that satisfaction is derived from the physical product performing its functions. As noted by Burk (1968, p.5), ". . . the concept of utility is basic to the standard theory of consumer behavior, and most of the formal economics of consumption is built on it."

Utility theory posits that consumers make choices so as to maximize their total utility, and that they will allocate expenditures among alternatives so that the utility of the last dollar spent on each is equal (Alchian 1953, Strotz 1953, Ellsburg 1954, Arrow 1963, Burk 1968). Economic utility theory further assumes that utility is a function of the quantity of goods consumed, and that consumption—and therefore utility—is constrained by product prices. It is posited that when the price of an alternative is increased, with income and other product prices held constant, the demand for that alternative decreases. Thus, we consider price to be a salient attribute contributing to functional value. A number of authors in marketing and consumer behavior have modeled the effects of price on product evaluation and utility judgments (Monroe 1976, Srinivasan 1982, Rao and Gautschi 1982, Archibald et al. 1983, Rao 1984, Erickson and Johansson 1985).

Utility models proposed in economics have been widely accepted and applied to a diversity of choice situations. For example, utility theory has been used in political science to explain voting behavior (Downs 1957, Frohlich et al. 1978, Chapman and Palda 1983), and it has been applied in marketing to the study of consumer preference and choice (Ferber 1973, Haines 1973, Hauser and Urban 1979, Silberg 1982). Further, comprehensive theories of buyer behavior appear to implicitly accept a utility theory perspective (Engel et al. 1968, Howard and Sheth 1969). However, utility theory has also been widely criticized. For example, George Katona (1951, 1953, 1963, 1975), a pioneer in the areas of consumption economics and economic psychology, criticized utility theory for its reliance on utility maximization as the sole determinant of choice. Katona argued that utility theory is a one-motive theory attempting to explain a multiple-motive phenomenon, and that the utility maximization objective generally operates under only the following limited conditions:

1. for infrequent purchases and purchases that are of major importance to the buyer

2. when the consumer has had an unsatisfactory or disappointing past experience with a similar purchase

3. in purchasing new products and in first-time purchase situations

4. when purchase is influenced by strong precipitating circumstances

Other theorists taking a psychological perspective have similarly recognized that the utility maximization model fails to reflect the multiple motives driving choice behavior (Simon 1963, Morgan 1980). This view is consistent with our theory, which recognizes five distinct values driving choice.

Attributes

The concept of *attributes* is also inherent in our definition of functional value because attributes are instrumental in determining an alternative's capacity to perform. It is widely recognized that an alternative's utility may be derived directly from its attributes or characteristics (Ferber 1973). In marketing Myers and Shocker (1981) have developed a typology of product attributes consisting of product referent attributes, task or outcome attributes, and user referent attributes. Product referent attributes refer to the physical characteristics and properties of products; task or outcome referent attributes refer to the results emanating from product use; and user referent attributes refer to how products represent their users, both to others and to the self.

Building on traditional economic utility theory, Lancaster (1971) formulated a utility maximization model of consumption demand giving particular attention to product attributes or characteristics. According to Lancaster, all goods possess objective characteristics, with product demand depending on these objective properties and sometimes on consumers' "technological know-how," knowledge of what the product can do and how to use it. Thus, product preference and demand are *indirect* or *derived* in that products are actually valued for their characteristics, with individuals differing in their preferences for various collections of attributes. Lancaster's work provides a basis for predicting the effect on product demand when product attributes or characteristics are altered, and it affords an approach for predicting new product preference and demand.

Similar to Lancaster, Rosen (1974) posited that a market exists for a particular product when that product possesses a bundle of characteristics that is valued by customers. Rosen modeled utility maximization as occurring over characteristics of goods as well as over quantities of goods, subject to the constraints of income. Influenced by Rosen's approach, Agarwal and Ratchford (1980), in marketing, developed a model to estimate the demand and supply functions of product attributes.

Other authors have suggested that it is actually consumers' attitudes and beliefs regarding product attributes, rather than product attributes themselves, that determine a product's value (Ratchford 1975, 1979). This view is consistent with attitude models proposed in social psychology (Rosenberg 1956, Fishbein 1967, Triandis 1971, Fishbein and Ajzen 1975).

In general, these models relate attitude toward an object to the perceived potential of the object for bringing about desired consequences. This perceived potential is often based on the existence of specific attributes. Further, the perceived potential may itself be regarded as an attribute.

The applicability of these models to market choice has been widely recognized. Marketing and consumer researchers have contributed a rich literature devoted to adapting, applying, and testing these models in consumer behavior contexts, as well as to developing new models (Bass and Talarzyk 1972; Wilkie and Pessemier 1973; Sheth 1974a; Bettman et al. 1975; Lutz 1975, 1977; Mazis et al. 1975; Ryan and Bonfield 1975; Holbrook 1977; Lutz and Bettman 1977; Green et al. 1981; Holbrook and Havlena 1988). In marketing and consumer behavior contexts, these models are frequently referred to as "multiattribute attitude models."

Needs

Authors across disciplines have regarded choice outcomes as resulting from efforts to satisfy a variety of intrinsic needs. Depending on their disciplinary focus, some have specifically identified consumer needs (Katona 1953, Galbraith 1958, Katona et al. 1971, Fennell 1975, Hanna 1980) while others have identified universal human needs (Murray 1938; Maslow 1943, 1954, 1970; Katz 1960; Alderfer 1969, 1972). In general, such classifications contain at least one category similar in domain to our functional value concept. As mentioned in Chapter 2, Maslow's physiological needs and safety needs, Katona's necessities need, and Katz's instrumental, adjustive, or utilitarian needs are subsumed in our functional value construct.

In general, it has been suggested that needs fall into two general categories: *biogenic* and *psychogenic*. Biogenic needs arise from physiological tension systems and include the physical drives of hunger, thirst, and sleep. Psychogenic needs are based on psychological tensions and are influenced by personality variables, social relations, and the like. Many consumption decisions are attempts to satisfy biogenic and psychogenic needs and therefore are functional in nature. For example, Scitovsky (1976) has suggested that consumers have needs both for "defensive products," which prevent pain, injury, and distress, and for "creative products," which provide positive satisfaction or gratification. Also advancing this view, Dichter (1971), a proponent of motivation research in consumer behavior, has stated that:

> . . . most aspects of human behavior have as their final goal adaptation to, and conquest of, the difficulties of life. First among those difficulties are physical protection, security, shelter, and satisfaction of hunger; secondarily, they include regulations and guides to make living together easier and to avoid hardship. (p. 2)

Consumer behavior theorists have explicitly considered consumer needs as they influence decision making. For example, Howard and Sheth (1969) have suggested that need arousal is an integral part of the motivation process in buying behavior. The arousal of a need pushes the consumer toward action believed to lead to its satisfaction or fulfillment. Fennell (1975) delineated five need-related situations influencing product and brand choice behavior: normal depletion, aversive, anticipated aversive, product-related aversive, and positive product-use situations. Normal depletion situations motivate the purchase of products needed to maintain or replenish the customary product supply. Aversive situations motivate the purchase of products effective in dealing with specific unpleasant situations, for example, headache remedies. Anticipated aversive situations motivate the purchase of products effective in preventing specific negative occurrences (e.g., fire extinguishers). Product-related aversive situations motivate the purchase of brands offering assurances against negative outcomes from use, such as products that offer a warranty. Finally, positive product-use situations motivate the purchase of products expected to facilitate enjoyable experiences.

Influenced by interdisciplinary efforts to identify and categorize human needs, Hanna (1980) proposed a typology of seven *consumer needs* as follows:

1. Physical safety: "The need to consume products so as to avoid harm or danger in their use, and to preserve clean air and water in the environment." (p. 94)

2. Material security: "The need to consume an adequate supply of material possessions." (p. 95)

3. Material comfort: "The need to consume a large and/or luxurious supply of material possessions." (p. 95)

4. Acceptance by others: "The need to consume products so as to be associated with a significant other or a special reference group." (p. 95)

5. Recognition from others: "The need to consume products so as to be acknowledged by others as having gained a high status in one's community." (p. 95)

6. Influence over others: "The need to feel one's impact on others' consumption decisions." (p. 96)

7. Personal growth: "The need to consume products so as to become one's own unique self." (p. 96)

Hanna's typology accounts for both biogenic and psychogenic needs. The needs for physical safety, material security, and material comfort are subsumed by our concept of functional value. Other needs identified by Hanna are encompassed by our concepts of social value and epistemic value.

To summarize, our concept of functional value has been influenced by interdisciplinary theory and research on utility, attributes, and needs. The concept of *utility* refers to the intrinsic satisfaction derived from using a product or service and is therefore pertinent to functional value. Introduced in economics, utility theory has been adopted and adapted by a diversity of disciplines to explain choice behavior. Similarly, theory and research on *attributes* is pertinent to functional value because attributes are instrumental in determining the performance of an alternative. Attributes have received considerable attention in economics, and they are a primary focus of multiattribute attitude models in social psychology and consumer behavior. Finally, authors across disciplines have focused on *needs* as influencing choice outcomes. Some authors—primarily in psychology—have focused on universal human needs, while others—primarily in economics and consumer behavior—have focused specifically on consumer needs.

SOCIAL VALUE

The *social value* of an alternative is derived from its association with one or more distinctive social groups. More specifically, social value results from identification with positively or negatively stereotyped demographic, socioeconomic, and cultural-ethnic groups. Products consumed visibly or publicly are often attributed such value. Further, social value is often engendered by marketing efforts. To illustrate, advertising for Virginia Slims cigarettes portrays its smokers as exclusively female, and as young, sophisticated, independent, and affluent. In contrast, Marlboro and Camel advertising portray their smokers as rugged, masculine, cowboy types. A consumer driven by social value will choose alternatives associated with those groups to which he or she belongs, identifies, or aspires.

Our concept of social value has been influenced by theory and research in social psychology, sociology and rural sociology, communications, anthropology, economics, and marketing and consumer behavior. Relevant research has focused on social class, symbolic value, reference groups, conspicuous and compensatory consumption, the normative component of attitude, and opinion leadership and diffusion of innovation. Table 3-2 provides an overview of work cited by discipline. As mentioned previously, Maslow's love and belongingness needs, Katona's fun and comfort needs, and Katz's value expressive needs all pertain to social value. Further, Hanna's (1980) acceptance, recognition, and influence needs are subsumed under our concept of social value.

Social Class

Interest in social class membership goes back at least as far as the nineteenth century to the writings of Karl Marx, who maintained that crucial status distinctions exist between those who own capital and those who do not (Marx 1966). Also contributing an economic perspective, Weber (1966) distinguished between the concept of *social class*, which is determined by wealth and occupation, and the concept of *social status*, which is determined by honor and prestige. However, Weber maintained that both phenomena originate in situations characterized by unequal distributions of power and that social class and social status are mutually perpetuating.

Several authors have sought to identify the attributes and behaviors distinguishing the various social classes within American society (Warner and Lunt 1941, Kahl 1953, Jain 1975, Coleman et al. 1978, Gilbert and Kahl 1982). Social classes have most commonly been distinguished in terms of demographic characteristics such as income, occupation, and education. However, scholars taking a sociological perspective have also identified them in terms of discrete membership groups, cultural homogeneity, contribution to the social welfare, and degree of privilege, prestige, and influence (Lasswell 1965, Jaher 1973).

As a pioneer in this area, W. Lloyd Warner (Warner and Lunt 1941) identified six American social classes: upper-upper, lower-upper, upper-middle, lower-middle, upper-lower, and lower-lower. He maintained that the groups are comprised of persons who possess equal community esteem, who socialize with one another, and who share behavioral expectations. Other popular views of the American class structure include the Coleman-Rainwater approach (Coleman et al. 1978) and the Gilbert-Kahl approach (Gilbert and Kahl 1982). As contrasted by Coleman (1983), the Gilbert-Kahl approach emphasizes economic status as creating class status, while the Coleman-Rainwater approach (1983) emphasizes popular imagery and how people interact with one another as equals, superiors, and inferiors.

A number of marketing and consumer researchers have investigated the efficacy of social class as a predictor of purchase and consumption behavior. Warner and his colleagues demonstrated during the 1940s that members of different social classes display different shopping and purchasing behavior (Coleman 1983). This sparked a great deal of interest and a general belief that social class differences impact economic behavior.

As a pioneer in this area, Martineau (1958b) reported notable psychological differences between members of various social classes, with these differences engendering distinctive store patronage, spending, and communications behaviors. Further, he found that the members of various social classes identified with very different symbols of social mobility,

Table 3-2   Social value: traditions, disciplines, authors

	Economics	Anthropology	Social psychology	Sociology, rural sociology, and communications	Marketing and consumer behavior
Social class	Marx 1966 Weber 1966			Warner/Lunt 1941 Kahl 1953 Caplovitz 1963 Lasswell 1965 Bishop/Masaru 1970 Jaher 1973 Coleman et al. 1978 Gilbert and Kahl 1982	Martineau 1958b Coleman 1961, 1983 Levy 1966 Rich/Jain 1968 Mathews/Slocum 1969 Peters 1970 Slocum/Mathews 1970	Myers et al. 1971 Myers/Mount 1973 Foxall 1975 Jain 1975 Hugstad 1981 Schaninger 1981
Symbolic value	Duesenberry 1948, 1949	Benedict 1934 Douglas/Isherwood 1979 Hamid 1972	Vitz/Johnston 1965 Secord 1968 Peterson/Curran 1976	Goffman 1951 Veblen 1953 Form/Stone 1957 Porter 1967 Blumberg 1974, 1980	Haire 1950 Evans 1959 Levy 1959a,b, 1981 Woods 1960 Sommers 1964 Grubb/Grathwohl 1967 Birdwell 1968 Dolich 1969 Grubb/Stern 1971 Landon 1974 Calder/Burnkrant 1977	Belk 1978, 1980 Hirschman 1981, 1985 Hirschman/Holbrook 1981 Holman 1981 Belk et al. 1982, 1984 Solomon 1983 Rook 1985 Holbrook/Grayson 1986 Mick 1986
Reference groups	Duesenberry 1948 Brady 1952 Alexis 1972	White 1949 Hall 1959 Hallowell 1955 Wallace 1961 McCracken 1986, 1988	Hyman 1942 Sherif 1959 Asch 1956, 1960 French/Raven 1959 Thibaut/Kelley 1959 Deutsch/Gerard 1960 Festinger 1960, 1968 Festinger et al. 1960 Siegel/Siegel 1960 Kelley 1966 Newcomb 1966	Merton 1957 Williams 1970 Hechter 1978	Bourne 1957 Stafford 1966 Venkatesan 1966 Arndt 1967, 1968 Engel et al. 1968 Witt 1969 Bauer/Cunningham 1970 Witt/Bruce 1970 Cocanougher/Bruce 1971 Sturdivant 1973 Burnkrant/Cousineau 1975 Moschis 1976	Park/Lessig 1977 Stafford/Cocanougher 1977 Bearden/Etzel 1982 Wallendorf/Reilly 1983 Hirschman 1985 Schaninger et al. 1985 Wilkes/Valencia 1985 Deshpande et al. 1986 Tan/Farley 1987

Table 3-2   (continued)

	Economics	Anthropology	Social psychology	Sociology, rural sociology, and communications	Marketing and consumer behavior
Conspicuous and compensatory consumption				Veblen 1899, 1953 Caplovitz 1963 Porter 1967 Brooks 1981	Bullock 1961 Akers 1968 Sturdivant 1968, 1973 Bauer/Cunningham 1970 — Sexton 1971 Ashby 1973 Andreasen 1975, 1982 Andreasen/Hodges 1977 Mason 1981
Normative component of attitude			Allport 1935 Heider 1946, 1958 Smith 1947 Rosenberg 1956 Abelson/Rosenberg 1958 Katz 1960 Triandis 1971 Fishbein/Ajzen 1975		Sheth 1974a Ryan 1982 Miniard/Cohen 1983
Opinion leadership and diffusion of innovation	Katona/Mueller 1954	Hawley 1946 Suttles 1951 Bliss 1952 Sharp 1952 Barnet 1953 Erasmus 1961 Erasmus et al. 1961 Heath et al. 1969		Lazarsfeld et al. 1944 Greenberg 1951 Apodaca 1952 Dobyns 1952 Spicer 1952 Lippitt et al. 1953 Duncan/Kreitlow 1954 Katz/Lazarsfeld 1955 Hoffer/Strangland 1958 Lionberger 1960 Rogers 1961, 1962, 1971, 1976, 1983 Coleman et al. 1966 Herzog 1968 Rogers/Svenning 1969 Rogers/Bhowmik 1971	Whyte 1955 Silk 1966 Arndt 1967, 1968 Robertson 1967, 1971 Robertson/Kennedy 1968 Howard/Sheth 1969 Robertson/Myers 1969 King/Summers 1970 Summers 1970, 1971 Montgomery/Silk 1971 Myers/Robertson 1972 Roberto 1972 Zaltman/Stiff 1973 — Ostlund 1974 Baumgarten 1975 Thorelli et al. 1975 Midgley 1976 Moschis 1976 Kiel/Layton 1981 LaBay/Kinnear 1981 Dickerson/Gentry 1983 Gatignon/Robertson 1985 Leonard-Barton 1985 Reingen/Kernan 1986 Feick/Price 1987

leading to divergent product preferences. Levy (1966) extended this work, positing that social class is a determinant of general lifestyle and therefore exerts a very broad and meaningful influence on consumption behavior. A number of subsequent studies have examined social class differences regarding product preference, store patronage, product knowledge, price awareness, leisure behavior, innovativeness, and the like (Caplovitz 1963, Levy 1966, Rich and Jain 1968, Mathews and Slocum 1969, Bishop and Masaru 1970, Foxall 1975, Schaninger 1981).

A few researchers argued during the early 1970s that income is stronger than social class as a predictor of consumer choice (Slocum and Mathews 1970, Myers et al. 1971, Myers and Mount 1973). Building on their earlier work, Schaninger (1981) found social class to be the stronger predictor of relatively inexpensive purchases that reflect consumers' lifestyles and values, and income to be the stronger predictor of relatively expensive purchases that are not visibly consumed. Further, Schaninger found the interaction of social class and income to be the best predictor of highly visible purchases that serve as status symbols.

Providing a different and highly influential perspective on social class, Coleman (1961) noted that each social class includes members with greater than average income for the class as well as members with relatively less income. These he termed the overprivileged and underprivileged members, respectively. Examining car buying behavior, Coleman found choice of automobile to depend less on either absolute income or social class than on relative status within a social class. His research showed the purchase of economy cars and low-priced compacts to be most prevalent among the underprivileged segments of all social classes, and the purchase of larger and more luxurious makes to be most prevalent among the overprivileged. Coleman's perspective received further empirical support in subsequent studies by Peters (1970), Schaninger (1981), and Hugstad (1981).

Symbolic Value

It has long been recognized that products may possess symbolic value in excess of their functional utility (Veblen 1899; Benedict 1934; Duesenberry 1948, 1949; Goffman 1951; Form and Stone 1957; Douglas and Isherwood 1979). For example, Woods (1960) asserted that where ego involvement with a product is high, significant importance is attributed to its symbolic content. Symbolic value has been variously defined, but the concept largely pertains to learned meanings and imagery.

While the notion that products serve as ubiquitous social cues has been challenged (Blumberg 1974, 1980), the premise that symbolic qualities impact product evaluation is widely accepted and underlies several streams of research in consumer behavior. These include research on the congruence between self-image and product or store image (Levy 1959a,b); research on the role of products in impression formation and as social stimuli (Belk 1978, Holman 1981, Solomon 1983); and research on symbolic consumption (Hirschman 1981, 1985; Hirschman and Holbrook 1981; Holbrook and Hirschman 1982; Belk et al. 1982; Belk et al. 1984; Rook 1985; Holbrook and Grayson 1986; Mick 1986).

As a seminal contributor to research on the symbolic meaning of products, Levy asserted that most products say something about the social world of those who consume them. As a result, purchase decisions necessarily involve an assessment of this symbolism. Levy suggested that products are judged favorably when they enhance or reinforce the individual consumer's self-concept and are frequently used in this way. Further, product symbolism is affected by social class membership (Sommers 1966). More recently, Levy (1981) has suggested that consumer protocols reveal the symbolic content of products and consumption behavior.

Based on the premise that products contain symbolic content, a number of authors have attempted to relate product choice to personality. For example, Secord (1968) advanced that people largely see products as extensions of themselves. While empirical work in this area has shown mixed results (Evans 1959, Vitz and Johnston 1965), a considerable amount of work has demonstrated a positive relationship between purchase and the congruence between product image and self-concept (Porter 1967, Birdwell 1968, Dolich 1969, Grubb and Stern 1971, Landon 1974). Further, Belk et al. (1982) and Solomon (1983) have suggested that consumers encode their own consumption behavior so as to clarify their self-concept.

It is apparent that if a product is to serve as a social symbol, it must achieve clear recognition as such (Grubb and Grathwohl 1967). A substantial amount of research on consumption encoding and decoding has concluded that the use of specific products conveys socially meaningful information. For example, in a classic study, Haire (1950) found consumers to form very different attributions about users of regular versus instant coffee. Subsequent studies have found similar results relevant to other highly visible products and behaviors (Hamid 1972; Peterson and Curran 1976; Calder and Burnkrant 1977; Belk 1978, 1980).

Reference Groups

Individual behavior is clearly influenced by group membership (Brady 1952, Merton 1957, Thibaut and Kelley 1957, Williams 1970, Hechter 1978). Further, it is not at all unusual for individuals to comply with the norms of groups to which they do not even belong (Duesenberry 1948). The concept of *reference group* was introduced to account for the influence of both membership and nonmembership groups.

Pioneering in this area, Hyman (1942) defined a reference group as any collective influencing the attitudes of those individuals using it as a reference point in evaluating their own situations. Sherif (1953) made more explicit the idea that group membership is not a requirement for such influence. The individual may merely aspire to group membership or may just identify with the group's values.

The phenomenon of reference group influence is clearly germane to consumer choice behavior (Engel et al. 1968, Stafford and Cocanougher 1977). Significant reference group influence has been found in choice situations involving highly visible, salient, and/or publicly consumed products (Bourne 1957, Venkatesan 1966, Witt 1969, Witt and Bruce 1970, Bearden and Etzel 1982). However, reference group influence has even been demonstrated in situations involving relatively "invisible" products (Stafford 1966). It has also been shown that consumers frequently put forth considerable effort to observe the consumption behavior of referent others, to determine how these others evaluate specific alternatives, and to use reference group members as sources of product information (Arndt 1967, 1968; Burnkrant and Cousineau 1975; Moschis 1976).

A number of sociologists have studied the dynamics of reference group influence from the group perspective, focusing on such issues as reference group functions and means of influence. Kelley (1966) identified two primary functions of reference groups as the normative function and the comparison function. Through the normative function, the group sets and enforces standards of behavior for the individual. Through the comparison function, the group provides a point of comparison against which the individual may evaluate him/herself or others. Relevant to means of influence, French and Raven (1959) proposed that a group may gain compliance through any or all of five bases of social power: reward power, coercive power, referent power, legitimate power, and expert power. Similarly, Park and Lessig (1977) identified in consumer behavior three types of group influence as informational, utilitarian, and value-expressive. A rich body of research exists in social psychology demonstrating the power of groups to gain compliance and conformity (Asch 1960; Deutsch and Gerard 1960; Festinger 1960, 1968; Festinger et al. 1960; Siegel and Siegel 1960; Newcomb 1966). In a classic study, Asch (1956) demonstrated that when confronted with an apparent discrepancy between personal judgments and group consensus, judgments were often expressed that were obviously contrary to personal perception. Going a step further, Deutsch and Gerard (1960) found that subjects avoided expressing judgments that conflicted with erroneous group consensus even when the group was not physically present.

Influenced by this literature, several authors in marketing have examined conformity as a motive in product and brand choice situations. A significant tendency toward conformity has been found in contexts involving group pressure and/or a high degree of group cohesion (Venkatesan 1966, Witt 1969). However, the tendency to conform has also been found in contexts involving informal and even socially distant groups (Stafford 1966; Cocanougher and Bruce 1971). The propensity to conform appears to vary significantly among individuals. For example, Park and Lessig (1977) found college students to be much more susceptible than homemakers to reference group influence.

Finally, cultural group influence may be regarded as a special case of reference group influence (Hallowell 1955, Hall 1959, Wallace 1961). Culture is commonly defined as a set of socially acquired behavior patterns common to the members of a society. White (1949) has suggested that culture is easily transmitted from individual to individual because of its highly symbolic nature. A number of authors have demonstrated the efficacy of cultural and subcultural identification as a determinant of consumer choice behavior (Akers 1968; Bauer and Cunningham 1970; Alexis 1972; Sturdivant 1973; Wallendorf and Reilly 1983; Hirschman 1985; Schaninger et al. 1985; Wilkes and Valencia 1985; Deshpande et al. 1986; McCracken 1986, 1988; Tan and Farley 1987).

Conspicuous and Compensatory Consumption

The phenomena of conspicuous consumption and compensatory consumption are further manifestations of the importance of social value. Both types of behavior generally occur as consumers seek to associate or disassociate with specific demographic, socioeconomic, or cultural-ethnic groups.

Conspicuous consumption occurs when individuals buy or use products with the express intent of communicating socially significant meanings to others (Porter 1967, Brooks 1981). Veblen (1899, 1953) originated the concept of conspicuous consumption, asserting that ". . . the members of each stratum accept as their ideal of decency the scheme of life in vogue in the next higher stratum, and bend their energies to live up to the ideal" (1953, p. 70). According to Mason (1981), conspicuous consumption highlights consumers' sensitivities to third party reactions. Conspicuous consumption may represent an ostentatious display of affluence as a symbol of social status, an effort to emulate the consumption style of social classes further up the hierarchy, an attempt to disprove the stereotype associated with one's own class status, or a deviant or nonconforming consumption style symbolizing the rejection of social or group norms.

Compensatory consumption occurs when individuals feel economically or socially deprived and seek compensation through extravagant spending and the acquisition of luxuries. Caplovitz (1963) has suggested that compensatory consumption is motivated by desires to offset limited upward social and occupational mobility. Compensatory consumption allows the individual to obtain some redress for the negative status of being poor and to derive some enhancement of self-worth. A number of authors studying the behavior of economically disadvantaged consumers have observed purchasing and consumption behavior that appears to be compensatory in nature (Bullock 1961; Caplovitz 1963; Akers 1968; Sturdivant 1968, 1973; Bauer and Cunningham 1970; Sexton 1971; Ashby 1973: Andreasen 1975, 1982; Andreasen and Hodges 1977).

Normative Component of Attitudes

Since the pioneering work of Allport in the 1930s, social psychologists have focused considerable attention on the nature and determinants of attitude. Allport (1935) defined *attitude* as a learned predisposition to respond to an object or class of objects in a consistently favorable or unfavorable way. Researchers focusing on determinants have recognized that attitudes include a social or normative component, that is, attitudes are influenced by the expectations of referent others.

As an early contributor to this area, Smith (1947) identified five functions of attitudes, with one of these being conformity. Through the conformity function, attitudes express identification with meaningful social groups. Katz (1960) suggested that attitudes are comprised of descriptive, evaluative, and normative beliefs. He theorized that attitudes substantially influenced by normative beliefs serve ego defensive and value expressive functions for the individual.

Many of the attitude-behavior models developed in social psychology and consumer behavior include normative components (Rosenberg 1956, Abelson and Rosenberg 1958, Triandis 1971, Sheth 1974a, Fishbein and Ajzen 1975, Ryan 1982, Miniard and Cohen 1983). For example, the Fishbein behavioral intention model (Fishbein and Ajzen 1975) portrays behavioral intention as dependent on attitude, normative beliefs (beliefs about what referent others think), and motivation to comply with normative beliefs.

Cognitive consistency models developed in social psychology similarly focus on normative influences. One example is Heider's balance theory (1946, 1958). According to the theory, if an individual holds a positive or negative attitude toward an attitude object while a referent other holds the opposite attitude, the subject individual will be in a state of imbalance. The individual will then attempt to reestablish balance by changing her or his attitude toward the object, by changing her or his attitude toward the referent other, or by attempting to change the referent other's attitude.

Opinion Leadership and Diffusion of Innovations

Certain members of any social system have more exposure than others to sources of information, including sources of product information (Thorelli et al. 1975, Feick and Price 1987). In their classic study of the 1940 presidential election, Lazarsfeld et al. (1944) observed that individuals with more access to information served as filters or transmitters for others, thereby intervening between the mass media and the opinions and choices of their cohorts. Since differential knowledge implies differential influence, the authors termed these individuals *opinion leaders* in the development of their influential "two-step flow hypothesis."

The concept of opinion leadership pertains to *informal* influence, as opposed to leadership through formal position or status (Rogers 1983). Interpersonal or word-of-mouth communication, often transmitted through opinion leaders, is frequently the most persuasive determinant of consumer choice (Katona and Mueller 1954, Katz and Lazarsfeld 1955, Whyte 1955, Arndt 1967, Howard and Sheth 1969, Robertson 1971, Baumgarten 1975, Kiel and Layton 1981, Reingen and Kernan 1986). It has been demonstrated that as much as 50 percent of this communication is initiated by consumers seeking information from those they regard as opinion leaders (Arndt 1968).

Numerous researchers in such varied disciplines as communications, consumer behavior, and rural sociology have tried to identify opinion leader characteristics that might be unique or at least distinguishing (Katz and Lazarsfeld 1955, Rogers 1962, Coleman et al. 1966, Robertson 1967, Herzog 1968, Robertson and Myers 1969, Rogers and Svenning 1969, Summers 1970, 1971). From a review of the existing literature, Robertson (1971) concluded that opinion leaders often demonstrate a higher than average degree of gregariousness and innovativeness. Contrary to hypothesis, however, he concluded that opinion leaders are of generally the same social status as their followers. Other hypothesized differences varied by product category. The consensus now is that opinion leaders and those they influence are generally similar in terms of demographics, background, attitude, and lifestyle (Rogers and Bhowmik 1970, Moschis 1976).

Rogers (1983) concluded that the status of an opinion leader is earned and maintained through technical competence, social accessibility, and conformity to system norms. Because opinion leaders conform to social norms, they serve as apt role models when other members of the social system are confronted with new consumption alternatives. Comparing opinion leaders with the general population, Rogers found opinion leaders to be more cosmopolitan and socially participative, to have more exposure to the mass media and more contact with change agents, and to be more innovative.

Whatever the corollaries of opinion leadership, it has been found that opinion leaders largely earn their status through involvement and expertise with, at most, a small set of related products (Silk 1966, King and Summers 1970, Montgomery and Silk 1971, Myers and Robertson 1972, Midgley 1976). Thus, the phenomenon of opinion leadership tends to be relatively product specific.

As an area related to opinion leadership, research on diffusion of innovations also demonstrates the importance of social value in consumer choice (Rogers 1976, Gatignon and Robertson 1985, Leonard-Barton 1985). Diffusion of innovations is the process by which new products, methods, and ideas are disseminated and accepted among individuals (Rogers 1962, 1971, 1983; Robertson 1967, 1971; Zaltman and Stiff 1973). It is evident that some consumers adopt new innovations more rapidly than others, and many believe this to be a relatively stable predisposition.

Rogers's (1962, 1971, 1983) well-known typology classifies consumers as innovators, early adopters, early majority, late majority, and laggards. Significant socioeconomic and psychographic differences have been observed between the early adopting and late adopting groups. In general, consumers in the early adopting groups appear to be more educated, upwardly mobile, venturesome, affluent, socially integrated, and status oriented (Duncan and Kreitlow 1954; Hoffer and Strangland 1958; Rogers 1961, 1962, 1971, 1983; Robertson and Kennedy 1968; LaBay and Kinnear 1981; Dickerson and Gentry 1983). However, Ostlund (1974) found perceptual variables to be far more powerful than personal characteristics in predicting early adoption.

Sociologists have furnished insight into factors that facilitate or inhibit the diffusion process. For example, studies in rural sociology have highlighted the crucial role of socially determined norms, tastes, and habits (Spicer 1952, Apodaca 1952). It is clear that new product introductions are most successful when change agents work *within* existing social structures (Greenberg 1951, Dobyns 1952, Erasmus 1961, Erasmus et al. 1978). Lionberger (1960) posited that practices that are compatible with existing social beliefs are more likely to be adopted quickly, and Lippitt et al. (1953) suggested that relationships between change agents and social systems initiate and propel the diffusion process. Similar observations have been reported in anthropology and marketing (Hawley 1946, Suttles 1951, Bliss 1952, Sharp 1952, Barnet 1953, Roberto 1972).

In conclusion, our concept of social value has been influenced by interdisciplinary theory and research on social class, reference groups, symbolic value, conspicuous and compensatory consumption, the normative component of attitude, and opinion leadership and diffusion of innovation. Seminal research has been advanced by the social sciences, but these concepts have also received substantial attention in other disciplines, particularly marketing and consumer behavior. Research on *social class* and *reference groups* is pertinent to social value because the social value of an alternative is derived through its association with such groups. Similarly, research on *symbolic value, conspicuous and compensatory consumption*, and the *normative component of attitude* illustrates how alternatives acquire social value and demonstrates the importance of social value in consumer choice. Finally, *opinion leadership and diffusion of innovation* research demonstrates how social value is communicated within and between social groups.

SUMMARY

This chapter has reviewed interdisciplinary literature pertaining to functional value and social value, affording an overview of the origins of these constructs and of the types of theory and research advanced. Concepts subsumed by our functional value and social value constructs have received wide recognition as drivers of consumer choice.

Our functional value construct has been influenced by theory and research on utility, attributes, and needs. Seminal work has been advanced by economics, consumption economics, and psychology (including social psychology). Further, marketing and consumer behavior researchers have utilized and refined these concepts in the specific context of consumer choice.

Similarly, our social value construct has been influenced by theory and research on social class, symbolic value, reference groups, conspicuous and compensatory consumption, the normative component of attitude, and opinion leadership and diffusion of innovation. These concepts largely originated in the social sciences—including sociology, rural sociology, and social psychology—and significant contributions relevant to consumer choice have been made by marketing and consumer behavior researchers.

Next, Chapter 4 reviews theory and research pertaining to emotional, epistemic, and conditional values. As contrasted with functional and social values, these values have received less attention as drivers of consumer choice. Nevertheless, a rich theoretical and research base exists.

4

EMOTIONAL, EPISTEMIC,
AND CONDITIONAL VALUES

This chapter completes the review of literature pertaining to the five values identified as drivers of market choice behavior. While Chapter 3 focused on functional and social values, this chapter focuses on emotional, epistemic, and conditional values. As noted in Chapter 3, functional and social values have traditionally been regarded as primary influences on market choice behavior. The three values discussed in this chapter have also received attention as determinants of market choice, but they do not represent the traditional focus.

As with the topics covered in Chapter 3, many of the topics relevant to emotional, epistemic, and conditional values have been researched extensively. Thus, it is not practical to provide an exhaustive review. Rather, this chapter, like Chapter 3, attempts to provide a flavor for the origins of our concepts and for the types of theory and research that have been advanced relevant to each. As a result, the references cited are limited to those that we consider to be seminal, highly influential, or representative of the wider base of research.

EMOTIONAL VALUE

As opposed to cognitive-based criteria, *emotional value* is derived from feelings or affective states. An alternative is perceived to possess emotional value when it precipitates or perpetuates specific and desired feelings.

Emotional value plays an influential role in many market choice situations (Olshavsky and Granbois 1979, Hirschman and Holbrook 1982, Havlena and Holbrook 1986, Peterson et al. 1986), engendering such actions as unplanned purchasing and impulse buying (Weinberg and Gottwald 1982, Rook 1987). Emotions driving market choice are often positive ones, such as loyalty, nostalgia, and excitement, but negative emotions like fear, guilt, and anger also motivate choice.

Our concept of emotional value has been influenced by theory and research in various branches of psychology—clinical, environmental, social, experimental, cognitive, and educational—and in marketing and consumer behavior. Pertinent areas of inquiry include motivation research and research on personality, marketing and promotional mix variables, nonverbal processing and hemispheral brain lateralization, and subliminal perception. Table 4-1 provides an overview of work cited by discipline. Further, as mentioned in Chapter 2, Maslow's love and belongingness needs, Katona's fun and comfort needs, and Katz's ego defensive and value expressive needs are also relevant to our concept of emotional value.

Motivation Research

Popular during the 1950s, motivation research was instrumental in advancing the view that consumer choice may be based on noncognitive and emotional motives expressed through product symbolism (Packard 1957, Levy 1959a,b, Dichter 1964). Most commonly associated with the work of Dichter (1947, 1958, 1960, 1964, 1971, 1979), motivation research examined consumer behavior from the perspective of Freudian psychology, emphasizing unconscious and subconscious motives (Freud 1966, Hall and Lindzey 1970) and seeking to understand those largely affective mechanisms that "bridge the world of objects and the world of the mind" (Dichter 1964, p. 385). Motivation research employs methods from clinical psychology, including depth interviewing and such projective techniques as word association, sentence completion, and picture interpretation (Smith 1954, Newman 1957, Dichter 1958, Vicary 1958, Kassarjian 1974, Sampson 1986).

Motivation researchers have advanced very interesting (although arguably unverifiable) findings relevant to a full range of product types (Dichter 1947, 1960, 1964; Smith 1954; Martineau 1957; Newman 1957; Packard 1957). For example, it has been posited that crunchy cereals allow release of subconscious aggression, that milk represents emotional comfort and security, that life insurance enhances feelings of male sexual potency, and that baking symbolizes the act of giving birth.

Packard (1957) examined efforts by advertisers during the 1950s to associate products with subconscious needs. Although sometimes humorous, many motivation research findings were successfully utilized. As one example, Dichter concluded that men subconsciously see a convertible automobile as a "substitute mistress," offering a socially and morally acceptable means of regaining feelings of youth and excitement. He convinced automobile manufacturers to appeal to consumers on that basis, and sales increased dramatically. Similarly, Dichter concluded that consumers subconsciously associate ice cream with uninhibited indulgence, and he convinced ice cream advertisers to depict it in lavish and overflowing portions. Again, sales increased.

Table 4-1 Emotional value: traditions, disciplines, authors

	Clinical, social, and personality psychology	Experimental, educational, cognitive and environmental psychology	Marketing and consumer behavior
Motivation research	Freud 1966 Hall/Lindzey 1970		Dichter 1947, 1958, 1960, 1964, 1971, 1979 Haire 1950 Smith 1954 Rothwell 1955 Martineau 1957, 1958a Newman 1957 Packard 1957 Politz 1958 Scriven 1958 Vicary 1958 Levy 1959a,b Wells/Tigert 1971 Sheth 1973b Wells/Beard 1973 Kassarjian 1974 Hirschman/Holbrook 1982 Sampson 1986
Personality	Freud 1966 Jung 1916 Adler 1928 Murray 1938 Horney 1945 Adorno et al. 1950 Erikson 1950 Riesman 1950 Eysenck 1953 Sullivan 1953 Taylor 1953 Fromm 1955 Edwards 1957 Guilford 1959 Steiner 1961 Cattell 1965 Marcus 1965 Ellenberger 1970 Hall/Lindzey 1970 Buss/Poley 1976		Haire 1950 Gardner/Levy 1955 Martineau 1957 Dichter 1958, 1964 Evans 1959, 1968 Levy 1959a,b Tucker/Painter 1961 Winick 1961 Westfall 1962 Kuehn 1963 Cox/Bauer 1964 Kamen 1964 Claycamp 1965 Kassarjian 1965, 1971 Vitz/Johnston 1965 Newman 1966 Wells 1966 Bell 1967 Cohen 1967, 1968 Kernan 1968 Massy et al. 1968 Jacoby 1971 Robertson/Myers 1969 Blake et al. 1970 Boone 1970 Donnelly 1970 Fry 1971 Sparks/Tucker 1971 Wells/Tigert 1971 Wiseman 1971 Alpert 1972 Donnelly et al. 1973 Greeno et al. 1973 Wells/Beard 1973 Horton 1974 Kassarjian/Sheffet 1975 Villani/Wind 1975 Webster 1975 Wells 1975 Woodside/Andress 1975 Wright 1975 Brooker 1976, 1978 Schaninger 1976 Mehrotra/Wells 1977 Becherer/Richard 1978 Mizerski/Settle 1979 Noerager 1979 Raju 1980 Schaninger/Sciglimpaglia 1981 Punj/Stewart 1983 Richins 1983 Holbrook et al. 1984 Holbrook 1986 Shimp/Sharma 1987 Lastovicka/Joachimsthaler 1988

Table 4-1   (continued)

	Clinical, social, and personality psychology	Experimental, educational, cognitive and environmental psychology	Marketing and consumer behavior
Marketing and promotional mix variables	Janis/Feshbach 1953 Goldstein 1959 Berkowitz/Cottingham 1960 Leventhal/Niles 1964, 1965 Leventhal et al. 1965 Leventhal/Watts 1966 Milgram 1970 Desor 1972	Esser 1972 Stokols 1972, 1976 Saegert 1973 Saegert et al. 1975	Martineau 1958c Lynch/Hartman 1968 Berry 1969 Ray/Wilkie 1970 Sternthal/Craig 1973, 1974 Fry/McDougall 1974 Kotler 1974 Beckwith/Lehmann 1975 Dichter 1975 Kelly/Solomon 1975 Jacoby/Olson 1977 Olson 1977 Burnett/Oliver 1979 Holbrook/Huber 1979 Harrell et al. 1980 Woodside/Motes 1980 Gorn 1982 Milliman 1982, 1986 Richmond/Hartman 1982 Zeithaml 1982 Zielske 1982 Holbrook 1983 Quelch/Cannon-Bonventre 1983 Aaker et al. 1986 Park/Young 1986 Westbrook 1987
Nonverbal processing and brain lateralization		Orstein 1972 Kimura 1973 Paivio/Begg 1974 Das et al. 1975 Paivio 1975, 1979 Deglin 1976 Bogen 1977 Broadbent 1977 Gazzaniga 1977 Lindsay/Norman 1977 Wittrock et al. 1977 Das et al. 1979 Geschwind 1979 McCallum 1979 McGee 1979 Wexler 1980	Krugman 1965, 1977, 1979 Hansen 1981 Hansen/Lundsgaard 1981 Holbrook/Moore 1981 Kassarjian 1982 Janiszewski 1988 Rothschild et al. 1988
Subliminal perception	Miller 1939, 1940, 1942 Bruner/Postman 1947, 1948 Zajonc 1968, 1980 Silverman 1976 Shevrin/Dickman 1980	Pierce/Jastrow 1884 Coover 1917 Collier 1940 McCleary/Lazrus 1949 McGinnies 1949 Lazarus/McCleary 1951 Bricker/Chapanis 1953 Voor 1956 Adams 1957 Bach/Klein 1957 McConnell et al. 1958 Naylor/Lawshe 1958 Barthol/Goldstein 1959 Byrne 1959 Dember 1960 Wiener/Schiller 1960 Bevan 1964 Spence 1964 Dixon 1971, 1981 Erdelyi 1974 Fowler et al. 1981	Brean 1958 DeFleur/Petranoff 1959 Hawkins 1970 Key 1973, 1976, 1980 George/Jennings 1975 Kelly 1979 Saegert 1979 Caccavale et al. 1982 Hart/McDaniel 1982 Moore 1982 Zajonc/Markus 1982 Zanot et al. 1983 Tsal 1985 Janiszewski 1988

While Dichter was the most visible of the motivation researchers, motivation research has been widely employed. The Advertising Research Foundation in 1953 published a directory of 82 firms offering motivation research services (Wells and Beard 1973), and both Smith (1954) and Newman (1957) summarize representative studies. For example, a study by the advertising agency of Weiss and Geller found women to be "deadly serious about their hair"; they were overwhelmingly unfavorable toward a test ad featuring identical mother/daughter hair styles with the headline "A Double Header Hit with Dad." Depth interviews revealed a deep resentment at the implied competition between mother and daughter. However, on a conscious level, subjects tended to deny such competition could exist (Smith 1954).

Similarly, Martineau (1958a) published the results of an inquiry into the meanings of automobiles. It was found that the automobile represents a powerful symbol of self-control, signifying personal mastery of basic impulses, and a socially acceptable outlet for self-assertion.

Finally, no discussion of motivation research would be complete without reference to the now classic study by Haire (1950) on instant coffee. Concerned with consumer resistance to this new product, nonusers were asked what they disliked, and most indicated the flavor. Then, a projective technique was used to indirectly ferret out deeper motives. Subjects were divided into two groups and given alternate shopping lists, identical except that one included instant coffee and the other included regular coffee. When asked to characterize the owners of the shopping lists, subjects revealed considerations far deeper than taste. While the instant coffee user was frequently characterized as lazy, a poor planner, not thrifty, and not a good wife, such negative characteristics were rarely attributed to the regular coffee user.

After a heyday during the 1950s, motivation research declined in popularity and, in retrospect, its long term contributions are disappointing. Nevertheless, its role in enhancing appreciation of the emotive aspects of consumption is recognized by contemporary authors. For example, Hirschman and Holbrook (1982, p. 93) credit motivation research as "an important precursor of research on hedonic consumption." In addition, motivation research is regarded as the forebear of lifestyle research (Wells and Tigert 1971, Wells and Beard 1973).

Several factors undoubtedly led to motivation research's rapid decline. Most notably, it has consistently been criticized as lacking rigor, validity, and verifiability (Rothwell 1955, Politz 1958, Scriven 1958). Further, as noted by Wells and Beard (1973), marketers eventually became tired of hearing about the unconscious; they recognized very real differences between situations typically encountered in clinical versus marketing settings. Similarly, Sheth (1973b) argued that intense loyalty to Freudian psychology limited the contribution of motivation research.

Personality

Personality pertains to persistent individual qualities resulting in relatively consistent responses to environmental stimuli (Kassarjian 1971). As noted by Newman (1966, p. 225):

> The notion that human behavior, including the buying of goods and services expresses personality, is commonly accepted.... One would expect, therefore, that different personalities are attracted to different kinds of products and brands.

The study of the relationship between personality and behavior dates back to ancient times. However, interest in consumer behavior was fostered by personality theories developed in the twentieth century beginning with the psychoanalytic theories of Freud and Jung (Jung 1916, Freud 1966, Ellenberger 1970, Hall and Lindzey 1970). According to Freudian theory, behavior results from stresses within the personality system consisting of the id (the source of unrestrained impulses), the superego (repository of traditional morals and values), and the ego (mediator between the id and ego). Psychoanalytic personality theory had substantial influence on consumer research during the 1950s, especially among motivation researchers (Haire 1950; Gardner and Levy 1955; Martineau 1957; Dichter 1958, 1964; Levy 1959a,b).

Disillusioned with the emphasis on the biological/libidinal basis of personality, many personality theorists broke with the Freudian tradition and took a more social perspective recognizing the interdependence of the individual and society (Adler 1928, Murray 1938, Horney 1945, Erikson 1950, Riesman 1950, Sullivan 1953, Fromm 1955). While greatly influencing marketing in general, very little consumer personality research has used psychosocial theory as its basis. Exceptions are studies based on Riesman's distinction between inner- and other-directedness (Kassarjian 1965, Donnelly 1970, Mizerski and Settle 1979); and Cohen's (1967, 1968) development of a scale to measure Horney's three orientations toward coping with anxiety: complaint, aggressive, and detached personality types (Woodside and Andress 1975, Noerager 1979).

The most popular approach to consumer personality research uses trait and factor theories (Kassarjian 1971). Traits are defined by Guilford (1959, p. 6) as "distinguishable, relatively enduring way[s] in which one individual differs from another." Thus, traits are considered to be individual difference variables (Buss and Poley 1976), and they are measured by personality scales.

Personality scales consist of two types: those measuring specific traits and general personality inventories. Well-known specific scales include the F-Scale to measure authoritarianism (Adorno et al. 1950) and Taylor's Manifest Anxiety Scale (1953). In contrast, general personality inventories assume that personality can be described by a small number of variables (Eysenck 1953, Guilford 1959, Cattell 1965). From a variety of behavioral measures, factors are distilled which account for a large portion of the variance and these are presumed to represent "personality."

The ready availability of standardized personality inventories fostered much interest in consumer behavior (Kassarjian 1971). Some of the more popular scales used to predict consumer behavior—especially product and brand choice—are the Edwards Personal Preference Schedule (Evans 1959, Claycamp 1965, Massy et al. 1968, Alpert 1972); the Gordon Personal Profile (Tucker and Painter 1961, Kernan 1968, Sparks and Tucker 1971, Greeno et al. 1973); the Thurstone Temperament Schedule (Westfall 1962, Kamen 1964, Wiseman 1971); and the California Personality Inventory (Vitz and Johnston 1965, Robertson and Myers 1969, Boone 1970).

In general, the results have been disappointing. Although most studies demonstrate some explained variance, correlations are usually too weak to allow for meaningful prediction. For example, in what has come to be regarded as a classic study, Evans (1959) used the Edwards Personal Preference Schedule (Edwards 1957) to determine if personality differences could be found between Ford and Chevrolet owners. Some of the variance in brand choice was explained, but Evans concluded that demographics provide better predictions. Many authors have reexamined the research, reaching largely the same conclusion (Steiner 1961; Winick 1961; Westfall 1962; Kuehn 1963; Marcus 1965; Evans 1968).

Several authors have offered reasons for the lackluster results derived from general personality tests (Wells 1966, Kassarjian 1971, Wells and Beard 1973, Horton 1974, Kassarjian and Sheffet 1975, Villani and Wind 1975, Brooker 1978). These include:

1. Standardized tests are used for purposes not intended.

2. Tests are arbitrarily modified without validation.

3. Analysis is performed without theoretical justification.

4. Other interrelated influences on behavior are ignored.

5. Relationships are oversimplified.

In contrast to the standardized tests, consumer researchers have also related *specific* personality traits to consumer behavior (Cox and Bauer 1964, Bell 1967, Blake et al. 1970, Jacoby 1971, Donnelly et al. 1973, Holbrook et al. 1984). Further, a recent trend has been to examine the influence of personality on behaviors other than brand and product choice. These include information acquisition (Schaninger and Sciglimpaglia 1981), response to advertising and design features (Wright 1975, Holbrook 1986), interaction style (Richins 1983), perceived risk (Schaninger 1976), and social consciousness (Webster 1975, Brooker 1976).

Given the criticisms of early personality research, it is encouraging that recent efforts have focused on developing tailor-made personality instruments (Holbrook 1986, Shimp and Sharma 1987); have related behavior to theoretically justified personality variables (Raju 1980, Richins 1983); and have sought to improve the reliability and validity of personality research (Lastovicka and Joachimsthaler 1988). Further, personality is more often used in conjunction with other predictor variables (Fry 1971, Becherer and Richard 1978, Punj and Stewart 1983). Psychographic research, integrating personality and lifestyle, represents one such effort (Wells and Tigert 1971, Wells 1975, Mehrotra and Wells 1977).

Marketing Mix and Promotional Mix Variables

It has been demonstrated that marketing and promotional mix variables arouse affective responses, generalizing to marketed products and influencing subsequent behavior (Westbrook 1987). Much work in this area is of an applied nature, demonstrating its direct relevance to marketing practice.

Advertising typically contains background features, such as music, color, and movement, which are used to engender affective responses. Further, ads often contain humorous, fear-oriented, and other appeals designed to arouse specific emotions. Substantial theoretical and applied research has focused on responses to advertising elements, with topics including warmth (Aaker et al. 1986); sex (Richmond and Hartman 1982); music (Park and Young 1986); image and mood appeals (Woodside and Motes 1980, Zielske 1982); humor (Lynch and Hartman 1968, Sternthal and Craig 1973, Kelly and Solomon 1975); and fear (Janis and Feshbach 1953; Goldstein 1959; Berkowitz and Cottingham 1960; Leventhal and Niles 1964, 1965; Leventhal et al. 1965; Leventhal and Watts 1966; Ray and Wilkie 1970; Sternthal and Craig 1974; Burnett and Oliver 1979). While the efficacy of these appeals and techniques is equivocal, there is no doubt that emotions are aroused that could be generalized from the ad to the product being advertised (Beckwith and Lehmann 1975, Holbrook and Huber 1979, Holbrook 1983).

Using the principles of classical conditioning, Gorn (1982) contended that when a *conditioned* stimulus such as a product is paired with a positively or negatively regarded *unconditioned* stimulus, for example, music, the conditioned stimulus will become endowed with positive or negative affect. Gorn showed subjects two ballpoint pen ads, varying only the pen color (the conditioned stimulus, neutrally perceived) and the background music (the unconditioned stimulus, universally liked or disliked). Consistent with hypothesis, the majority selected the color pen paired with the liked music. Gorn suggested that unconditioned stimuli often influence preference and choice.

Atmospherics, the creation of favorable atmosphere at the point of purchase, have also been found to generate generalized affect. Research suggests that such atmospheric variables as lighting, background music, color, layout, and degree of crowding influence affect and, hence, buying decisions (Martineau 1958c; Berry 1969; Kotler 1974; Harrell et al. 1980; Quelch and Cannon-Bonventre 1983; Milliman 1982, 1986). Further, impressions are formed immediately upon experiencing an atmosphere; once formed, they are extremely difficult to change.

Crowding is among the most well researched atmospheric variables. Crowding is defined both as a physical state of high density and as a psychological state of stimulus overload (Desor 1972, Esser 1972). It has been demonstrated to engender negative affect, often generalizing to the source of stimulation and leading to avoidance behavior (Stokols 1972, 1976; Harrell et al. 1980).

Using the concept of overload, Milgram (1970) suggested that when the amount and rate of environmental input exceeds an individual's capacity to cope, behavioral adaptation strategies are enacted. Possible strategies include decreased time with each stimulus input (e.g., less exploratory and comparison shopping), disregard of low priority items (e.g., less browsing), and limited social interaction (e.g., with store personnel or other shoppers). Saegert (1973) found consumers shopping under crowded conditions less able to recall details about store layout and merchandise than consumers shopping in low density situations. Saegert et al. (1975) found that subjects performing a task under high density conditions described themselves as tense and confused, whereas those in low density conditions described themselves as pleased and relaxed.

Although engendering somewhat less research interest, it has also been suggested that *pricing* and *packaging* contribute to generalizable affect. Various emotional meanings and affective responses have been demonstrated to result from pricing cues (Fry and McDougall 1974, Jacoby and Olson 1977, Olson 1977, Zeithaml 1982). Product packaging is capable of communicating affective meanings through shape, color, illustration, and the like (Dichter 1975, Quelch and Cannon-Bonventre 1983).

Nonverbal Processing and Hemispheral Brain Lateralization

Because emotional value is noncognitive by nature, research pertaining to *nonverbal* or visual information processing is also relevant. Research in cognitive psychology suggests different modes of information processing for verbal versus nonverbal inputs. Further, the two processes lead to different types of response outputs, with pictorial processing engendering more emotive, affective, or noncognitive outputs.

The "dual coding hypothesis" (Paivio and Begg 1974; Paivio 1975, 1979) suggests that pictures tend to be perceived, processed, and stored *simultaneously* in an "imagery system," while words tend to be perceived, processed, and stored *sequentially* in an independent "verbal system." A similar proposition was advanced by Das et al. (1975, 1979) who, by factor analyzing aptitude test responses, found primarily verbal abilities to cluster together, presumably due to a shared reliance on sequential processing skills, and primarily spatial abilities to cluster together, presumably due to a shared reliance on simultaneous processing skills.

Directly related to research on nonverbal processing is a significant body of work on *hemispheral brain lateralization*, or the specialized functioning of the two sides of the human brain (Orstein 1972, Kimura 1973, Bogen 1977, Lindsay and Norman 1977, Geschwind 1979, McCallum 1979, McGee 1979, Wexler 1980, Hansen 1981, Hansen and Lundsgaard 1981, Rothschild et al. 1988). Considerable evidence suggests that the left hemisphere plays the dominant role in verbal information processing and is the center for logical, abstract, and conceptual thinking, while the right hemisphere plays the principal role in visual information processing and is the center for creative, intuitive, and imaginal thinking. While the left hemisphere provides the capacity to perceive consciously and report on these perceptions, information processed by the right hemisphere is often perceived unconsciously and is difficult to verbalize.

Under normal conditions, the two hemispheres work together, interacting through the connecting corpus callosum and allowing for rich mental ability. However, the specialized functioning of each of the brain hemispheres has been clearly observed in clinical settings where one side of a patient's brain has been temporarily inhibited or permanently impaired (Deglin 1976, Gazzaniga 1977, Wittrock et al. 1977). Further, even under normal conditions, one hemisphere is more likely to dominate depending on the nature of the task, and some theorists believe that individuals may be either left or right brain dominated (Rothschild et al. 1988).

Models of consumer judgment have traditionally assumed left brain thinking. It has been suggested, however, that right brain processes dominate where learning occurs in low involvement contexts and where evaluative judgments depend on aesthetics, taste, symbolic meaning, sensory experience, and other highly subjective or emotive phenomena (Krugman 1965, 1977, 1979; Hansen and Lundsgaard 1981; Hansen 1981; Holbrook and Moore 1981; Kassarjian 1982).

Building on Broadbent's "two-step theory of perception" (1977), Hansen (1981) advanced an integrative model of left and right brain information processing. According to his theory, material from advertising and other information sources is encoded and stored holistically or pictorially in the right hemisphere. Then, through the interaction of the two hemispheres, these holistic images are decoded. Information relating to salient attributes is processed and stored in the left hemisphere, and unedited holistic images continue to be stored in the right hemisphere. Finally, when faced with a buying decision, the individual may rely either on holistic images stored in the right hemisphere or on coded attributional information stored in the left.

In a more recent study, Rothschild et al. (1988) demonstrated through electroencephalograph (EEG) measures that hemispheric dominance may shift when subjects are exposed to verbal and nonverbal components of television commercials. The researchers found the right hemisphere to be more responsive to visual, musical, and abstract cues and the left hemisphere more responsive to verbal and concrete cues. Similarly, Janiszewski (1988), studying attitude formation toward unattended stimuli, found pictorial ads to be more preferred when placed to the left of a picture search task, thus inviting right hemispheral processing, and verbal ads to be more preferred when placed to the right, inviting left hemispheral processing.

Subliminal Perception

Subliminal perception pertains to the influence of stimuli presented below the threshold of conscious recognition or awareness (Dember 1960, Hart and McDaniel 1982). Subliminal stimuli include visual inputs presented for very brief durations, auditory inputs presented through accelerated speech or at low volume levels, and imbedded or hidden images or words in pictorial material (Moore 1982). Because subliminal perception does not involve cognitive awareness, it is affective by nature and therefore pertinent to emotional value.

A rich tradition of experimentation suggests that the threshold for conscious awareness or recognition is higher than the absolute threshold for effective perception, and that discrimination can occur without awareness (Pierce and Jastrow 1884; Miller 1939, 1940; McCleary and Lazarus 1949; McGinnies 1949; Lazarus and McCleary 1951; Adams 1957; McConnell et al. 1958; Nayler and Lawshe 1958; Bevan 1964; Dixon 1971, 1981; Erdelyi 1974; Janiszewski 1988). Further, substantial evidence suggests that subliminal stimuli are capable of producing psychological effects. Most notably, such stimuli can influence conscious perception, affective judgments, physiological drives, and emotions (Coover 1917; Collier 1940; Miller 1942; Bach and Klein 1957; Byrne 1959; Spence 1964; Zajonc 1968, 1980; Hawkins 1970; Silverman 1976; Zajonc and Markus 1982). Nevertheless, research on subliminal perception has always been controversial and subject to methodological criticism (Bruner and Postman 1947, 1948; Bricker and Chapanis 1953; Voor 1956; Wiener and Schiller 1960; Tsal 1985).

Awareness of subliminal stimuli was aroused in the late 1950s with the publicity surrounding an experiment by James M. Vicary (Brean 1958). Over a six-week period, more than 45,000 unsuspecting theater patrons were presented with two filmed messages; "Eat Popcorn" and "Drink Coca-Cola" flashed for a fraction of a second at five-second intervals. By comparing receipts during the test period with those from a previous period, it was reported that popcorn sales increased by 58 percent and Coca-Cola sales increased by 18 percent. The dramatic results led to ethical questions concerning the manipulative potential of subliminal advertising. However, because Vicary failed to provide even the most rudimentary scientific controls, many external factors may have influenced his results (McConnell et al. 1958, Barthol and Goldstein 1959). Further, subsequent efforts to replicate the findings did not succeed, and Vicary himself did not make available scientific data to support his conclusions.

Public interest in subliminal perception subsided for more than a decade until the issue was once again brought to the forefront by Key (1973, 1976, 1980). In his popular books, Key claimed to "document" the use of masked erotic and other emotionally charged cues in ads. He claimed that such cues are effective because they are not pronounced enough to produce selective attention and other defense mechanisms, but they are strong enough to arouse unconscious desires. However, the idea that subliminal advertising is as widespread as claimed by Key is questionable, and research on perception does not support his concerns about its potential consequences (Moore 1982). Laboratory experiments involving masked stimuli have, at best, demonstrated only very mild effects and no effect on brand recall or consumption behavior (Kelly 1979, Fowler et al. 1981).

Even though subliminal advertising has aroused public concern (Zanot et al. 1983), evidence suggests that its power is severely limited (Barthol and Goldstein 1959, Byrne 1959, Dixon 1971, Moore 1982). Although capable of producing psychological effects, most research indicates that subliminal messages produce very little or no behavioral change and have virtually no effect in directing consumers toward particular brands (DeFleur and Petranoff 1959, Hawkins 1970, George and Jennings 1975, Shevrin and Dickman 1980, Caccavale et al. 1982, Hart and McDaniel 1982). However, subliminal messages have been used to deter shoplifting, reduce anxiety, and motivate employees ("Secret Voices" 1979, Danzig 1980, Maxwell 1980). Saegert (1979), reviewing work in psychology, suggests that subliminal messages may influence consumers' specific desires, but only those already predisposed to act are likely to be affected.

To recapitulate, areas pertinent to our concept of emotional value include motivation research, personality, research on marketing and promotional mix variables, nonverbal processing and hemispheral brain lateralization, and subliminal perception. All share a concern with affective, as opposed to cognitive, determinants of behavior. *Motivation research* applied the concepts and techniques of clinical psychology to consumer behavior. The study of *personality* originated in clinical/personality psychology, and it has received substantial attention in consumer behavior. *Marketing and promotional mix variables* are widely researched in marketing, and researchers in consumer behavior and psychology have contributed specific findings. Finally, interest in *subliminal perception* and *nonverbal processing and hemispheral brain lateralization* originated in psychology, and the potential relevance to advertising is recognized by marketing and consumer researchers.

EPISTEMIC VALUE

The *epistemic value* of an alternative is derived from its capacity to provide novelty, arouse curiosity, and/or satisfy knowledge-seeking aspirations. Such utility is often derived from stimuli that are unfamiliar and somewhat ambiguous or complex.

As commonly defined, epistemic behavior involves the acquisition of general knowledge for future use. This is in contrast to the search for immediately useful information. A consumer driven by epistemic value may shop and even purchase without a current functional or other need. Much browsing, window shopping, and other recreational shopping is motivated by epistemic value. For example, a consumer without a specific need for new clothing may simply have a desire for something "new" or "different," or may just want to see what is currently in fashion. New technology and "gadgets" often appeal for the same reasons. While epistemic needs are usually defined as pertaining to curiosity and the desire for knowledge, we also include desires for novelty and complexity.

Our concept of epistemic value has been influenced by theory and research in personality and social psychology; in experimental, educational, and environmental psychology; in sociology and communications; in anthropology and economics; and in marketing and consumer behavior. Pertinent research areas include exploratory, variety-seeking, and novelty-seeking behavior; optimal arousal and stimulation; and innovativeness. Table 4-2 provides an overview of work cited by discipline. Further, as mentioned in Chapter 2, Maslow's self-actualization need, Katona's spiritual and artistic needs, and Katz's knowledge needs are all consistent with epistemic behavior. Hanna's personal growth need is also consistent with our concept.

Exploratory, Variety-Seeking, and Novelty-Seeking Behavior

The desire for novelty, variety, and exploration are well documented as motivating human behavior (Huizinga 1950; Cattell 1957; Stephenson 1967; Harrison 1968; Zuckerman 1971, 1979; Faison 1977, Jeuland 1978; Rogers 1979; Lancy 1980; Wallendorf and Zinkhan 1980; Raju 1981; Wallendorf et al. 1981; Holbrook and Hirschman 1982; McAlister and Pessemier 1982; Kahn et al. 1986); this desire has even been demonstrated to motivate animal behavior (Harlow et al. 1950, Butler 1954, Berlyne 1966). Thus, it is not surprising that curiosity and the simple desire to try something new underlie many consumer choices.

It has been suggested that exploratory, novelty-seeking, and variety-seeking motives activate product search, trial, and switching behaviors. For example, Katz and Lazarsfeld (1955) found that consumers often purchase new brands simply because they desire a change, and a study by Haines (1966) found 15 percent of respondents indicated that they had bought a product simply because it was new. Cox (1967) found a substantial amount of brand switching to be associated with satiation.

Howard and Sheth (1969) recognized that buying behavior is sometimes motivated by epistemic needs; they termed this phenomenon the "psychology of complication." Causal relationships were hypothesized between "stimulus ambiguity" (a function of novelty, complexity, and incongruity) and "arousal" (meaning alertness, excitedness, and wide-awakeness) and between arousal and increased attention to stimuli. Based on these relationships, exploratory behavior, termed "overt search," was predicted.

The early work of Howard and Sheth (1969) was closely followed by contributions from other consumer researchers. Also originating a comprehensive theory of buying behavior, Hansen (1972) suggested that consumer choice results from both deliberation and exploration. Whereas deliberation involves previously available information, exploration involves the acquisition and assessment of new information. Copley and Callom (1971) found a small amount of stimulus ambiguity to increase product search among industrial buyers, and they explained this finding in terms of curiosity. Venkatesan (1973) suggested that consumers attempt to maintain an optimal level of stimulation, with novelty-seeking and variety-seeking serving to ameliorate conditions of understimulation.

Hirschman (1980a) suggested that novelty-seeking consists of both exploratory behavior and variety-seeking behavior. Exploratory behavior relates to the search for new and potentially discrepant information, and variety-seeking behavior relates to the alternating of choice among known stimuli. Hirschman (1980a,b) further suggested that novelty-seeking serves a very practical purpose. Faced with an unpredictable future, many

Table 4-2   Epistemic value: traditions, disciplines, authors

	Anthropology and economics	Environmental psychology	Personality and social psychology	Experimental and educational psychology	Sociology and communications	Marketing and consumer behavior
Exploratory, variety-seeking, and novelty-seeking behavior	Huizinga 1950 Lancy 1980		Cattell 1957 Hunt 1963 Berlyne 1966 Harrison 1968	Harlow et al. 1950 Butler 1954	Katz/Lazarsfeld 1955 Stephenson 1967	Haines 1966 Cox 1967 Howard/Sheth 1969 Copley/Callom 1971 Hansen 1972 Venkatesan 1973 Faison 1977 Jeuland 1978 Rogers 1979 Hirschman 1980a,b Wallendorf/Zinkhan 1980 Raju 1981 Wallendorf et al. 1981 Holbrook/Hirschman 1982 McAlister/Pessemier 1982 Kahn et al. 1986
Optimal arousal and stimulation		Mehrabian/Russell 1973, 1974	Frenkel-Brunswick 1949 Barron 1952, 1953 Eysenck 1953, 1973 Berlyne 1960, 1963, 1966, 1969, 1970, 1971 Bieri 1961 Fiske/Maddi 1961 Maddi 1961, 1968 Cattell 1966 Dent/Simmel 1968 Kish/Busse 1968 Bone/Montgomery 1970 Philipp/Wilde 1970 Kish/Donnenwerth 1972 Segal 1973 Waters 1974	Bexton et al. 1954 Dember/Earl 1957 Dember et al. 1957 Howard 1961 Garlington/Shimota 1964 Zuckerman et al. 1964 Acker/McReynolds 1965, 1967 Farley/Farley 1967 Zuckerman/Link 1968 Davies et al. 1969 Loft 1971 Looft/Baronowski 1971 Coombs/Avrunin 1977 Zuckerman 1971, 1979		Driver/Streufert 1965 Howard/Sheth 1969 Venkatesan 1973 Mittelstaedt et al. 1976 Faison 1977 Cacioppo/Petty 1979 Raju 1980, 1981 Wallendorf/Zinkhan 1980 Sawyer 1981 Wallendorf et al. 1981 Belch 1982 Joachimsthaler/Lastovicka 1984 Rethans et al. 1986 Cox/Cox 1988

Table 4-2   (continued)

	Anthropology and economics	Environ-mental psychology	Personality and social psychology	Experimental and educational psychology	Sociology and communi-cations	Marketing and consumer behavior
Innovativeness	Barnet 1953 Robinson 1961				Rogers 1961, 1962, 1971, 1983 Bendix 1967 Gusfield 1967 Rogers/ Shoemaker 1971 Smith/Inkeles 1975 Suzman 1977 Armer/Isaac 1978 Fischer 1978	Robertson/Myers 1969 Jacoby 1971 Robertson 1971 Donnelly/Etzel 1973 Mazis/Sweeney 1973 Szybillo 1973 Craig/Ginter 1975 Leavitt/Walton 1975 Fromkin 1976 Midgley/Dowling 1978 Hirschman 1980a Wallendorf/Zinkhan 1980

consumers routinely seek out information which, although not presently useful, could very well assume future importance. A good example is constant attention to interest rates during an unpredictable economy. Then, having this stored information, consumers are better equipped to handle new and novel problems as they arise. As a contrasting point of view, in social psychology, Hunt (1963) contended that novel stimuli are necessarily incongruent with previous cognitions and suggested that heightened attention to these stimuli serves as a means of resolving the incongruence.

Optimal Arousal and Stimulation

It is clear that minimal levels of stimulation are necessary for normal human functioning. For example, it has been found that people will hallucinate (a form of involuntary self-stimulation) when environmental stimulation is dramatically reduced (Bexton et al. 1954). However, psychological research and theory goes beyond this, suggesting that individuals are motivated by the need to maintain an *optimal* level of arousal, stimulation, or complexity. This implies that individuals are therefore *attracted* to novel and complex stimuli (Dember and Earl 1957; Dember et al. 1957; Berlyne 1960, 1966, 1970; Fiske and Maddi 1961; Maddi 1961, 1968; Garlington and Shimota 1964). This view is largely accepted in marketing and consumer behavior, and it has direct implications for consumer choice behavior (Howard and Sheth 1969, Venkatesan 1973, Raju 1980, Wallendorf and Zinkhan 1980, Wallendorf et al. 1981; cf., Joachimsthaler and Lastovicka 1984).

One of the most significant contributors to the study of optimal stimulation and arousal has been Berlyne (1960, 1963, 1966, 1970, 1971). According to Berlyne, the level of arousal experienced by an individual is a function of the properties or "arousal potential" of the environmental stimuli with which he or she is confronted. Berlyne contended that individuals are driven to maintain an optimal or intermediate level of stimulation. Below the optimal point, the individual seeks additional arousal. Beyond the optimal point, arousal potential is overwhelming and the individual seeks to reduce the level of stimulation.

Berlyne's "two-factor theory" (1970) suggests two possible effects from repeated exposure to stimuli. The first, "positive habituation," increases positive affect because the repeated exposure moves the higher-than-optimal arousal potential back toward the optimal level. The second, "tedium," decreases positive affect as the repeated exposure moves the arousal potential to a lower-than-optimal level. To illustrate, Berlyne found liking for complex stimuli to increase with repeated exposure, and liking of simple stimuli to decrease. Thus, Berlyne saw the relationship between arousal potential and preference as curvilinear, or "inverted U-shaped."

A large number of researchers in psychology and consumer behavior similarly view the relationship between stimulation and the propensity toward arousal, liking, or preference as inverted U-shaped, M-shaped, single-peaked, curvilinear, or some variant of these (Eysenck 1953, 1973; Venkatesan 1973; Coombs and Avrunin 1977; Faison 1977; Cacioppo and Petty 1979; Raju 1980, 1981; Sawyer 1981; Belch 1982, Rethans et al. 1986, Cox and Cox 1988). While these authors may disagree on the *precise* nature of the functional relationship, there does seem to be consensus that it is nonmonotonic with one or more optimal points in the intermediate range.

Driver and Streufert (1965) applied the principles of "incongruity theory" to optimal stimulation. According to this theory, an individual experiences incongruity when information received disagrees with one or more stored concepts. As explained by the authors, an individual comes to expect a certain level of incongruity on the basis of past experience. A greater or lesser amount results in discomfort and a drive to restore the expected level.

Research in psychology and consumer behavior has suggested that arousal-seeking and stimulation-seeking tendencies vary significantly across individuals (Frenkel-Brunswick 1949; Barron 1952, 1953; Bieri 1961; Howard 1961; Dent and Simmel 1968; Kish and Busse 1968; Davies et al. 1969; Looft 1971; Zuckerman 1971, 1979; Kish and Donnenwerth 1972). A number of instruments have been developed for measuring these and similar attributes (Zuckerman et al. 1964; Acker and McReynolds 1965, 1967; Zuckerman and Link 1968; Looft and Baranowski 1971; Mehrabian and Russell 1973, 1974; Waters 1974). Attempts have been made to relate stimulation-seeking and arousal-seeking proclivities to other psychological traits. Authors such as Maddi (1961) and Berlyne (1970) have suggested that optimal stimulation and variety-seeking behavior are related to flexibility, breadth of interest, tolerance for ambiguity, and preference for complexity versus simplicity. Optimal stimulation has also been found to be positively related to extroversion, and to be negatively related to neuroticism, anxiety, rigidity, and dogmatism (Cattell 1966; Farley and Farley 1967, Bone and Montgomery 1970, Philipp and Wilde 1970, Mehrabian and Russell 1973, Segal 1973, Raju 1980).

Preferred levels of stimulation and arousal have been found to directly affect consumption and buying behavior. For example, Raju (1980) found that, as compared with those preferring less stimulation, consumers with high optimal stimulation levels exhibited a greater desire to receive information, to experience unfamiliar alternatives, and to alternate experience among familiar alternatives. Mittelstaedt et al. (1976) found consumers with high optimal stimulation levels to be more aware of new products and retail facilities, and more likely to evaluate, try, and eventually adopt new products. Further, these consumers generally let a shorter amount of time lapse between awareness and trial. The authors suggested that consumers who prefer a high level of stimulation may evaluate new products by trying them, whereas others evaluate products prior to trial.

Innovativeness

Innovativeness, in a consumer behavior context, refers to the propensity to adopt *new products and services*. As discussed by Hirschman (1980a):

> If there were no such characteristics as innovativeness, consumer behavior would consist of a series of routine buying responses to a static set of products. The inherent willingness of a consuming population to innovate is what gives the marketplace its dynamic nature. On an individual basis, every consumer is, to some extent, an innovator; all of us over the course of our lives adopt some objects or ideas that are new in our perception. (p. 283)

It appears that the "willingness to innovate" discussed by Hirschman is motivated, at least in part, by epistemic value.

Rogers and Shoemaker defined consumer innovativeness as "the degree to which an individual is relatively earlier in adopting an innovation than other members of a social system" (1971, p. 27); Midgley and Dowling defined it as "the degree to which an individual is receptive to new ideas and makes innovation decisions independently of the communicated experience of others" (1978, p. 236). Szybillo (1973) suggested that the tendency to buy new products results from a desire for self-expression, and Fromkin (1976) suggested that innovativeness expresses a desire to see the self as differing in a socially acceptable way from peers. In economics, Robinson (1961) noted that the consumer who possesses scarce commodities is afforded an acceptable means of expressing individuality.

Hirschman (1980a), reviewing several definitions of innovativeness, noted the close relationship between innovativeness and novelty seeking:

> ... these definitions [of innovativeness] reveal that they are closely related to the constructs of inherent and actualized novelty seeking. The desire to seek out the new and different (i.e., inherent novelty seeking) is conceptually indistinguishable from the willingness to adopt new products (i.e., inherent innovativeness). Especially when one defines products in their broad sense, it becomes apparent that new products may constitute new information. ... Thus, a consumer who expresses a willingness to adopt a new product is necessarily also expressing a desire for novel information. ... (p. 284)

It is clear that some individuals are generally more innovative—open to new products, experiences, and ideas—than are others (Barnet 1953;

Rogers 1961, 1962, 1971, 1983; Bendix 1967; Gusfield 1967; Donnelly and Etzel 1973; Smith and Inkeles 1975; Suzman 1977; Armer and Isaac 1978; Fischer 1978; Wallendorf and Zinkhan 1980). Further, innovativeness has been conceptualized as a relatively enduring personality trait (Robertson and Myers 1969, Jacoby 1971, Craig and Ginter 1975, Leavitt and Walton 1975). Robertson (1971) related innovativeness to venturesomeness, and Mazis and Sweeney (1973) related it to tolerance for ambiguity. As summarized by Rogers (1983), innovativeness has also been found to be positively related to the ability to deal with abstractions, the ability to cope with uncertainty, and favorableness toward change, education, and science.

As shown, our concept of epistemic value has been influenced by interdisciplinary theory and research on exploratory, variety-seeking, and novelty-seeking behavior; optimal arousal and stimulation; and innovativeness. These areas all share in common a concern with the human tendency to seek out new and varied experience. *Exploratory, variety-seeking, and novelty-seeking behavior* and *optimal arousal and stimulation* have been studied in various branches of psychology, and their relevance to consumer choice is widely recognized in marketing and consumer behavior. *Innovativeness* has received attention in sociology and communications, and it has been recognized by marketing and consumer researchers to impact the propensity of consumers to try new products.

CONDITIONAL VALUE

The *conditional value* of an alternative is derived from its capacity to provide *temporary functional or social value* in the context of a specific and transient set of circumstances or contingencies. An alternative selected on the basis of conditional value acquires utility from its association with the antecedent situation. It simply does not possess the same degree of utility outside that situation. In other words, the alternative provides *extrinsic* rather than intrinsic utility. Thus, when a choice is driven by conditional value, the outcome is contingent on antecedent circumstances that may cause the consumer to deviate from her or his typical or planned behavior.

It should be emphasized that conditional value is *necessarily* transient in nature. An alternative offering conditional value frequently has little worth to the consumer until faced with the specific set of circumstances that give rise to its purchase. For example, prior to the onset of a specific illness, a consumer generally has no need or desire for the prescription medicine used in its treatment. Further, he or she rarely has use for it after recovery. As an example involving social value, a Christmas tree offers considerable value in December as a symbol of the celebration of

Christmas, but its display at any other time of year actually denotes negative social value.

Even when an alternative does provide utility independent of the specific situation, *conditional value* is created by the *pressure* of that situation. For example, a consumer may prefer a particular brand of beer and plan to purchase it. However, finding another acceptable brand at a special sale price, the consumer may purchase that brand instead, thereby obtaining conditional functional value from the temporarily reduced price. A conditional functional value could also be obtained when a price is high if, for example, the beer is being purchased for guests and the consumer buys a more expensive imported brand in honor of the special occasion.

Our concept of conditional value has been influenced by theory and research from environmental psychology and geography, experimental and educational psychology, social psychology, sociology, economics, and marketing and consumer behavior. Pertinent research areas include the effects of situational contingencies, classifications of situational characteristics, and research specifically focusing on antecedent states, physical surroundings, social surroundings, task definition, and temporal perspective. Table 4-3 (pages 72–73) provides an overview of the work cited.

Effects of Situational Contingencies

Situational analysis is an area of increasing interest to consumer researchers. Recognizing that behavior often cannot be accurately predicted on the basis of attitude or intention alone, a number of researchers during the 1970s began to investigate the predictive ability of situational factors (Belk 1973, 1974, 1975a,b; Sheth 1974a; Park 1976; Bearden and Woodside 1977). There appears now to be general agreement that choice behavior is affected by the situation antecedent to purchase (Sheth 1973a, Russell and Mehrabian 1976, Cote et al. 1985).

Sells (1963), in experimental psychology, proposed that the total variance of any response depends in part on the stimulus characteristics of the environment or situation. Similarly, Rokeach (1968), in social psychology, maintained that behavior toward an object depends both on attitude toward the object and attitude toward the situation.

As a major contributor to research on situational effects, Belk (1974) defined the situation as:

> . . . all those factors particular to a time and place of observation which do not follow from a knowledge of personal (intra-individual) and stimulus (choice alternative) attributes, and which have a demonstrable and systematic effect on current behavior. It should be noted that this definition describes situation in terms of observable aggregate effects rather than in terms of similarities in individual perceptions of situations. (p. 156)

Credit for advancing the idea that consumer choice is dependent on situational factors should go to John Howard. In his classic textbook, Howard (1963) recognized the importance of "stimulus dynamism," a concept borrowed from learning theory. As advanced by Hull (1943), stimulus dynamism explains learning that takes place as a result of experience with a given situation.

Howard and Sheth (1969) extended Howard's earlier work by defining the construct *inhibitors* as external or "noninternalized" forces that impede buyers' preferences. Specifically, Howard and Sheth saw inhibitors as limiting the power of attitude to determine actual behavior. The authors identified two classes of inhibitors as those coming from the buyer's immediate environment and those carried on from past environments.

The concept of inhibitors was more formally developed by Sheth (1974a) in his model of attitude-behavior relationship. Sheth conceptualized inhibitors as both *anticipated situations* and *unexpected events*. Anticipated situations are conditions predicted by the consumer to exist at the time of purchase, and unexpected events are antecedent and contiguous occurrences that unpredictably impinge at the time of purchase. Thus, Sheth saw behavioral intention as a function of anticipated situations as well a function of attitude and social norms. Behavior was seen as a function of unexpected events as well as behavioral intention (cf., Fishbein and Ajzen 1975). The inclusion of the variable "facilitating conditions" in Triandis's attitude-behavior model (1971) represents a similar perspective.

A growing base of empirical research exists relevant to situational effects and consumer choice. Providing substantial impetus for further research, an early experiment conducted by Sandell (1968) found nearly 40 percent of choice variance explained by the interaction between situation and alternative, and another nearly 30 percent was explained by the three-way interaction between situation, alternative, and individual. In social psychology, Bishop and Witt (1970) examined situational effects as they impact choice of leisure activities.

Belk (1973, 1974) adapted the Behavioral Differential Inventory developed by Triandis, and he used it to assess situational effects relevant to choice of snack foods, meats, and movies. He found situational main effects and interactions to explain 15 to 20 percent of variance in choice of snack foods, and nearly 35 percent of variance in choice of meats. However, he found little situational effect in choice of movies. Thus, Belk concluded that situational effect varies by product class.

A study by Bearden and Woodside (1977) demonstrated that purchase intention can depend both on attitude toward the choice object and on situational considerations. While attitude was found to explain a large amount of variance in purchase intention, predictive ability was increased significantly when the consumption situation was also considered.

Table 4-3   Conditional value: traditions, disciplines, authors

	Experimental and educational psychology	Sociology	Social psychology	Environmental psychology and geography	Marketing and consumer behavior
Effects of situational contingencies	Hull 1943 Sells 1963		Rokeach 1968 Triandis 1971 Bishop/Witt 1970	Russell/Mehrabian 1976	Howard 1963 Sandell 1968 Howard/Sheth 1969 Belk 1973, 1974, 1975a,b Sheth 1973a, 1974a Park 1975 Vincent/Zikmund 1976 Bearden/Woodside 1977 Srivastava et al. 1978 Miller/Ginter 1979 Dickson 1982 Hornik 1982 Cote et al. 1985
Classifications of situational characteristics	Sells 1963 Wolf 1966 Frederickson 1972		Sherif/Sherif 1956 Sargent et al. 1958 Bellows 1963 Allen 1965 Moos 1973	Kasmar 1970	Belk 1975a Srivastava et al. 1978 Belk 1979
Antecedent states			Kelley 1957 Weiner 1986	Mehrabian/Russell 1973, 1974	Fennell 1975 Lutz/Kakkar 1975 Mizerski et al. 1979 Hanna 1980 Reibstein et al. 1980 Holbrook/Hirschma 1982 Zajonc/Markus 1982 Andreasen 1984 Gardner 1985 Zaichkowsky 1985 Laurent/Kapferer 1985 Batra/Ray 1986 Havlena/Holbrook 1986 Peterson et al. 1986 Edell/Burke 1987 Goldberg/Gorn 1987 Holbrook/Batra 1987 Folkes 1988
Physical surroundings		Durkheim 1951 Kerner Comm. 1968	Griffitt 1970 Milgran 1970 Griffitt/Veitch 1971 Moos 1976 Bell 1981	Auliciums 1972 Stokols 1972, 1976 Saegert 1973 Saegert et al. 1975 Altman/Wohlwill 1976 Holahan 1978 Schneider et al. 1980 Breen-Lewis/Wilding 1984 Howarth/Hoffman 1984	Harrell et al. 1980

Table 4-3 (continued)

	Economics	Experimental and educational psychology	Sociology	Social psychology	Environmental psychology and geography	Marketing and consumer behavior
Social surroundings		Sells 1963		Sherif/Sherif 1956 Sargent et al. 1958 Rokeach 1968 Triandis 1971	Lewin 1935, 1936	Ferber/Lee 1974 Sheth 1974b Davis 1976 Nicosia/Mayer 1976 Wind 1976 Calder/Burnkrant 1977 Szybillo et al. 1979 Filiatrault/Ritchie 1980 Thomas 1982 Zielinski/Robertson 1982 Krishnamurthi 1983 Spiro 1983 Qualls 1987
Task definition	Katona 1975 Morgan 1980				Barker 1966	Robinson et al. 1967 Howard/Sheth 1969 Webster/Wind 1972 Sheth 1973a Belk 1976 Lussier/Olshavsky 1979 Johnston/Bonoma 1981 Sherry 1983 Wilton/Myers 1986 Engel et al. 1986
Temporal perspective					Folkard 1979 Breen-Lewis/Wilding 1984	Howard 1963 Howard/Sheth 1969 Schary 1971 Jacoby et al. 1976 Berry 1979 Voss/Blackwell 1979 Holman/Wilson 1980, 1982 Feldman/Hornik 1981 Graham 1981 Holbrook/Lehmann 1981 Nickols/Fox 1983 Gross 1987 Hirschman 1987 Hornik 1988

Similarly, Cote et al. (1985) found behavior-intention inconsistency to be partially attributable to unexpected situations.

Miller and Ginter (1979) examined situational effects on choice of fast food. Consistent with hypothesis, they found both purchase levels and perceptions of the alternative fast-food establishments to vary significantly by choice situation (weekday lunch, snack during shopping trip, or rushed evening meal). The importance of various attributes (convenience, speed of service, menu variety, and popularity with children) also varied by situation. Other empirical research has found buying situation to impact perceived risk (Vincent and Zikmund 1976); usage situation to influence perception of product markets (Srivastava et al. 1978); and situational variables to affect consumers' selection of judgment models (Park 1976) and consumers' time allocation, particularly to discretionary activities (Hornik 1982).

Recognizing that situational contingencies affect choice behavior, Dickson (1982) developed the concept of "person-situation market segmentation." He argued that effective market segmentation requires knowledge of the "what, when, where, how, and why" of demand. More specifically, because demand results from the interaction of the individual with the environment, market segmentation needs to consider both the person and the situation faced by the person. Dickson recommended segmenting markets into consumer groups (such as demographic groups or socioeconomic groups) within consumption or usage situations.

Classifications of Situational Characteristics

A number of authors from various branches of psychology have attempted to provide comprehensive taxonomies of situational characteristics. Some have focused primarily on the social situation (Sherif and Sherif 1956, Sargent et al. 1958, Bellows 1963, Allen 1965), while others have attempted to identify universal situational characteristics (Sells 1963, Wolf 1966, Kasmar 1970, Frederickson 1972, Moos 1973). All have identified characteristics that are pertinent to consumer choice behavior.

Based on a review of earlier work, Belk (1975a, p. 159) suggested the following situational taxonomy as specifically relevant to consumer behavior:

1. *Antecedent States*: "These are momentary moods (such as acute anxiety, pleasantness, hostility, and excitation) or momentary conditions (such as cash on hand, fatigue, and illness) rather than chronic individual traits. These conditions are further stipulated to be immediately antecedent to the current situation. . . ."

2. *Physical Surroundings*: "These features include geographical and institutional location, decor, sounds, aromas, lighting, weather, and visible configurations of merchandise or other material surrounding the stimulus object."

3. *Social Surroundings*: "Other persons present, their characteristics, their apparent roles, and interpersonal interactions occurring are potentially relevant examples."

4. *Task Definition*: ". . . include an intent or requirement to select, shop for, or obtain information about a general or specific purchase. In addition, task may reflect different buyer and user roles anticipated by the individual."

5. *Temporal Perspective*: ". . . may be specified in units ranging from time of day to season of the year. Time may also be measured relative to some past or future event for the situational participant. This allows conceptions such as time since last purchase, time since or until meals or payday, and time constraints imposed by prior or standing commitments."

Finally, Srivastava et al. (1978) worked toward the development of a product-specific usage-situation taxonomy, an approach also advocated by Belk (1979). The authors concluded that a parsimonious classification can be constructed on the basis of behavioral criteria.

Not surprisingly, at least a moderate base of research exists relevant to each of the situational categories delineated by Belk (1975a). The following sections provide a limited review of research pertinent to each.

Antecedent States. Antecedent states refer to the consumer's internal or psychological condition at, or immediately preceding, the time of choice. These states may be considered synonymous with the *psychological situation*. As proponents of increased focus on the psychological situation, Lutz and Kakkar (1975) defined it as:

> . . . an individual's internal responses to, or interpretations of, all factors particular to a time and place of observation which are not stable intra-individual characteristics or stable environmental characteristics, and which have a demonstrable and systematic effect on the individual's psychological processes and/or his overt behavior. (p. 441)

Influenced by the work of Mehrabian and Russell (1973, 1974) in environmental psychology, Lutz and Kakkar envisioned the external situation as being mediated by three internal state variables: pleasure, arousal, and dominance.

Lutz and Kakkar (1975) replicated Belk's (1974a,b) empirical work on external situational effects, specifically examining the explanatory power of the three internal state variables. The authors found explanatory power to be increased substantially when internal state variables were included.

Other research relevant to antecedent states includes inquiry into consumer mood states (Gardner 1985), level of involvement (Laurent and Kapferer 1985, Zaichkowsky 1985), attributions (Kelley 1967, Mizerski et al. 1979, Weiner 1986, Folkes 1988), openness to change (Andreasen 1984), motives (Fennell 1975, Hanna 1980), and emotion or affective states (Reibstein et al. 1980, Holbrook and Hirschman 1982, Zajonc and Markus 1982, Batra and Ray 1986, Havlena and Holbrook 1986, Peterson et al. 1986, Edell and Burke 1987, Goldberg and Gorn 1987, Holbrook and Batra 1987). It is apparent that temporary psychological states strongly influence consumer choice.

Physical Surroundings.   Behavioral and affective response to physical surroundings has aroused interest across disciplines (Altman and Wohlwill 1976, Holahan 1978). For example, the effects of ambient temperature have been investigated by scholars in sociology, social psychology, and environmental psychology.

The French sociologist Emile Durkheim found during the late nineteenth century that the suicide rate in Europe followed a definite seasonal pattern. A significantly greater number of suicides occurred during the hot summer months than during any other time of year (Durkheim 1951, Moos 1976). Similarly, in the United States, the National Advisory Commission on Civil Disorders (Kerner Commission, 1968) found that in 90 percent of riot incidents, violence erupted on days on which temperatures reached into the nineties. In contrast, temperatures on the preceding days had been only in the eighties. Griffitt (1970), in social psychology, found a negative relationship between ambient temperature, interpersonal attraction, and other interpersonal affect. He inferred that a broad class of social behaviors may be negatively affected by high temperatures.

Bell (1981) reviewed and analyzed research on the effects of ambient temperature, concluding that very high temperatures are associated with discomfort, narrow attention span, and either increased or decreased arousal. In turn, these states foster reduced levels of attraction, helping behavior, performance, and aggression. Schneider et al. (1980) similarly found temperature to affect helping behavior. Howarth and Hoffman (1984) related ten affective variables to eight weather variables, finding temperature, humidity, and hours of sunshine to significantly affect mood and degree of anxiety, concentration, and skepticism. Aulicieums (1972) found work efficiency and performance to be favorably affected by cool, mild, and dry weather.

Other work relevant to the physical situation has focused on such variables as population density (Griffitt and Veitch 1971), noise (Breen-Lewis and Wilding 1984), and crowding (Milgram 1970; Stokols 1972,

1976; Saegert 1973; Saegert et al. 1975; Harrell et al. 1980). For example, Griffitt and Veitch (1971) found population density to negatively impact interpersonal affect (measured in terms of liking versus disliking other persons). A series of six volumes edited by Altman and Wohlwill (1976) demonstrates the breadth of research on the physical environment and its influence on behavior. Integrating work across disciplines and research traditions, the series provides an excellent overview of theoretical perspectives and empirical work.

Social Surroundings. A number of researchers from various branches of psychology have focused specifically on social situational effects. Early contributions include those of Sherif and Sherif (1956) and Sargent et al. (1958), identifying social situational characteristics that impact behavior. Among the most significant is the work of Kurt Lewin (1935, 1936), a psychologist well known for his "field theory." Lewin viewed the individual and the environment as interdependent. He argued that behavior is a function of the antecedent situation or "life space" of the individual, defining life space as the totality of the individual's world as he or she perceives it.

Another significant contributor, Sells (1963), in experimental psychology, examined the effects of environmental setting on both individual and group behavior, proposing that behavior results from interaction with the physical and social environments. Sells' work in developing a set of situational measurement scales represents a notable contribution. Finally, in social psychology, both Rokeach (1968) and Triandis (1971) are well-known proponents of situational focus, with their attention being primarily on the social environment.

A number of consumer researchers have called for greater attention to social phenomena and sociological perspectives on consumer behavior (Nicosia and Mayer 1976, Zielinski and Robertson 1982). Further, consumer research has given attention to such relevant topics as interpersonal influence (Calder and Burnkrant 1977, Thomas 1982) and family member influence (Ferber and Lee 1974, Sheth 1974b, Davis 1976, Wind 1976, Szybillo et al. 1979, Filiatrault and Ritchie 1980, Krishnamurthi 1983, Spiro 1983, Qualls 1987).

Task Definition. Observers of economic behavior have traditionally focused on the buying task. For example, Katona (1975), in consumption economics, observed that situational influences, as opposed to personal characteristics, foster seemingly "irrational" purchasing behavior. According to Katona:

> The instances in which people purchased major household goods without taking alternatives into consideration and with practically no information seeking or discussion were not determined by age, education, or income of the buyers. (p. 23)

Katona went on to delineate those task situations in which this seemingly irrational behavior occurred:

> The first was the presence of a special opportunity to make a purchase as perceived by the buyer. Availability of a desired article through friends, or through "sales," or through a persuasive salesman are examples of situations in which some people proceeded without careful deliberation. . . . Urgent need was another situation in which the absence of careful deliberation was found. When people felt they could not afford to wait, their purchasing process differed substantially from decision making in other circumstances. (p. 23)

Influenced by Katona's work, Morgan (1980) similarly expressed the idea that economic behavior is impacted by the task situation.

Also relevant to task definition, Barker (1968), in environmental psychology, discussed the "behavioral setting" as an influence on behavior. He defined the behavioral setting as being bounded by a complete sequence of behavioral patterns and, in turn, defined these behavioral patterns as expected actions in given situations.

A number of authors in marketing and consumer behavior have specifically focused on judgment and buying task definitions (Robinson et al. 1967, Howard and Sheth 1969, Webster and Wind 1972, Sheth 1973a, Lussier and Olshavsky 1979, Johnston and Bonoma 1981, Wilton and Myers 1986); significant research attention has been given to the tasks of problem recognition, product search, evaluation, and purchase (Engel et al. 1986). Further, a few have focused on more specific tasks, such as gift buying (Belk 1976, Sherry 1983).

Temporal Perspective.   Finally, temporal perspectives or temporal situations have been demonstrated to affect behavior. Howard (1963) suggested that an individual consumer under time pressure is likely to engage in vigorous product search, with this search likely to be less effective, more stereotyped, and more wrought with perceptual bias than search not impacted by such time pressure. Expanding on this idea, Howard and Sheth (1969) included "time pressure" as an exogenous variable in their theory of buyer behavior. The authors hypothesized that buyers under time pressure are less likely than others to try new brands.

Folkard (1979), in psychology, examined the relationship between retention and the time of day at which material is presented. He concluded that time of day effects may be mediated by spontaneous shifts in mode of cognitive processing. Subjects appeared to place more reliance on maintenance processing in the morning and engage in more elaborate processing in the evening. Similarly, Breen-Lewis and Wilding (1984) examined the effects of time of testing on recall, finding that test expectations had no effect on recall in the morning but did in the afternoon. Hornik (1988), in consumer behavior, examined the effects of time of day on advertising recall and recognition, finding that immediate recognition and recall declined across the day and that delayed recognition scores were significantly higher in the late afternoon than in the early morning. However, time of day had no effect on purchase intention.

The consumer behavior literature has also given attention to such relevant topics as time scarcity, time allocation, and temporal perception (Schary 1971, Jacoby et al. 1976, Feldman and Hornik 1981, Graham 1981, Holbrook and Lehmann 1981, Nickols and Fox 1983, Gross 1987, Hirschman 1987). It is suggested that the temporal situation directly affects product choice and shopping strategies (Berry 1979; Voss and Blackwell 1979; Holman and Wilson 1980, 1982).

This section has shown how our concept of conditional value has been influenced by interdisciplinary theory and research on situational contingencies and situational characteristics. Common to these topics is a concern with antecedent circumstances that impact subsequent behavior. Research on the *effects of situational contingencies* has been advanced in consumer behavior and psychology. Demonstrating that behavior cannot be accurately predicted on the basis of attitude or intention alone, such research has led to efforts to develop *classifications of situational characteristics*. Situational influences on consumer choice have been identified as *antecedent states* (internal or psychological conditions), *physical surroundings* (physical or atmospheric features), *social surroundings* (presence of others who influence choice), *task definition* (the nature and requirements of the choice task), and *temporal perspective* (the structure and constraints of time). Relevant interdisciplinary research exists pertinent to each.

SUMMARY

This chapter has provided an overview of interdisciplinary literature pertaining to emotional value, epistemic value, and conditional value. As contrasted with functional and social values, the values discussed in this chapter have traditionally received less recognition as drivers of market choice. However, as evidenced by a growing body of literature, concepts subsumed by these values are receiving increased attention.

Our emotional value construct has been influenced by motivation research, personality, research on marketing and promotional mix variables, nonverbal processing and hemispheral brain lateralization, and subliminal perception. Researchers in various branches of psychology and in marketing and consumer behavior have advanced substantial contributions.

Similarly, our epistemic value construct has been influenced by theory and research on exploratory, variety-seeking, and novelty-seeking behavior; on optimal arousal and stimulation; and on innovativeness. The bulk of research has been contributed by authors working in various branches of psychology, in sociology and communications, and in marketing and consumer behavior.

Finally, our conditional value construct has been influenced by theory and research on situational contingencies, including antecedent states, physical surroundings, social surroundings, task definition, and temporal perspective. Pertinent work has been advanced from various branches of psychology (including experimental, educational, environmental and social psychology), sociology, geography, economics, and marketing and consumer behavior.

Next, Chapter 5 discusses operationalization and data collection. Considerations involved in measuring each of the five values are discussed, and a standardized or "generic" questionnaire format is provided. Further, sample questionnaires are provided and recommendations are offered pertaining to measurement and data collection.

PART 2
GUIDANCE FOR
APPLICATIONS

5
OPERATIONALIZATION
AND DATA COLLECTION

This chapter provides guidance for operationalizing the theory. It supplies essential tools so that the reader may collect data relevant to choice situations of interest. Examples are provided to clarify how the theory works in practice.

MEASUREMENT

In operationalizing the theory, we have developed a standardized or "generic" questionnaire format as well as a standardized procedure for adapting the format to any specific market choice situation. The procedure and format have been utilized in approximately 200 applications focusing on a diversity of choice situations. As examples, the theory has been applied to "buy versus no-buy" or "use versus do not use" choices regarding food stamps, bowling, cocaine, X-rated movies, computer dating, and sporting events attendance; to product type choices involving alternative types of automobiles (e.g., sports cars, luxury cars), music (e.g., classical, jazz), and television shows (e.g., detective shows, situation comedies); and to brand choice situations involving such products as toothpaste, aspirin, chewing gum, cereal, pens, and automobiles.

Although a generic questionnaire format has been developed, the specifics associated with each choice situation are unique. Thus, measurement is choice- or application-specific. The *specific* questions to be asked will vary from one choice situation to the next.

For example, the decision whether to buy a home—a "buy versus no-buy" choice—involves a different set of considerations as compared with the decision to buy a condominium versus a single-family home—a product type decision. The "buy versus no-buy" decision might be based on such functional concerns as the desire to build equity and the desire for more space, or on emotional value pertaining to financial security and family stability. On the other hand, the product type decision might be based on functional value pertaining to size, location, and cost, or on social value relating to the "type of people" who live in condominiums versus single-family homes. Furthermore, both of these decisions differ considerably from a "brand" choice between two condominiums of comparable cost in the same neighborhood. "Brand" choice might be based on functional value pertaining to floor plans, size, available financing, and amenities and fixtures; or on conditional value pertaining to expected move-in date, special incentives, and the like.

Specific values likely to be considered in a particular choice situation, and which therefore should be included in the questionnaire, may be determined by interviewing consumers during the pilot study phase of the research. As discussed later in this chapter, focus group interviews are recommended. The following sections describe the measurement of the five values.

Functional Value

Functional value is measured on a profile of *product attributes* relating to pertinent functional, utilitarian, or physical *benefits and problems*. For example, in a brand choice study involving two competing automobile makes, focus group interviews with car buyers indicated that such functional attributes as fuel efficiency, roominess, and engine size had influenced their choices. Thus, items pertaining to these attributes were included in the survey questionnaire.

It must be emphasized that only *salient* attributes should be included in the questionnaire. Products typically feature many functional attributes that are *not* pertinent to consumer decision making because they do not suggest meaningful benefits or problems. For example, in the automobile study, consumers interviewed did not express concern about the carburetion systems in the two cars or whether their engines featured timing belts or timing chains.

The number and content of salient functional attributes is unique to each situation. However, a few generalizations based on our experience in applying the theory may be offered. We caution the reader to be aware that these are indeed *broad* generalizations, with the disclaimer that there are many "exceptions to the rule."

We have found that "buy versus no-buy" decisions often involve only a few underlying dimensions relevant to functional value. In contrast, product type choices generally involve more, and brand choices even more. To illustrate, the decision to buy a video camcorder (a "buy versus no-buy" choice) might involve just a few concerns relating to application and price. However, the decision to buy a *standard* Super VHS versus a *compact* Super VHS, a product type decision, might involve concerns pertaining to design and convenience as well as to price and application. Finally, the decision to buy an RCA versus a Panasonic compact camcorder, a brand choice, might involve concerns with service and terms of warranty, as well as with application, price, design, and convenience.

We have also found decisions pertaining to durable goods to generally involve a greater number of functional concerns than decisions pertaining to nondurable goods. This is particularly true at the brand level, but the observation also holds at the product type level. The observation has face validity in that durable goods often involve a greater financial and performance risk. The purchase of a durable good frequently represents a major investment, and one that the consumer may have to live with for years. For example, the purchase of a mattress or a freezer may be a "once in a lifetime" event, while the purchase of paper clips or rubber bands may be so free of risk that the choice between brands depends only on availability and/or price. Of course, the number and content of functional criteria also varies by product within product class. To illustrate, orange juice and face soap are both nondurable goods, but their purchase is based on very different underlying functional values.

Social Value

Social value is measured on a profile of *social imagery* representing the association of choice alternatives with specific demographic, socioeconomic, and cultural-ethnic groups. Again, salient associations can be determined through focus group interviews. Demographic groups pertain to distinctions on the basis of age, sex, marital status, family size, and the like. Socioeconomic groups refer to aggregates of people sharing the same general level of financial status, occupational status, social class status, and so on. Cultural-ethnic groups pertain to regional, national, racial, religious, and lifestyle distinctions.

Visibly consumed products almost invariably become associated with social groups and the stereotypes that consumers hold about them. Thus, it is clearly advantageous for marketers to proactively identify their products with positively regarded groups. The fact that marketers recognize this is evident from recent advertising messages. For example, it is apparent that Pepsi has endeavored to become associated with youth ("the taste of a new generation"), that Canada Dry has sought to become identified with maturing baby boomers ("for when your tastes grow up"), and that Perrier has aimed to be associated with health-conscious consumers ("nature's first soft drink").

The image or stereotype that an individual consumer associates with a particular social group may be either positive or negative, and will depend on his or her experience and socialization. Various segments of the population may hold very different stereotypes about the same group. Thus, it is very important to obtain social value information directly from the population of interest. To illustrate, some urban dwellers may regard farmers as "backward" or as "hicks," whereas others see them as the "backbone" of society and as having "good solid values." Conversely, farmers may regard urban and suburban dwellers as generally "snobbish" and "soft," whereas people living in the cities are unlikely to hold such negative stereotypes. Further, even the most commonly shared and deeply entrenched stereotypes change over time. For example, Americans have traditionally revered youth and viewed the aging process as negative. However, attitudes are shifting as the median age continues to rise and as the influential "baby boomer" group settles into middle age.

Emotional Value

Emotional value is measured on a profile of *personal feelings*, representing the *emotions* aroused by choice alternatives. Emotions associated with market offerings commonly include such feelings as excitement, comfort, nostalgia, sentimentality, hedonism, romance, self-esteem, guilt, and fear. However, it is safe to say that virtually any emotion may be aroused in a consumer choice context.

In contrast with the other values in our theory, emotional value has no underlying cognitive structure and therefore may be difficult to describe. However, we have found that consumers are usually able to specify the emotions aroused, even though they may not understand why they feel as they do. For example, a consumer may recognize that a particular brand of beer makes him feel "good about himself," but he may not be able to say why. Again, the profile of personal feelings should be generated from focus group interviews with target consumers.

It is not at all unusual for an alternative to arouse more than one emotion. Further, these multiple emotions may be conflicting. To illustrate, the decision to buy a house may simultaneously arouse such positive feelings as excitement, pride, and optimism and such negative feelings as anxiety and fear of being "trapped" or "tied down." Alternatively, it is not at all uncommon for alternatives to engender one overwhelming emotion, such that other potential feelings do not surface. For example, a handgun may arouse such fear that other feelings are rendered irrelevant.

Finally, very low involvement products associated with primarily functional value rarely arouse emotions. Examples include nails, paper clips, and string. In contrast, products associated with social and epistemic value are usually more involving and likely to also be associated with emotional value. Again, these generalizations are offered with the disclaimer that there are exceptions to every rule.

Epistemic Value

Epistemic value is measured by questionnaire items referring to *curiosity* and the perceived satisfaction of *novelty* and *knowledge* needs. Products provide epistemic value by offering something new, different, and interesting. As with the other values, it is recommended that the epistemic value items be generated through focus group interviews. Further, generic statements pertaining to curiosity, novelty, and knowledge may be included on the questionnaire.

The ability of an alternative to provide epistemic value may result from its being a distinctive new product or innovation, or from its simply being new or different to the experience of the consumer. Both offer a change of pace from the usual pattern of consumption. The experience of a new innovation or technology clearly provides epistemic value. Examples within the past decade include cellular phones, compact disks, and DAT recorders. However, it is important to recognize that a product does not have to be objectively new to provide epistemic value. Even buying a different brand of breakfast cereal can provide a "lift" in terms of novelty, variety, and exploration.

It is largely because consumers seek epistemic value that manufacturers introduce "new and improved" formulations, that new scents are added to laundry and household cleaning products, that soft drinks and food products come out in new flavors, and so on. Further, epistemic value supports the continual introduction of new brands onto the market, and the phenomenon of passing fads and fashions in everything from music, to clothing, to restaurant cuisines. Concern with "what's hot" indicates that choices are being driven by epistemic value.

Conditional Value

Conditional value is measured on a profile of *situational contingencies* contributing to *temporary* functional and social utility. These contingencies represent circumstances antecedent to and influencing choice, often causing the consumer to deviate from her or his planned or typical pattern of behavior. A profile of situational contingencies may be operationalized from information obtained through focus group interviews.

Conditional value involves both *functional* and *social* utility. Conditional functional value is created by circumstances that increase the need for an alternative's physical or utilitarian attributes, or that enhance the benefits derived from these attributes. For example, many consumers take extra Vitamin C while suffering from a cold, take a taxi only when it is raining, and buy gasoline with a credit card only when they have forgotten to get cash at the bank.

Like conditional functional value, conditional social value is created by situational contingencies. Further, it involves a desire to fit in with a salient social group. For example, a consumer may drink alcohol only when coworkers suggest going out for drinks after work, may attend church only when staying with more actively religious relatives, and may wear a Hawaiian shirt only when visiting the Hawaiian Islands.

More than one dimension of conditional value may be associated with any given purchase. Indeed, it often takes a number of concurrent contingent circumstances to evoke a change in purchasing behavior. To illustrate, a consumer may go into a supermarket intending to purchase only milk and bread. However, passing the butcher section, she may notice an expensive cut of meat on sale. The sale price itself creates conditional value but not enough to influence her to purchase the meat if she has no need for it. However, realizing that on the weekend she will be entertaining her in-laws, who have fairly upscale tastes, she may decide to purchase the meat for the special dinner and also take advantage of the sale price.

FORMAT AND WORDING OF MEASUREMENT INSTRUMENTS

Questionnaire Format

A generic questionnaire format for measuring the five values is presented in Exhibit 5-1. Introductory paragraphs and scaling are included for each question. The generic format may be adapted for any specific market choice situation of interest. Exhibit 5-2 shows how the format was adapted for a study pertaining to mass transit use.

Exhibit 5-1 Generic questionnaire format

[Functional Value]

Please indicate whether you agree or disagree that the following benefits or problems are associated with (*write in the alternative you are studying*).

(*Write in the alternative you are studying.*)   AGREE   DISAGREE

1. (*List the benefits and problems*   1. _____   _____
2.   *generated by your focus groups.*)   2. _____   _____

	AGREE	DISAGREE
3.	3. _____	_____
.	.	.
.	.	.
.	.	.
n.	*n.* _____	_____

[Social Value]

Not everybody (*write in the alternative you are studying*). Which of the following groups of people do you believe are most and least likely to *(write in the alternative you are studying)*.

	MOST LIKELY	LEAST LIKELY
1. (*List the social imagery items*	1. _____	_____
2. *generated by your focus groups.*)	2. _____	_____
3.	3. _____	_____
.	.	.
.	.	.
.	.	.
n.	*n.* _____	_____

[Emotional Value]

People sometimes (write in the alternative you are studying) for personal and emotional reasons. Please indicate whether you personally experience any of the following feelings associated with your decision to (*write in the alternative you are studying*).

	YES	NO
1. (*List the emotion items generated*	1. _____	_____
2. *by your focus groups.*)	2. _____	_____
3.	3. _____	_____
.	.	.
.	.	.
.	.	.
n.	*n.* _____	_____

[Epistemic Value]

Some people (write in the alternative you are studying) because they are curious about it, or simply bored with whatever else they are doing. Do you (*write in the alternative you are studying*) for any of the following reasons?

(*List epistemic items generated by your focus groups, as well as appropriate generic epistemic items such as the following:*)

	YES	NO
1. I am curious about it.	1. _____	_____
2. I am bored with (*other alternative*).	2. _____	_____
3. I like a change of pace.	3. _____	_____
4. I like to do things that are new and different.	4. _____	_____
5. I want to learn about it.	5. _____	_____
.	.	.
.	.	.
.	.	.
n.	*n*. _____	_____

[Conditional Value]

Certain conditions motivate people to behave differently than their regular behavior or habit. Do you believe that the following conditions might cause you to change your behavior to (write in the alternative you are studying)?

	YES	NO
1. (*List the situational contingencies*	1. _____	_____
2. *generated by your focus groups.*)	2. _____	_____
3.	3. _____	_____
.	.	.
.	.	.
.	.	.
n.	*n*. _____	_____

NOTES: The alternative specified may pertain to a "buy versus no-buy" or "use versus do not use" choice (e.g., smoking cigarettes), a product type choice (e.g., smoking filtered versus nonfiltered cigarettes), or a brand choice (e.g., smoking Marlboros versus Virginia Slims).

Randomize the order of positive and negative items within each section.

Exhibit 5-2   Adaptation of the generic questionnaire format to mass
transit example ("use versus do not use" decision)

[Functional Value]

Please indicate whether you agree or disagree that the following benefits or
problems are associated with the use of mass transit.

Using Mass Transit . . .	AGREE	DISAGREE
1. provides reliable transportation.	1. _____	_____
2. gets me where I want to go.	2. _____	_____
3. is inconvenient.	3. _____	_____
4. saves energy.	4. _____	_____
5. takes too much time.	5. _____	_____
6. eliminates parking problems.	6. _____	_____
7. is unsafe.	7. _____	_____
8. is safer than driving.	8. _____	_____
9. saves money.	9. _____	_____
10. is uncomfortable in hot or cold weather.	10. _____	_____
11. deprives me of my privacy.	11. _____	_____

[Social Value]

Not everybody uses mass transit. Which of the following groups of people
do you believe are most and least likely to use mass transit?

	MOST LIKELY	LEAST LIKELY
1. College students	1. _____	_____
2. Senior citizens	2. _____	_____
3. Office workers	3. _____	_____
4. Blacks	4. _____	_____
5. Poor people	5. _____	_____
6. High school students	6. _____	_____

	MOST LIKELY	LEAST LIKELY
7. Derelicts	7. _____	_____
8. Homemakers	8. _____	_____
9. Apartment dwellers	9. _____	_____
10. Professionals	10. _____	_____
11. Yuppies	11. _____	_____

[Emotional Value]

People sometimes use or do not use mass transit for personal and emotional reasons. Please indicate whether you personally experience any of the following feelings associated with your decision to use or not use mass transit.

	YES	NO
1. I feel relaxed when I use mass transit.	1. _____	_____
2. I feel *afraid* when I use mass transit.	2. _____	_____
3. I feel *guilty* when I drive rather than use mass transit.	3. _____	_____
4. I feel *uneasy* when I use mass transit.	4. _____	_____
5. I feel *socially responsible* when I use mass transit.	5. _____	_____
6. I feel *bored* when I use mass transit.	6. _____	_____
7. I feel *jumpy* when I use mass transit.	7. _____	_____
8. I feel *nervous* when I drive rather than use mass transit.	8. _____	_____
9. I feel *sophisticated* when I drive rather than use mass transit.	9. _____	_____
10. I feel *intruded on* when I use mass transit.	10. _____	_____
11. I feel *impatient* when I use mass transit.	11. _____	_____
12. I feel *depressed* when I use mass transit.	12. _____	_____
13. I feel *independent* when I drive rather than use mass transit.	13. _____	_____

[Epistemic Value]

Some people have used mass transit because they were curious about it, or simply bored with whatever else they were doing. Do you use mass transit or have thoughts of using mass transit for any of the following reasons?

	YES	NO
1. I am curious about it.	1. _____	_____
2. I am bored with driving.	2. _____	_____
3. I like a change of pace.	3. _____	_____
4. I like to do things that are new and different.	4. _____	_____
5. I am curious about people who use mass transit.	5. _____	_____

[Conditional Value]

Certain conditions motivate people to behave differently than their regular behavior or habit. Do you believe that the following conditions might cause you to change your behavior to use or not use mass transit?

	YES	NO
1. Bad weather	1. _____	_____
2. Car breakdown	2. _____	_____
3. Destination is far away	3. _____	_____
4. Feel lazy	4. _____	_____
5. Need to save money	5. _____	_____
6. Unusually heavy traffic	6. _____	_____
7. High gas prices	7. _____	_____
8. Not so busy at work	8. _____	_____
9. Have no money	9. _____	_____
10. Must work longer hours	10. _____	_____

This generic format has been developed and tested through the completion of approximately 200 studies. The wording of the introductory paragraphs and the scaling have been demonstrated to be unambiguous, nonbiasing, and easily understood. Further, the format is amenable to telephone surveys, mail surveys, and personal interviews, both interviewer-administered and self-administered. Thus, it is flexible and can be utilized within a broad range of time and budgetary constraints.

The format of the introductory paragraphs allows the user to simply insert words describing the alternative of interest, that is, the brand, product type, or behavior being studied. Thus, it is not necessary to develop unique wording; very minor rewording may be appropriate depending on the choice situation of interest. As shown in Exhibits 5-1 and 5-2, the questionnaire is scaled on a binary basis: for each question there are only two possible answers—yes/no, agree/disagree, or most likely/least likely. We believe this affords a number of benefits. First, the binary scaling closely approximates the way people often think. It has been demonstrated that opinion formation is often in yes-no or either-or terms (Thurstone and Clave 1929; Thurstone 1959; Guttman 1941, 1944; Coombs 1952, 1964). Second, the binary scaling forces the respondent to take a position in answering each question. Each item provides maximum information because subjects are not allowed to give noncommittal responses. Third, the binary scaling affords simplicity. The questionnaire is easy to understand and to complete, facilitating respondent cooperation and accuracy. Finally, the binary scaling allows the researcher to create ratio scaled variables. Ratio scales are amenable to a variety of analytical techniques, and they are necessary if the specific analytical techniques described in Chapter 6 are to be used.

Item Generation

Statements following the introductory paragraphs must be developed on an application-specific basis. However, bias is minimized by systematically incorporating statements from focus group interviews directly into the questionnaire. This procedure insures that wording will be familiar, meaningful, and unambiguous to respondents.

The procedure begins with preliminary information from a small group of consumers sampled from the population of interest. Interviews are preferably conducted in focus group settings, and questions are asked relevant to functional, social, emotional, epistemic, and conditional values.

The focus group technique brings together several respondents from the population of interest to be interviewed as a group. These group interviews often generate stimulating discussion, with the comments of one respondent triggering the thoughts of others so that the result is a "snowballing effect." The discussion is guided by the researcher or a professional moderator. Much has been written about focus group methodology, including recommended procedures (Goldman and McDonald 1987, Krueger 1988). We wish to emphasize that the moderator should attempt to facilitate a free flow of discussion, encourage input from all participants, probe for further clarification and elaboration when necessary, and avoid "leading" or biasing the respondents by suggesting "appropriate" responses.

The number of focus groups is dependent on the number of alternatives being studied. Two focus groups are required in "buy versus no-buy" studies and in studies involving two brands or product types; three focus groups are required in studies involving three brands or product types, and so on. Based on our experience, we recommend that each focus group be comprised of five to ten individuals. This size is large enough to generate a variety of responses but small enough to be manageable. Thus, in a "buy versus no-buy" study, for example, five to ten users are brought together in one focus group, and five to ten nonusers are brought together in another.

We recommend that a standard series of questions be asked of each focus group. This series of questions, delineated in Exhibit 5-3, consists of two questions for each of the five values in the theory. For each value, respondents are asked one question pertaining to themselves (e.g., brand A users and brand B users are each asked questions about themselves) and one question pertaining to each of the other groups (e.g., brand A users are asked questions about brand B users, and brand B users are asked questions about brand A users). The questions are applicable in studies pertaining to buy versus no-buy choices (product users and product nonusers are interviewed), product type choices (product type A users and product type B users are interviewed), and brand choices (brand A users and brand B users are interviewed).

Exhibit 5-3 Focus group questions

[Functional Value]

Product Users, Product Type A Users, or Brand A Users:

1. What are some of the benefits and problems that you associate with (*identify the alternative you are studying*)?

2. What are some of the benefits and problems that you think a nonuser associates with (*identify the alternative you are studying*)?

Product Nonusers, Product Type B Users, or Brand B Users:

1. What are some of the benefits and problems that you associate with (*identify the alternative you are studying*)?

2. What are some of the benefits and problems that you think a user associates with (*identify the alternative you are studying*)?

[Social Value]

Product Users, Product Type A Users, or Brand A Users:

3. Which groups of people do you believe are both most and least likely to (*identify the alternative you are studying*)?

4. Which groups of people do you think a nonuser believes are both most and least likely to (*identify the alternative you are studying*)?

Product Nonusers, Product Type B Users, or Brand B Users:

3. Which groups of people do you believe are both most and least likely to (*identify the alternative you are studying*)?

4. Which groups of people do you think a user believes are both most and least likely to (*identify the alternative you are studying*)?

[Emotional Value]

Product Users, Product Type A Users, or Brand A Users:

5. What feelings are aroused by your decision to (*identify the alternative you are studying*)?

6. What feelings do you think are aroused by a nonuser's decision not to (*identify the alternative you are studying*)?

Product Nonusers, Product Type B Users, or Brand B Users:

5. What feelings are aroused by your decision not to (*identify the alternative you are studying*)?

6. What feelings do you think are aroused by a user's decision to (*identify the alternative you are studying*)?

[Epistemic Value]

Product Users, Product Type A Users, or Brand A Users:

7. What triggered your decision to (*identify the alternative you are studying*)?

8. What do you think triggers a nonuser's decision not to (*identify the alternative you are studying*)?

Product Nonusers, Product Type B Users, or Brand B Users:

7. What triggered your decision not to (*identify the alternative you are studying*)?

8. What do you think triggers a user's decision to (*identify the alternative you are studying*)?

[Conditional Value]

Product Users, Product Type A Users, or Brand A Users:

9. Are there any circumstances or situations that would cause you to stop (*identify the alternative you are studying*)?

10. Are there any circumstances or situations that you think would cause a nonuser to start (*identify the alternative you are studying*)?

Product Nonusers, Product Type B Users, or Brand B Users:

9. Are there any circumstances or situations that would cause you to start (*identify the alternative you are studying*)?

10. Are there any circumstances or situations that you think would cause a user to stop (*identify the alternative you are studying*)?

_____

Because responses to these questions will be utilized as questionnaire items, it is imperative to record them *verbatim*. This procedure facilitates the development of questionnaire items that "speak the language" of the survey subjects. Reliable and valid research findings depend on questionnaire items that are meaningful and unambiguous to respondents, so appropriate wording is critical. It is suggested that focus group sessions be tape recorded and transcribed to facilitate these efforts.

Item Selection

Once focus group responses have been generated, they must be converted into potential questionnaire items. Transcripts of the focus group sessions can be content analyzed, identifying responses that reflect salient concerns. Those engendering the most agreement, discussion, and enthusiasm should certainly be used. Final questionnaire items should be phrased as closely as possible to the verbatim responses and inserted into the generic format (Exhibit 5-1).

Background Information

As illustrated in Exhibits 5-4 and 5-5, Part One of the questionnaire serves to identify each respondent's group membership: (product user versus nonuser, or user of a certain product type or brand versus the user of a different product type or brand). Thus, this section measures the dependent variable for the discriminant analysis (Chapter 6). This section can be readily adapted by the user to his or her own topic of research.

Exhibit 5-4   Sample questionnaire: A survey of church attendance

---

This is an academic study about church attendance. The results of this study will be used for academic research only, and your responses will be kept strictly confidential.

We are interested in your own personal feelings and opinions. *There are no right or wrong answers.*

On each page you will find several different kinds of statements about church attendance. All you have to do is put an X in the spaces that reflect your own personal feelings and opinions.

PLEASE NOTE:

1. Check only one answer per statement.

2. When you are finished, please check to be sure you have not omitted any answers.

THANK YOU VERY MUCH!

- -

Questionnaire No. ⎯⎯⎯⎯⎯

PART ONE

1. Do you consider yourself to be a regular churchgoer?
   Yes ⎯⎯⎯⎯
   No ⎯⎯⎯⎯

2. How often do you attend church services?
   Never   ⎯⎯⎯⎯
   Only occasionally   ⎯⎯⎯⎯
   About once a month   ⎯⎯⎯⎯
   Nearly every week   ⎯⎯⎯⎯

3. Which of the following church related activities are you presently involved in?

None _____

Athletic activities _____

Choir _____

Mens' club _____

Womens' club _____

Adult education _____

Sunday school _____

Other_____
        (please specify)

4. Do you contribute money to your church on a regular basis?

Yes _____

No _____

5. Do you believe that religion plays an important role in your personal life?

Yes _____

No _____

6. Did you regularly attend church when you were a child?

Yes _____

No _____

7. Did you participate in any church-related activities when you were a child?

Yes _____

No _____

8. To what extent do you think your past background and experience have determined your choice to attend or not attend church services?

To a very
small extent _____ _____ _____ _____ _____ _____ _____ To a very
large extent

9. Please indicate the extent to which you are familiar with church services.

Not at all
familiar _____ _____ _____ _____ _____ _____ _____ Extremely
familiar

10. How interested are you in church services?

Not at all
interested _____ _____ _____ _____ _____ _____ _____ Very
interested

PART TWO

Please indicate whether you agree or disagree that the following benefits or problems are associated with church services attendance:

Attending church services . . .	AGREE	DISAGREE
1. makes me a better person.	1. _____	_____
2. benefits my position in the community.	2. _____	_____
3. is in the best interests of my children.	3. _____	_____
4. takes too much time.	4. _____	_____
5. gives direction to my goals in life.	5. _____	_____
6. helps me get to heaven.	6. _____	_____
7. is a good investment for future benefits.	7. _____	_____
8. sometimes creates conflicts with my own beliefs.	8. _____	_____

PART THREE

Not everybody attends church services. Which of the following groups of people do you believe are most and least likely to attend church services?

	MOST LIKELY	LEAST LIKELY
1. Women	1. _____	_____
2. Rich people	2. _____	_____
3. College students	3. _____	_____
4. Families with young children	4. _____	_____
5. Older people	5. _____	_____
6. Conservatives	6. _____	_____
7. Community leaders	7. _____	_____
8. Poor people	8. _____	_____
9. Blacks	9. _____	_____
10. Homebodies	10. _____	_____
11. The middle class	11. _____	_____
12. Families with teenagers	12. _____	_____

PART FOUR

Certain conditions motivate people to behave differently than their regular behavior or habit. Do you believe that the following conditions might cause you to change your behavior to attend or not attend church services?

	YES	NO
1. Bad weather	1. _____	_____
2. Church's stand on political or community issues	2. _____	_____
3. Major religious holiday	3. _____	_____
4. Family problems	4. _____	_____
5. Baptisms, confirmations, christenings, and other important religious ceremonies	5. _____	_____
6. Death or illness in family	6. _____	_____
7. Working on Sundays	7. _____	_____
8. Transportation problems	8. _____	_____
9. Too busy with other things	9. _____	_____
10. Terminal illness	10. _____	_____

PART FIVE

People sometimes attend or do not attend church services for personal and emotional reasons. Please indicate whether you personally experience any of the following feelings associated with your decision to attend or not attend church services.

	YES	NO
1. I feel guilty when I do *not* attend church services.	1. _____	_____
2. I feel *dissatisfied* when I attend church services.	2. _____	_____
3. I feel *bored* when I attend church services.	3. _____	_____
4. I feel *uncomfortable* when I attend church services.	4. _____	_____
5. I feel *happy* when I attend church services.	5. _____	_____
6. I feel *peaceful* when I attend church services.	6. _____	_____

	YES	NO
7. I feel *angry* when I attend church services.	7. _____	_____
8. I feel *fearful* when I do *not* attend church services.	8. _____	_____
9. I feel *spiritual* when I attend church services.	9. _____	_____
10. I feel *good about myself* when I attend church services.	10. _____	_____
11. I feel *intelligent* when I do *not* attend church services.	11. _____	_____
12. I feel *sophisticated* when I do *not* attend church services.	12. _____	_____
13. I feel *interested* when I attend church services.	13. _____	_____

PART SIX

Some people attend church because they are curious about it, or simply bored with whatever else they are doing. Do you attend or have thoughts of attending church services for any of the following reasons?

	YES	NO
1. To see what it is like	1. _____	_____
2. Bored with other Sunday activities	2. _____	_____
3. As a change of pace to break the monotony of my routine	3. _____	_____
4. To learn more about others who attend church services	4. _____	_____
5. To keep an eye on what is going on in church	5. _____	_____
6. To keep up with changes in religious practice	6. _____	_____
7. To learn more about religion	7. _____	_____
8. To learn more about God	8. _____	_____

To facilitate accurate measurement of the dependent variable, the questionnaire should include a variety of items pertaining to group membership (Haley and Gatty 1971). This allows responses to be verified for consistency, and it serves as a validity check. For example, in the church attendance questionnaire presented in Exhibit 5-4, a respondent indicating that she or he is a regular churchgoer (Question 1) might also be expected to respond affirmatively to questions pertaining to frequent attendance (Question 2), participation in church activities (Question 3), familiarity with church services (Question 9), and so on. While it is unreasonable to expect affirmative answers to all such questions, if the subject's responses appear inconsistent, there can be no confidence in their validity, and they should be discarded.

Multiple measures of the dependent variable also provide useful classification information. For example, in the church attendance example, it might be informative to examine the value differences of those who attend church every week versus those who attend only occasionally. It is also recommended that demographic, socioeconomic, and psychographic information be collected. Because value structures are frequently mediated by such variables, background information of this type may be very useful for market segmentation and target marketing.

Pretesting

The final phase in the preparation of the data collection instrument is the pretest. Most basic marketing research texts provide adequate discussions of pretesting (Green and Tull 1978, Boyd et al. 1981). We emphasize that pretesting should use an *identical* procedure to that selected for the main study. For example, if the survey data are to be collected through interviewer-administered personal interviews, pretest data should be collected in the same manner. In this way, problems with the survey setting and procedures, as well as with the survey instrument, can be detected.

DATA COLLECTION

Once the measurement instrument is finalized, a large representative sample from the population of interest is selected and survey data are collected. The operationalization of our theory requires that data be collected from both users and nonusers in a "buy versus no-buy" study, from users of competing brands in a brand choice study, and from users of competing product types in a product type choice study. These data are then used to identify value differences between the groups. For example, the study of mass transit ridership (Exhibit 5-2) included both respondents who use mass transit and respondents who do not.

Sampling

The survey sample should be selected so as to include an approximately equal number of respondents from each group of interest—for example, product users versus nonusers. While sample size necessarily depends on budgetary constraints and population characteristics, we recommend that no fewer than 100 respondents be sampled from each group being studied. A large sample size minimizes the threat of sampling bias, even when several incomplete or inaccurate questionnaires must be discarded.

Similarly, the optimal sampling *method* depends on the nature of the application, the degree of generalization required, and budgetary constraints. Numerous resources exist that describe and discuss strengths and weaknesses of the various types of samples, such as simple random sampling, stratified random sampling, systematic sampling, and cluster sampling (Sudman 1976, Kalton 1983, Scheaffer et al. 1986). We emphasize that the sample must be representative of the population of interest, and that any random sampling procedure may be appropriate. Stratified, systematic, and cluster sampling designs are often more efficient than simple random sampling because they require a smaller sample size, and are therefore less costly.

Alternative Methods of Data Collection

The operationalization of our theory is amenable to the full range of data collection methods: mail survey, telephone interview, and personal interview (both written self-administered and oral interviewer-administered). As discussed in almost any basic text on marketing research, each is associated with various strengths and weaknesses (Green and Tull 1978, Churchill 1979). Thus, the user can select the method that is most suitable to his or her own needs and budget. Telephone interviews and mail surveys are often less expensive than personal interviews, particularly if the subject population is geographically dispersed. Further, given the highly structured nature of our operationalization and questionnaire format, many of the limitations typically associated with telephone and mail surveys are not applicable.

Coding

Once data have been collected, they should be checked for completion and consistency and then coded to facilitate data analysis. Coding involves translating the raw data into numbers, and it is discussed in virtually every basic research text (Green and Tull 1978, Churchill 1979).

Exhibit 5-5 presents a coded questionnaire pertaining to marketing research use versus nonuse by small businesses. Throughout the questionnaire, the positive responses are coded as 1 and the negative responses are coded as 0. To illustrate, a "yes" response relevant to a *positive* value—for example, "Can identify customer needs"—is coded as 1, and a "no" answer is coded as 0. However, a "yes" response relevant to a *negative* value, such as "Is too costly", is coded as 0, and a "no" answer is coded as 1. In measuring the dependent variable (Part One), possible responses are numbered consecutively.

Exhibit 5-5   Sample Questionnaire: A survey of marketing research use for small businesses

---

This is an academic study about marketing research. We are interested in finding out the extent to which small businesses use marketing research. The results of this study will be used for academic research only, and your responses will be kept strictly confidential.

We are interested in your own personal feelings and opinions. *There are no right or wrong answers.*

On each page you will find several different kinds of statements about marketing research. All you have to do is put an X in the spaces that reflect your own personal feelings and opinions.

PLEASE NOTE:

1. Check only one answer per statement.

2. When you are finished, please check to be sure you have not omitted any answers.

THANK YOU VERY MUCH!

- -

Questionnaire No. _____

Industry _____

PART ONE

1. Have you ever used marketing research?
    Yes _____ (1)
    No   _____ (0)

2. Have you been involved in any of the following research-related activi-
   ties? (Check as many as apply.)
   Pricing research   _____ (1)
   Advertising research   _____ (2)
   Business economic research   _____ (3)
   Product research   _____ (4)
   Sales research   _____ (5)
   Other _____ (6)
              (please specify)

3. Have you used any of the following specific kinds of marketing research?
   (Check as many as apply.)
   Journal demographics   _____ (1)
   Syndicated services (e.g., Nielsen) _____ (2)
   Internal records   _____ (3)
   Magazine demographics   _____ (4)
   Professional studies   _____ (5)
   Special industry publications   _____ (6)
   Other _____ (7)
              (please specify)

4. To what extent do you think marketing research can be of help to your
   business?

   To a very   To a very
   small extent ____ ____ ____ ____ ____ ____ ____ large extent
                 (1)   (2)   (3)   (4)   (5)   (6)   (7)

5. To what extent do you think marketing research is used by small
   businesses?

   To a very   To a very
   small extent ____ ____ ____ ____ ____ ____ ____ large extent
                 (1)   (2)   (3)   (4)   (5)   (6)   (7)

6. Please indicate the extent to which you are familiar with marketing
   research services?

   Not at all   Very
   familiar   ____ ____ ____ ____ ____ ____ ____ familiar
                 (1)   (2)   (3)   (4)   (5)   (6)   (7)

7. How interested are you in using marketing research?

   Not at all   Very
   interested   ____ ____ ____ ____ ____ ____ ____ interested
                 (1)   (2)   (3)   (4)   (5)   (6)   (7)

8. Do you plan to use marketing research in the future?
   Yes _____ (1)
   No   _____ (0)

9. What is the most you would be willing to spend on one marketing research study?
   Less than $500   _____ (1)
   $500–$1,000   _____ (2)
   $1,001–$2,000   _____ (3)
   $2,001–$5,000   _____ (4)
   $5,001–$10,000   _____ (5)
   More than $10,000   _____ (6)

PART TWO

Please indicate whether you agree or disagree that the following benefits or problems are associated with the use of marketing research.

Marketing Research ...	AGREE	DISAGREE
1. is too costly.	1. ____ (0)	____ (1)
2. is not necessary because I do my own informal data gathering.	2. ____ (0)	____ (1)
3. is often too complicated to understand.	3. ____ (0)	____ (1)
4. can help me make better business decisions.	4. ____ (1)	____ (0)
5. can help me understand my customers.	5. ____ (1)	____ (0)
6. is not necessary because I use my own judgment in business decisions.	6. ____ (0)	____ (1)
7. can help me improve the quality of my product or service.	7. ____ (1)	____ (0)
8. can help me develop new products or services.	8. ____ (1)	____ (0)
9. can identify customer needs.	9. ____ (1)	____ (0)
10. is too time consuming.	10. ____ (0)	____ (1)
11. can help me develop better advertising and promotions.	11. ____ (1)	____ (0)
12. only tells me what I know anyway.	12. ____ (0)	____ (1)
13. can help me compete in the marketplace.	13. ____ (1)	____ (0)

Marketing Research ...	AGREE	DISAGREE
14. can help me increase sales.	14. _____ (1)	_____ (0)
15. takes too long. By the time I have the information, it's too late.	15. _____ (0)	_____ (1)
16. can help me identify market trends.	16. _____ (1)	_____ (0)
17. can keep me in touch with what my competitors are doing.	17. _____ (1)	_____ (0)
18. often provides information that is not accurate.	18. _____ (0)	_____ (1)

PART THREE

Not all businesses use marketing research. Which of the following types of businesses do you believe are most and least likely to use marketing research?

	MOST LIKELY	LEAST LIKELY
1. Large corporations	1. _____ (1)	_____ (0)
2. Small businesses	2. _____ (1)	_____ (0)
3. Large franchises	3. _____ (1)	_____ (0)
4. Family-owned businesses	4. _____ (1)	_____ (0)
5. Department stores	5. _____ (1)	_____ (0)
6. Small retail stores	6. _____ (1)	_____ (0)
7. Expanding businesses	7. _____ (1)	_____ (0)
8. Local businesses	8. _____ (1)	_____ (0)
9. Chain stores	9. _____ (1)	_____ (0)
10. Service organizations	10. _____ (1)	_____ (0)

PART FOUR

Certain conditions motivate business people to behave differently than their regular behavior or habit. Do you believe that the following conditions might cause you to change your behavior to use or not to use marketing research?

	YES	NO
1. A sudden decrease in sales for no apparent reason	1. _____ (1)	_____ (0)
2. Close competitors begin to use marketing research	2. _____ (1)	_____ (0)
3. Budget cuts	3. _____ (1)	_____ (0)
4. Entering a new market	4. _____ (1)	_____ (0)
5. Less money due to major unexpected expenses	5. _____ (1)	_____ (0)
6. Steady sales growth over an extended period of time	6. _____ (1)	_____ (0)
7. A special deal on marketing research	7. _____ (1)	_____ (0)
8. More money available due to other cutbacks	8. _____ (1)	_____ (0)
9. A change in customer demographics or life-style	9. _____ (1)	_____ (0)
10. A sudden demand for my product due to regulatory change, scientific finding, or other occurrence	10. _____ (1)	_____ (0)
11. Opening a new store or location	11. _____ (1)	_____ (0)
12. Introducing a new product	12. _____ (1)	_____ (0)
13. A windfall profit from an investment	13. _____ (1)	_____ (0)

PART FIVE

Business people sometimes use or do not use marketing research for personal and emotional reasons. Is your decision to use or not use marketing research influenced, at least in part, by any of the following feelings?

	YES	NO
1. I am *afraid* of not being able to understand the results of a marketing research study.	1. _____ (0)	_____ (1)
2. I feel *secure* that marketing research will benefit my business.	2. _____ (1)	_____ (0)
3. I feel a certain *reluctance* when I think about using marketing research.	3. _____ (0)	_____ (1)

		YES	NO
4.	I *enjoy* marketing research.	4. _____ (1)	_____ (0)
5.	Making major decisions *without* marketing research is too *risky*.	5. _____ (1)	_____ (0)
6.	In general, I have a *negative* feeling toward marketing research.	6. _____ (0)	_____ (1)
7.	Spending money on marketing research feels *wasteful*.	7. _____ (0)	_____ (1)
8.	I am *fascinated* by marketing research that can help my business.	8. _____ (1)	_____ (0)
9.	I *distrust* marketing research.	9. _____ (0)	_____ (1)
10.	I feel that marketing research *undermines* my business judgment.	10. _____ (0)	_____ (1)
11.	I feel *uncomfortable* with marketing research people.	11. _____ (0)	_____ (1)
12.	Doing marketing research before I make a final decision is *reassuring*.	12. _____ (1)	_____ (0)
13.	I am *bored* by marketing research.	13. _____ (0)	_____ (1)
14.	*Not* having marketing research makes me *uneasy*.	14. _____ (1)	_____ (0)

PART SIX

Some business people have used marketing research because they were curious about it and its potential benefits. Have you used or had thoughts of using marketing research for any of the following reasons?

		YES	NO
1.	Associates told me about their experience with marketing research.	1. _____ (1)	_____ (0)
2.	I was approached by a person from a professional marketing research firm.	1. _____ (1)	_____ (0)
3.	I saw an interesting advertisement/brochure about marketing research.	3. _____ (1)	_____ (0)
4.	Alternative solutions to my business problems always interest me.	4. _____ (1)	_____ (0)

	YES	NO
5. I was curious about what marketing research might show me about my business.	5. _____ (1)	_____ (0)
6. I read an interesting article about marketing research in a trade/business publication.	6. _____ (1)	_____ (0)
7. I was curious to see what marketing research might do for my business.	7. _____ (1)	_____ (0)
8. I got interested in marketing research when I learned about it in school/at a professional seminar.	8. _____ (1)	_____ (0)
9. I like to keep up with the latest business tools.	9. _____ (1)	_____ (0)
10. Anything that can tell me more about my customers is interesting to me.	10. _____ (1)	_____ (0)

SUMMARY

This chapter has provided guidance for operationalizing the theory. Using the guidelines and tools provided in this and the following chapter, readers may utilize the theory to determine which values drive specific market choices of interest.

Issues involved in measuring each of the five values were discussed in this chapter, as are issues of questionnaire design (formatting, item generation, item selection, background information, pretesting) and data collection (sampling, alternative methods, coding). Functional value is measured on a profile of product attributes; social value on a profile of social imagery; emotional value on a profile of personal feelings; epistemic value on a profile of items referring to curiosity, novelty, and knowledge; and conditional value on a profile of situational contingencies. To aid readers who are interested in applying the theory, we have provided a standardized or "generic" questionnaire format and a procedure for generating *specific* questionnaire items through focus group interviews. Further, sample questionnaires are provided.

Next, Chapter 6 discusses data analysis, demonstrating how to determine which values drive specific market choices. The recommended analytical technique is discriminant analysis, with independent variables developed through factor analysis. The analytic procedure is illustrated using data from an actual study of voter choice.

6

DATA ANALYSIS

This chapter discusses data analysis, demonstrating how to determine from survey data which values drive specific consumer choices. The recommended analytical technique is *discriminant analysis*, a multivariate statistical method. This technique is briefly described and its use is demonstrated with data pertaining to voter choice. It is recommended that independent or "discriminator," variables be derived through *factor analysis*.*

STATISTICAL ANALYSIS

In applying the theory, data obtained from respondents are analyzed through *discriminant analysis*. Procedural details and the mathematical theory underlying this multivariate statistical technique are discussed, for example, in books on multivariate methods (Hair et al. 1979, Jackson 1983) and in books specifically on discriminant analysis (Klecka 1980).

As described by Klecka (1980):

Discriminant analysis is a statistical technique which allows the researcher to study the differences between two or more groups of objects with respect to several variables simultaneously. (p. 7)

Further, as noted by Jackson (1983):

The discriminant procedure involves starting with a set of observations

---

*An alternative approach is to use individual questionnaire items as independent variables. For the sake of parsimony and to minimize upward bias in "goodness-of-fit," only items that maximally distinguish between groups should be used (Darlington 1968). In studies involving two groups, maximally distinguishing items may be selected by performing a series of pairwise t-tests and retaining as independent variables those items with statistically significant t-values ($p < .05$ is a typical "rule of thumb"). In studies involving more than two groups, items may be selected by performing a multi-group F ratio test on each item.

The individual items approach has the advantage of being very simple to implement. However, it is less statistically pure than the factor analytic approach. The most serious limitation is that the values may receive unequal weighting as a function of questionnaire design rather than as a function of their relative importance.

whose group memberships are known. That initial set of data is used to fit (or calibrate) a relationship which can be used to classify other observations whose group memberships are not known. Thus, investigators must begin the procedure knowing what groups are relevant for their analysis. . . . For each observation, investigators must have information on group membership and also on the values of one or more *discriminator* variables which can be used to establish a classification rule. (p. 89)

Discriminant analysis is ideally suited to our theory's operationalization because analysis begins with *known groups*, such as buyers/nonbuyers, users/nonusers, product type A/product type B users, and brand A/brand B users. In applying the theory, the objective is to classify these known groups on the basis of values driving choice, the independent or "discriminator" variables. Discriminant analysis accomplishes this by *maximizing between-group variance* and *minimizing within-group variance* to create mutually exclusive and collectively exhaustive groups. As noted by Hair et al. (1979):

Discriminant analysis involves deriving the linear combination of the two (or more) independent variables that will discriminate best between the *a priori* defined groups. This is achieved by the statistical decision rule of maximizing the between-group variance relative to the within-group variance. (p. 85)

Statistical packages such as SPSS (Statistical Package for the Social Sciences) and SAS (Statistical Analysis System) provide algorithms for classifying respondents into two or more groups. Multigroup discriminant analysis may be used when the objective is to compare the value structures of users of three or more brands (e.g., Crest, Colgate, and Aquafresh toothpastes) or product types (e.g., luxury cars, sports cars, and compacts). For the sake of simplicity, we demonstrate the use of two-group discriminant analysis.

Once groups have been distinguished, discriminant analysis allows the researcher to determine which variables account for the greatest discrimination. Those values that discriminate significantly are associated with large coefficients, and this information often suggests strategy implications. For example, the finding that users of a particular product associate it with positive emotional value might suggest that relevant emotions be emphasized in advertising. Similarly, the finding that nonusers associate it with very negative functional value might suggest that effort should be made to disassociate the product from negative attributes.

The accuracy or predictive power associated with a discriminant model may be evaluated by comparing *predicted* versus *actual* group memberships, as reported in the survey instrument. In operationalizing the theory, such "classification analysis" provides an indication of the theory's predictive validity.

INDEPENDENT VARIABLES

The independent variables serving as input to the discriminant analysis are best derived through *factor analysis*. Factor analysis is a data reduction technique used to simplify the dependence structure of a set of items by identifying combinations of correlated items called *factors*. Information on operational procedure and the statistical theory underlying factor analysis is readily available (Kim and Mueller 1978ab, Hair et al. 1979, Johnson and Wichern 1982, Jackson 1983). As noted by Hair et al. (1979):

> The general purpose of factor analytic techniques is to find a way of condensing (summarizing) the information contained in a number of original variables into a smaller set of new composite dimensions (factors) with a minimum loss of information. That is, to search for and define the fundamental constructs or dimensions assumed to underlie the original variables. (p. 218)

More simply stated, the objective of factor analysis is "to represent a set of variables in terms of a smaller number of variables" (Kim and Mueller 1978b, p. 9). As described by Jackson (1983):

> Factor analysis is a technique for analyzing the internal structure of a set of variables. The basic idea is that the members of a set of variables, each of which has been observed or measured for a number of observations, have some, though not all, of their structure determined by certain underlying, unobservable common constructs or *factors*. Investigators use factor analysis to help them identify such underlying constructs in sets of variables. (p. 131)

In applying the theory, the factors derived represent the underlying dimensions of the theory values. Typically, two or more factors are derived relevant to each value. This use of factor analysis affords a number of advantages in data analysis. First, it facilitates statistical purity. The technique throws out error variance, ensuring that only systematic variance is reflected in the independent variables. Second, the dimensions underlying each value are identified. While it is anticipated that the values contributing to choice are multidimensional, their structures are not known *a priori*. Third, individual items comprising each factor are differentially weighted. Thus, their *relative* contributions are identified in the factor analysis output. Finally, the directionality of each item's influence (whether the influence is positive or negative) is indicated by the factor analysis output.

A disadvantage of factor analysis is that the factors must be interpreted and labelled, introducing a degree of subjectivity. This is complicated by the fact that sometimes too many factors are derived, making the output difficult to interpret and contributing to upward bias in terms of goodness-of-fit. However, this disadvantage may be ameliorated by using a stepwise procedure in the discriminant analysis.

DEMONSTRATION OF DATA ANALYSIS

The remainder of this chapter illustrates the data analysis procedure using results from a survey pertaining to voter choice (Newman 1981). The study examines values motivating voters to support Jimmy Carter or Edward Kennedy in the 1980 Illinois Democratic presidential primary. Thus, the study calls for two-group discriminant analysis, with the dependent variable being voter behavior. We demonstrate the development of independent variables through factor analysis. Further, the predictive power of the discriminant model is evaluated through classification analysis.

Because this is not a typical marketing application, Newman (1981) modified the theory values to fit the voter choice situation. Specifically, both emotional value and conditional value are divided into two domains. Thus, in this application, seven values are operationalized rather than the usual five. The seven values are defined as follows (Newman and Sheth 1985):

1. **Functional Value—Issues and Policies:**
   Refers to a list of salient issues and policies along four dimensions: economic policy, foreign policy, social policy, and leadership characteristics; represents the perceived value a candidate possesses in these salient criteria that represent the rational or functional purposes of the candidate's platform.

2. **Social Value—Social Groups:**
   Refers to all relevant primary and secondary reference groups likely to be supportive of the candidates being studied.

3. **Emotional Value—Personal Feelings:**
   Represents the emotional dimension of voting; refers to affective feelings such as hope, responsibility, patriotism, etc. aroused by the candidate.

4. **Emotional Value—Candidate Characteristics:**
   Refers to the image of the candidate based on salient personality traits that are thought to be characteristic of the candidate.

5. **Conditional Value—Current Events:**
   Refers to the set of issues and policies that develop during the course of a campaign; includes the domestic and international situations that would cause the voter to switch his/her vote to another candidate. The candidate acquires utility or value because of certain issue and policy stands s/he makes that affect different situations.

6. **Conditional Value—Candidate Events:**
   Refers to situations in the personal life of the candidate that would cause the voter to switch his/her vote to another candidate. The candidate acquires utility or value because of certain personal or family events that precede the voter's decision.

7. **Epistemic Value—Nonspecific Issues:**
   Refers to reasons that would justify the perceived satisfaction of curiosity, knowledge, and exploratory needs offered by the candidate as a change of pace (something new, different).

The questionnaire used to measure these values is provided in Exhibit 6-1.

Exhibit 6-1 Political choice questionnaire

This is an academic survey designed to study voting behavior. On the following pages you will find statements about the *Democratic* party candidates running in the Illinois Primary on March 18, 1980 for the Democratic Presidential nomination. *The survey should be filled out with reference to the Primary Election only. (None of the statements should be associated with the coming General Election in November.)*

The results of this study will be used for academic research only. Your responses will be kept *strictly confidential.*

Please carefully read the instructions at the beginning of each section. Simply put an X in the spaces that reflect your own personal feelings and opinions about the candidate you plan to vote for in this primary.

PLEASE NOTE:

1. Check only one answer per statement.

2. When you are finished, please check to be sure you have not omitted any answers.

THANK YOU VERY MUCH!

Questionnaire No. _____

PART ONE

This section lists a series of questions about your political interests. For each question, please put an X in the appropriate space. Be sure to make *only one X for each question.*

1. Whom do you plan to vote for in the Illinois Primary on March 18?
   a. Jimmy Carter   _____
   b. Edward Kennedy   _____
   c. Other _____
                                    (please specify)

2. Generally speaking, do you think of yourself as a:
   a. Democrat   _____
   b. Independent   _____   (If Independent, skip to #4.)
   c. Other _____
                                    (please specify)

3. If you think of yourself as a Democrat, please indicate how strongly you feel as one.

   A very   A very
   strong   weak
   Democrat   ____ ____ ____ ____ ____ ____ ____ Democrat
                   (1)   (2)   (3)   (4)   (5)   (6)   (7)
   (Skip to #5.)

4. If you think of yourself as an Independent, please indicate which party you consider yourself closer to.
   Democrat   ____ ____ ____ ____ ____ ____ ____ Republican
                   (1)   (2)   (3)   (4)   (5)   (6)   (7)

5. Please indicate which one of the following statements is most accurate (please indicate only one).
   a. Both parents were Democrats   _____
   b. Both parents were Republicans   _____
   c. Parents had different partisanship   _____

6. Please indicate which one of the following statements best describes your present political position (please check only one).
   a. I have never changed from one party to another.   _____
   b. I was a Republican, but changed to the Democratic party.   _____
   c. I was a Republican, but changed to an Independent.   _____
   d. Other _____
                                    (please specify)

7. How likely are you to vote in this election according to your party
   preference?

   Very   Very
   likely   _____ _____ _____ _____ _____ _____ _____ unlikely
              (1)   (2)   (3)   (4)   (5)   (6)   (7)

8. How interested are you in the Illinois Primary?

   Very   Very
   interested _____ _____ _____ _____ _____ _____ _____ uninterested
                 (1)   (2)   (3)   (4)   (5)   (6)   (7)

9. How concerned are you over the outcome of the Illinois Primary?

   Very   Very un-
   concerned _____ _____ _____ _____ _____ _____ _____ concerned
                (1)   (2)   (3)   (4)   (5)   (6)   (7)

10. How effective do you believe your vote will be in determining the out-
    come of this election?

    Very   Very
    effective _____ _____ _____ _____ _____ _____ _____ ineffective
                 (1)   (2)   (3)   (4)   (5)   (6)   (7)

11. Do you consider yourself (please indicate only one):
    a. Conservative _____
    b. Moderate   _____
    c. Liberal   _____

PART TWO: ISSUES AND POLICIES

(When answering, please think of the candidate you plan to vote for.)

This section lists a number of statements about the issues in this primary.
Please indicate whether you agree or disagree that *each* of the following
issues is advocated by your candidate.

I believe that my candidate will try to . . .

A. ECONOMY	AGREE	DISAGREE
1. reduce inflation by instituting wage and price controls.	1. _____	_____
2. reduce inflation by imposing tight fiscal constraints.	2. _____	_____
3. reduce inflation by balancing the budget.	3. _____	_____

	AGREE	DISAGREE
4. reduce inflation by imposing gasoline rationing.	4. _____	_____
5. make it easier to afford a house by lowering interest rates.	5. _____	_____
6. cut taxes for individuals.	6. _____	_____
7. impose windfall profits taxes on oil companies.	7. _____	_____
8. decontrol oil and gasoline prices.	8. _____	_____
9. give assistance to low- and middle-income families to cushion the impact of higher energy prices.	9. _____	_____

B. FOREIGN POLICY

	AGREE	DISAGREE
1. increase defense spending.	1. _____	_____
2. keep us out of a war.	2. _____	_____
3. improve our relationship with Russia by supporting SALT II.	3. _____	_____

C. SOCIAL ISSUES

	AGREE	DISAGREE
1. reinstate the draft.	1. _____	_____
2. increase our energy supply by building more nuclear plants.	2. _____	_____
3. provide federal aid for abortions.	3. _____	_____
4. institute a national health program.	4. _____	_____
5. call for women to register for the draft.	5. _____	_____
6. protect human rights.	6. _____	_____

D. LEADERSHIP

	AGREE	DISAGREE
1. strengthen the nation morally and ethically.	1. _____	_____
2. be able to deal with Congress.	2. _____	_____

	AGREE	DISAGREE
3. carry out his campaign promises.	3. _____	_____
4. surround himself with trusted/knowledge-able people.	4. _____	_____

PART THREE: SOCIAL GROUPS

(When answering, please think of the candidate you plan to vote for.)

This section lists a number of groups of people who are likely to be supportive of the candidates. Which of the following groups do you believe are most and least likely to vote for your candidate.

Groups most and least likely to support my candidate:	MOST LIKELY	LEAST LIKELY
1. Minorities	1. _____	_____
2. The "silent majority"	2. _____	_____
3. Senior citizens	3. _____	_____
4. Traditional Democrats	4. _____	_____
5. Chicago politicians	5. _____	_____
6. Students	6. _____	_____
7. Underprivileged people	7. _____	_____
8. Liberals	8. _____	_____
9. Rich people	9. _____	_____
10. Downstate voters	10. _____	_____
11. Farmers	11. _____	_____
12. Blue-collar workers	12. _____	_____
13. Independents	13. _____	_____
14. Environmentalists	14. _____	_____

PART FOUR: PERSONAL FEELINGS TOWARD YOUR CANDIDATE

(When answering, please think of the candidate you plan to vote for.)

People sometimes vote for a particular candidate for personal and emotional reasons. Is your decision to vote for your candidate influenced, at least in part, by any of the following feelings?

Voting for my candidate would make me feel . . .   YES   NO

1. patriotic. 1. _____   _____
2. confident. 2. _____   _____
3. satisfied. 3. _____   _____
4. optimistic. 4. _____   _____
5. involved. 5. _____   _____
6. excited. 6. _____   _____
7. hopeful. 7. _____   _____
8. relieved. 8. _____   _____
9. responsible. 9. _____   _____

PART FIVE: CANDIDATE CHARACTERISTICS

(When answering, please think of the candidate you plan to vote for.)

This section lists several personality traits considered important for a candidate. Is your decision to vote for your candidate influenced, at least in part, by any of the following characteristics?

I believe that my candidate is . . .   YES   NO

1. decisive. 1. _____   _____
2. a family man. 2. _____   _____
3. honest. 3. _____   _____
4. cool under pressure. 4. _____   _____
5. charismatic. 5. _____   _____
6. articulate. 6. _____   _____
7. idealistic. 7. _____   _____
8. hard-driving. 8. _____   _____
9. self-confident. 9. _____   _____
10. a man with a good sense of humor. 10. _____   _____
11. innovative in implementing policies. 11. _____   _____
12. level-headed. 12. _____   _____
13. experienced. 13. _____   _____
14. stable. 14. _____   _____

	YES	NO
15. able to get things done.	15. _____	_____
16. a man with a sense of purpose.	16. _____	_____
17. compassionate.	17. _____	_____

PART SIX: CURRENT EVENTS: DOMESTIC AND INTERNATIONAL

(When answering, please think of the candidate you plan to vote for.)

Certain situations motivate people to change their behavior. Do you believe that the following conditions might cause you to switch to another candidate?

I would switch my vote to another candidate if . . .	YES	NO
1. the Soviets invade another country.	1. _____	_____
2. the U.S. decides to attend the Olympics in Moscow.	2. _____	_____
3. the hostages in Iran are released.	3. _____	_____
4. the Afghanistan situation worsens.	4. _____	_____
5. gasoline prices rise above $2/gallon.	5. _____	_____
6. another U.S. Embassy is overtaken.	6. _____	_____
7. economists predict that a deep recession is coming.	7. _____	_____
8. the inflation rate rises above 20% per year.	8. _____	_____
9. the present administration flip-flops on another major policy vote.	9. _____	_____

PART SEVEN: EVENTS CONCERNING YOUR CANDIDATE

(When answering, please think of the candidate you plan to vote for.)

This section lists a series of hypothetical situations about the candidates. Do you believe that the following conditions would influence you to vote for another candidate?

I would switch my vote to another candidate if I knew that my candidate . . .	YES	NO
1. had to oppose Ronald Reagan in the November election.	1. _____	_____

	YES	NO
2. had to oppose George Bush in the November election.	2. _____	_____
3. evaded his taxes.	3. _____	_____
4. was involved in a political scandal.	4. _____	_____
5. had lied to the press.	5. _____	_____
6. was having extra-marital romantic affairs.	6. _____	_____
7. had no chance of winning the Democratic nomination.	7. _____	_____
8. got caught drinking while driving.	8. _____	_____
9. knew about wrongdoing in his personal staff.	9. _____	_____
10. was going to drop out of the race.	10. _____	_____
11. would hurt the country by his actions or statements.	11. _____	_____

PART EIGHT: NONSPECIFIC ISSUES ABOUT YOUR CANDIDATE

(When answering, please think of the candidate you plan to vote for.)

People sometimes vote for a particular candidate because they are curious about him or her, or just fed up with the present administration. Have any of the following reasons influenced you to vote for your candidate?

I am voting for my candidate because ...	YES	NO
1. of my party loyalty.	1. _____	_____
2. of the mediocrity of the other candidates.	2. _____	_____
3. of a bandwagon effect.	3. _____	_____
4. of his standing in the polls.	4. _____	_____
5. I want a change in the present administration.	5. _____	_____
6. of his media coverage.	6. _____	_____
7. my spouse influenced me.	7. _____	_____
8. of his magnetic personality.	8. _____	_____

Independent Variables

To derive independent variables, a separate factor analysis is performed for each value domain. Thus, the present application calls for seven factor analyses. Factors demonstrated to contribute significantly to explained variance are retained as potential independent variables. A factor's contribution to explained variance is indicated by the magnitude of its *eigenvalue*. Large eigenvalues indicate significant contribution.

To determine what is "large," a *scree test* is recommended. The scree test simply plots the eigenvalues from largest to smallest, as demonstrated in Figure 6-1. The choice criterion specifies that factors associated with eigenvalues above the "elbow" (the point at which the curve begins to straighten out) be retained. Therefore, in this hypothetical example, the first three factors should be retained. Another common procedure is to use the "rule of thumb" that factors associated with eigenvalues of more than 1.0 be retained.

Figure 6-1   Hypothetical scree test

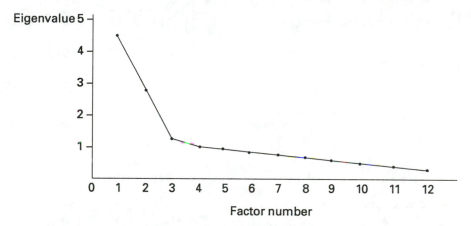

Another essential aspect of factor analysis is *factor rotation,* a procedure undertaken to facilitate the interpretation of factors. A number of rotation procedures exist and are based on different underlying assumptions. In applying our theory, *varimax* rotation is recommended. Consistent with the theory, varimax rotation assumes independence among factors. Thus, the algorithm highlights unique contributions by extracting orthogonal dimensions.

Factor structures derived using the scree test and varimax rotation methods are presented in Tables 6-1 through 6-7. As shown, a total of 36 factors are selected as potential independent variables. Had the "rule of thumb" method been used, the number of potential independent variables would be 28.

Table 6-1   Rotated factor structure in voter choice: Functional value
(issues and policies)

I believe that my candidate will . . .	Factors				
	1	2	3	4	5
ECONOMY					
1. reduce inflation by instituting wage and price controls.	.19	.39	−.36	−.56	.06
2. reduce inflation by imposing tight fiscal constraints.	.30	−.09	.17	.21	.13
3. reduce inflation by balancing the budget.	.20	.01	.16	.35	.04
4. reduce inflation by imposing gasoline rationing.	.07	.11	−.10	−.42	.23
5. make it easier to afford a house by lowering interest rates.	.17	.69	−.15	−.09	−.03
6. cut taxes for individuals.	.11	.58	.01	−.04	−.03
7. impose windfall profits taxes on oil companies.	.01	−.02	.07	.04	.27
8. decontrol oil and gasoline prices.	.01	−.26	.15	.28	.15
9. give assistance to low- and middle-income families to cushion the impact of higher energy prices.	.13	.10	−.00	−.05	.33
FOREIGN POLICY					
10. increase defense spending.	−.04	−.04	.64	.18	−.07
11. keep us out of a war.	.33	.12	−.18	.35	.35
12. improve our relations with Russia by supporting Salt II.	−.01	−.28	−.03	−.00	.54
SOCIAL ISSUES					
13. reinstate the draft.	−.03	−.03	.63	.03	.01
14. increase our energy supply by building more nuclear plants.	−.04	−.22	−.43	.28	−.00
15. provide federal aid for abortions.	−.04	−.13	−.33	−.07	.36
16. institute a national health program.	.24	.30	−.13	−.17	.28
17. call for women to register for the draft.	−.11	−.22	.31	.00	.19
18. protect human rights.	.32	.11	.00	.35	.37

Table 6-1   (continued)

I believe that my candidate will . . .	Factors				
	1	**2**	**3**	**4**	**5**
LEADERSHIP					
19. strengthen the nation morally and ethically.	.48	.09	.13	.25	.14
20. be able to deal with Congress.	.76	.22	−.11	−.13	.02
21. carry out his campaign promises.	.73	.15	−.08	−.02	.05
22. surround himself with trusted/ knowledgeable people	.74	.09	−.14	−.02	.02
eigenvalue	3.18	2.74	1.86	1.34	1.12
% variance explained	17.4	12.5	8.6	6.1	5.1

Table 6-2   Rotated factor structure in voter choice: Social value (social groups)

Groups most and least likely to support my candidate	Factors						
	1	**2**	**3**	**4**	**5**	**6**	**7**
1. Minorities	−.04	.24	.60	.18	−.07	−.00	.04
2. The "silent majority"	.40	.22	−.20	−.28	.12	−.00	−.12
3. Senior citizens	.93	.22	.08	−.17	−.11	−.33	.10
4. Traditional Democrats	.16	.68	.05	−.07	−.04	−.05	−.12
5. Chicago politicians	−.23	.18	.09	−.36	−.18	−.03	.12
6. Students	−.05	−.38	.24	.55	.19	.02	.11
7. Underprivileged people	−.14	.02	.77	.11	−.04	−.23	.13
8. Liberals	−.21	−.11	.13	.60	.12	−.11	.15
9. Rich people	.20	.00	−.14	−.11	−.02	.55	.09
10. Downstate voters	.59	.10	−.04	−.34	.17	.19	.00
11. Farmers	.63	.04	−.11	−.02	−.11	.17	−.07
12. Blue-collar workers	.05	.66	.16	−.05	.03	.02	.05
13. Independents	−.01	−.00	−.08	.06	.71	−.00	.13
14. Environmentalists	−.05	−.05	.14	.22	.17	.08	.56
eigenvalue	3.16	2.04	1.37	1.08	1.05	.87	.76
% variance explained	22.6	14.6	9.9	7.8	7.5	6.2	5.5

Table 6-3　Rotated factor structure in voter choice: Emotional value (personal feelings)

Voting for my candidate would make me feel . . .	Factors				
	1	2	3	4	5
1. patriotic.	.20	.18	.07	.38	.26
2. confident.	.34	.23	.30	.62	.11
3. satisfied.	.49	.17	.34	.24	.08
4. optimistic.	.65	.09	.12	.11	.29
5. involved.	.15	.57	.00	.13	.40
6. excited.	.23	.05	.30	.10	.53
7. hopeful.	.57	.20	.10	.24	.07
8. relieved.	.15	.10	.66	.13	.15
9. responsible.	.17	.72	.16	.17	−.02
eigenvalue	3.58	1.02	.86	.82	.74
% variance explained	39.8	11.4	9.6	9.2	8.3

Table 6-4　Rotated factor structure in voter choice: Emotional value (candidate characteristics)

I believe that my candidate is . . .	Factors						
	1	2	3	4	5	6	7
1. decisive.	.46	.44	.06	.09	.10	.03	−.01
2. a family man.	−.01	−.06	.18	.16	−.03	.73	.02
3. honest.	.01	−.03	.54	.10	.09	.45	.12
4. cool under pressure.	.03	.18	.61	.29	.04	.13	−.09
5. charismatic.	.59	.20	.09	−.07	.02	−.10	.24
6. articulate.	.50	.13	.25	.03	.01	−.06	.08
7. idealistic.	.05	−.05	.10	.06	.00	.04	.64
8. hard-driving.	−.06	.50	−.12	−.06	.38	.15	.16
9. self-confident.	.02	.24	.14	.19	.48	−.03	.03

Table 6-4 (continued)

I believe that my candidate is . . .	Factors						
	1	2	3	4	5	6	7
10. a man with a good sense of humor.	.65	−.01	−.07	.09	.09	.16	−.16
11. innovative in implementing policies.	.47	.41	−.01	.00	.12	−.05	.04
12. level-headed.	.12	.07	.45	.55	.08	.23	.04
13. experienced.	.10	.36	.14	.04	.02	−.04	−.13
14. stable.	.02	.05	.06	.81	.07	.10	.05
15. able to get things done.	.34	.69	−.05	.08	.11	−.12	−.02
16. a man with a sense of purpose.	.20	.05	.16	.01	.73	−.00	−.05
17. compassionate.	.08	−.05	.42	−.03	.15	.02	.16
eigenvalue	3.54	2.38	1.40	1.26	1.05	1.01	.95
% variance explained	20.9	14.0	8.3	7.4	6.0	6.2	5.6

Table 6-5 Rotated factor structure in voter choice: Conditional value (current events)

I would switch my vote to another candidate if . . .	Factors		
	1	2	3
1. the Soviets invade another country.	.26	.87	.22
2. the U.S. decides to attend the Olympics in Moscow.	.20	.54	.22
3. the hostages in Iran are released.	.12	.34	.68
4. the Afghanistan situation worsens.	.33	.51	.37
5. gasoline prices rise above $2/gallon.	.68	.18	.34
6. another U.S. Embassy is overtaken.	.62	.54	.20
7. economists predict that a deep recession is coming.	.66	.15	.40
8. the inflation rate rises above 20%.	.78	.23	.07
9. the present administration flip-flops on another major policy vote.	.59	.30	−.02
eigenvalue	4.69	1.13	.79
% variance explained	52.1	12.6	8.8

Table 6-6   Rotated factor structure in voter choice: Conditional value (candidate events)

I would switch my vote to another candidate if I knew that my candidate . . .	Factors			
	1	2	3	4
1. had to oppose Ronald Reagan in the November election.	.02	.01	−.01	.22
2. had to oppose George Bush in the November election.	.02	−.05	.09	−.01
3. evaded his taxes.	.68	.14	.06	.15
4. was involved in a political scandal.	.72	.23	−.00	.00
5. had lied to the press.	.28	.42	−.03	.10
6. was having extra-marital romantic affairs.	.09	.73	.01	−.10
7. had no chance of winning the Democratic nomination.	−.04	−.01	.45	.00
8. got caught drinking while driving.	.16	.62	−.00	.26
9. knew about wrongdoing in his personal staff.	.16	.28	−.11	.42
10. was going to drop out of the race.	.21	.00	.69	−.03
11. would hurt the country by his actions or statements.	.35	.03	.20	.33
eigenvalue	2.61	1.47	1.13	1.03
% variance explained	23.7	13.4	10.4	9.4

Within the factor structures, numerical values corresponding to individual questionnaire items are referred to as *factor loadings*. Large factor loadings, those having absolute value of .40 or more, are boxed in the tables and used in interpretation. Referring to Table 6-1 (functional value) as an example, Factor 1 (eigenvalue = 3.18) explains 17.4 percent of the functional value variance. This factor loads high on items reflecting the belief among Kennedy supporters that Kennedy can "deal with Congress" (.76), "surround himself with trusted/knowledgeable people" (.74), "carry out his campaign promises" (.73), and "strengthen the nation morally and

Table 6-7   Rotated factor structure in voter choice: Epistemic value (nonspecific issues)

I am voting for my candidate because . . .	Factors				
	1	2	3	4	5
1. of my party loyalty.	.09	.01	.08	−.00	.35
2. of the mediocrity of the other candidates.	.01	.10	.03	.42	.00
3. of a bandwagon effect.	.76	.16	−.19	.03	.24
4. of his standing in the polls.	.70	−.03	.26	.00	.07
5. I want a change in the present administration.	.04	.53	−.12	.22	−.01
6. of his media coverage.	.31	.31	.09	−.26	.05
7. my spouse influenced me.	.04	.03	.53	.02	.11
8. of his magnetic personality.	.03	.44	.28	.02	.03
eigenvalue	1.86	1.23	1.12	1.01	.92
% variance explained	23.3	15.5	14.0	12.7	11.6

ethically" (.48). Thus, Factor 1 is interpreted as a "leadership" variable. Similarly, on the basis of their respective factor loadings, Factor 2 is interpreted as an "economic policies" variable, Factor 3 is interpreted as a "defense policies" variable, Factor 4 is interpreted as an "inflation" variable, and Factor 5 is interpreted as a "foreign policy" variable. The factors underlying the other values may be similarly interpreted on the basis of their factor loadings.

Discriminant Analysis

The factors derived now are input into the discriminant analysis. Thus, they serve as independent variables. Because a large number of factors are derived, a stepwise procedure is recommended to facilitate parsimony. As shown in Table 6-8, 20 of the 36 factors are retained as independent variables by the stepwise procedure.

Table 6-8   Results of stepwise discriminant analysis of political choice
factors

Variable description/Factor number/Value domain	Coefficients: Carter/Kennedy	Mean responses by group	
		Carter	Kennedy
1. Functional value (3) Issues and policies (defense spending, draft, nuclear buildup)	−.57	.33	−.79
2. Epistemic value (2) Nonspecific issues (change, magnetic personality)	.52	−.29	.53
3. Social value (4) Social groups (students, liberals)	.43	−.25	.74
4. Epistemic value (4) Nonspecific issues (mediocrity of other candidates)	.40	−.12	.17
5. Emotional value (1) Candidate characteristics (decisive, articulate, charismatic)	.36	−.29	.61
6. Functional value (2) Issues and policies (lower interest rates, cut taxes)	.32	−.17	.62
7. Social value (1) Social groups ("silent majority," seniors, farmers)	−.32	.31	−.33
8. Social value (2) Social groups (traditional Democrats, blue-collar workers)	−.28	.18	−.51
9. Emotional value (3) Candidate characteristics (honest, cool under pressure)	.23	−.05	.16
10. Epistemic value (3) Nonspecific issues (influenced by spouse)	−.23	.08	−.21
11. Conditional value (1) Current events (economy worsens, policy flip-flop)	−.21	.16	−.44
12. Social value (7) Social groups (environmentalists)	.19	−.08	.20
13. Emotional value (6) Candidate characteristics (a family man)	−.18	.01	−.01
14. Social value (3) Social groups (minorities, underprivileged people)	.15	−.05	.49
15. Social value (6) Social groups (rich people)	.14	−.03	−.01

Table 6-8   (continued)

Variable description/Factor number/Value domain	Coefficients: Carter/Kennedy	Mean responses by group	
		Carter	Kennedy
16. Emotional value (1) Personal feelings (satisfied, optimistic, hopeful)	–.14	.00	.25
17. Conditional value (3) Current events (release of hostages in Iran, recession coming)	.13	.07	–.01
18. Emotional value (2) Candidate characteristics (hard-driving, able to get things done)	–.11	.19	–.39
19. Social value (5) Social groups (Independents)	–.10	–.01	–.31
20. Functional value (5) Issues and policies (relations with U.S.S.R.)	–.09	.05	.15
Group means		–1.10	3.82

eigenvalue	Wilks' lambda	chi-squared	df	significance
4.27	.18	305.96	20	.0000

As shown, the most discriminating variable is a functional value factor pertaining to beliefs about Carter's position on defense issues (coefficient = –.57). Next is an epistemic value factor reflecting both a desire on the part of Kennedy supporters for a change in administration and attraction to Kennedy's "magnetic" personality (coefficient = .52). Also discriminating the two groups, and therefore likely to influence voter choice, are factors reflecting the association of Kennedy with students and liberals (social value, coefficient = .43); concern among Kennedy supporters over the "mediocrity of other candidates" (epistemic value, coefficient = .40); and feelings that Kennedy is decisive, articulate, and charismatic (emotional value, coefficient = .36).

Table 6-9 demonstrates the predictive ability of the theory through classification analysis, comparing voting behavior predicted by the model with actual voting behavior reported by respondents after the election. As shown, 97 percent of respondents are correctly classified. More specifically, 98 percent of respondents actually voting for Carter and 93 percent of respondents voting for Kennedy are correctly classified. This is particularly impressive given that it is *actual behavior* rather than merely intention that is predicted in this application.

Table 6-9   Predictive validity: Classification analysis of voter behavior

Actual (reported) voter behavior	Predicted voter behavior		Voters
	Carter	Kennedy	
Carter	89 (98%)	2 (2%)	91
Kennedy	2 (7%)	28 (93%)	30

Correctly classified: 97%

SUMMARY

This chapter has described the data analysis procedure used in applying the theory. As discussed, *discriminant analysis* is the recommended analytical technique. Discriminant analysis highlights differences between two or more *known* groups. Independent (discriminator) variables are derived through *factor analysis*. The analytic procedure is illustrated with an application involving voter behavior, and the results demonstrate the theory's excellent predictive ability.

Next, Chapter 7 demonstrates three applications of the theory, all pertaining to choices involving cigarette smoking. Data collection instruments used in actual studies are provided, and data are analyzed with discriminant analysis using independent variables derived through factor analysis.

PART 3
THE THEORY OF
CONSUMPTION VALUES
IN USE

7

APPLICATIONS
OF THE THEORY

This chapter illustrates three applications of the theory—all pertaining to market choices involving cigarette smoking. In the first, pertaining to the choice between smoking and not smoking (a "use versus do not use" decision), the values of smokers and nonsmokers are examined. The second application pertains to choice of product type by exploring the values differentiating smokers of filtered and nonfiltered cigarettes. Finally, the third application, which pertains to brand choice, examines the values differentiating Marlboro smokers and Virginia Slims smokers. As in the previous chapter, data are analyzed using discriminant analysis, with independent variables derived through factor analysis. Because cigarettes are a familiar product category and everyone is either a smoker or a nonsmoker, readers will be able to assess the face validity of our findings by comparing the results with their own intuition and choice values.

In this chapter, a "split-half" procedure is used for evaluating predictive validity. By incorporating a "holdout sample," the procedure minimizes the upward bias that may result when the same data are used both to construct and to validate a model. Thus, the split-half procedure provides a conservative estimate of predictive validity.

TO USE OR NOT USE—SMOKERS
VERSUS NONSMOKERS

The survey instrument developed to measure the values influencing the choice of whether to *smoke* is presented in Exhibit 7-1. Items were derived through focus group interviews with smokers and nonsmokers, and the questionnaire was administered to 185 respondents. After data cleaning, 168 questionnaires were retained, specifically, 71 usable questionnaires from the smokers sample, and 97 from the nonsmokers sample.

Exhibit 7-1 A survey of cigarette smoking—smokers versus nonsmokers

This is a survey to study cigarette smoking behavior. The results of this study will be used for academic research only, and your responses will be kept strictly confidential.

We are interested in your own personal feelings and opinions. *There are no right or wrong answers.*

On each page you will find several different kinds of statements about cigarette smoking. All you have to do is put an X in the spaces that reflect your own personal feelings and opinions.

PLEASE NOTE:

1. Check only one answer per statement.

2. When you are finished, please check to be sure you have not omitted any answers.

THANK YOU VERY MUCH!

PART ONE

	YES	NO
1. Do you consider yourself a regular cigarette smoker?	_____	_____

2. How much do you smoke?

Not at all	_____
Less than one pack a week	_____
More than one pack a week	_____
Less than one pack a day	_____
More than one pack a day	_____

	YES	NO
3. Have you ever engaged in any of the following behaviors?		
a. Smoked cigarettes and then stopped smoking	_____	_____

	YES	NO
b. Stopped smoking cigarettes and then started again	_____	_____
c. Always smoked cigarettes regularly	_____	_____
d. Never smoked cigarettes regularly	_____	_____

4. Would you ever consider switching your behavior by smoking cigarettes if you don't now, or by not smoking cigarettes if you do now?   _____   _____

5. Do you think your past habits and experiences have determined your choice to smoke or not smoke cigarettes?   _____   _____

6. Are you very familiar with smoking cigarettes?   _____   _____

7. Are you interested or involved in smoking cigarettes?   _____   _____

8. Are you very committed to smoking (or not smoking) cigarettes?   _____   _____

9. Do you consider smoking cigarettes very important?   _____   _____

PART TWO

Please indicate whether you agree or disagree that the following benefits or problems are associated with smoking cigarettes:

Smoking cigarettes . . .	AGREE	DISAGREE
1. is an addictive habit.	1. _____	_____
2. stops nervousness.	2. _____	_____
3. causes heart and lung disease.	3. _____	_____
4. annoys other people.	4. _____	_____
5. is relaxing.	5. _____	_____
6. helps me fit into a situation.	6. _____	_____
7. is something to keep me busy.	7. _____	_____

PART THREE

Not everybody smokes cigarettes. Which of the following groups of people do you believe are most and least likely to smoke cigarettes?

	MOST LIKELY	LEAST LIKELY
1. Insecure people	1. _____	_____
2. People with parents who smoke	2. _____	_____
3. Athletes	3. _____	_____
4. Health enthusiasts	4. _____	_____
5. Low-income people	5. _____	_____
6. People with strict parents	6. _____	_____
7. People under a lot of pressure	7. _____	_____
8. People who frequent bars	8. _____	_____
9. Students	9. _____	_____
10. Professional people	10. _____	_____
11. High achievers	11. _____	_____

PART FOUR

Certain conditions motivate people to behave differently than their regular behavior or habit. Do you believe that the following conditions might cause you to change your behavior to start or stop smoking cigarettes?

	YES	NO
1. Personal health complications	1. _____	_____
2. Large sums of money	2. _____	_____
3. Need of a stimulant	3. _____	_____
4. Everyone else is smoking.	4. _____	_____
5. Pressure from loved ones	5. _____	_____
6. Lack of money	6. _____	_____
7. Excessive stress	7. _____	_____
8. Physically threatened	8. _____	_____
9. Concerned about my children's health	9. _____	_____

PART FIVE

People sometimes smoke cigarettes for personal and emotional reasons. Please indicate whether you personally experience any of the following feelings associated with your decision to smoke or not smoke cigarettes.

	YES	NO
1. I feel *satisfied* when I smoke.	1. _____	_____
2. I feel *anxious* when I do not smoke.	2. _____	_____
3. I feel *accepted* when I smoke.	3. _____	_____
4. I feel *intelligent* when I do not smoke.	4. _____	_____
5. I feel *sexy* when I smoke.	5. _____	_____
6. I feel *angry* when I do not smoke.	6. _____	_____
7. I feel *confident* about not smoking.	7. _____	_____
8. I feel *safe* when I do not smoke.	8. _____	_____

PART SIX

Some people smoke cigarettes because they are curious about them, or simply bored with whatever else they are doing. Do you smoke or have thoughts of smoking for any of the following reasons?

	YES	NO
1. Need to eat less	1. _____	_____
2. Many friends started smoking	2. _____	_____
3. Because my parents smoke	3. _____	_____
4. Seeing advertisements	4. _____	_____
5. Rebellion against authority figures	5. _____	_____
6. Cost of cigarettes went down	6. _____	_____
7. Simply curious about smoking	7. _____	_____
8. Want to learn more about smoking	8. _____	_____

Factors discriminating between smokers and nonsmokers are derived through factor analysis. These represent potential independent variables to serve as input to the discriminant model. Data from 86 percent of subjects (145 randomly selected respondents) are used in constructing the discriminant model, while data from the other 14 percent (23 respondents) are retained as a holdout sample.

Rotated factor structures for the five values, using varimax rotation to derive orthogonal dimensions, are presented in Tables 7-1 through 7-5. As contrasted with the voter choice example in Chapter 6, which used the scree test method to select potential independent variables, the "rule of thumb" method is used in this application. Thus, only factors associated with eigenvalues of more than 1.0 are retained. As shown in Tables 7-1 through 7-5, 13 factors are retained. Large factor loadings, those with an absolute value of .40 or more, are boxed and used in interpreting the factors.

Table 7-1 Rotated factor structure in use or not use cigarettes: Functional value

Smoking Cigarettes ...	Factors		
	1	2	3
1. is an addictive habit.	−.07	.00	.86
2. stops nervousness.	.65	.06	−.42
3. causes heart and lung disease.	.04	.74	.37
4. annoys other people.	−.02	−.82	−.28
5. is relaxing.	.55	−.31	−.34
6. helps me fit into a situation.	.79	.05	−.02
7. is something to keep me busy.	.78	.01	.09
eigenvalue	2.20	1.32	1.02
% variance explained	31.4	18.9	14.5

As shown in Table 7-1, three functional value factors are extracted. Factor 1 reflects perceived benefits of smoking: "helps me fit into a situation," "is something to keep me busy," "stops nervousness," and "is relaxing." Factor 2 reflects perceived problems associated with smoking: "annoys other people," and "causes heart and lung disease." Factor 3 reflects concern over the addictive nature of smoking, and shows that some respondents feel that smoking does not stop nervousness. Similarly,

Table 7-2 Rotated factor structure in use or not use cigarettes:
Social value

Groups most and least likely to smoke cigarettes	Factors			
	1	2	3	4
1. Insecure people	.10	.05	.65	.36
2. People with parents who smoke	.06	.06	.70	−.04
3. Athletes	.06	.78	−.15	.03
4. Health enthusiasts	−.06	.78	.24	−.06
5. Low-income people	.06	−.09	.27	.67
6. People with strict parents	−.03	.01	−.14	.68
7. People under a lot of pressure	.49	−.37	.16	.21
8. People who frequent bars	.66	−.12	.11	−.02
9. Students	.60	.06	.00	−.39
10. Professional people	.67	.22	−.17	.18
11. High achievers	.34	.25	−.58	.38
eigenvalue	1.72	1.65	1.38	1.30
% variance explained	15.7	15.0	12.5	11.8

Table 7-2 shows four significant social value factors. High loadings are associated with groups believed to be most and least likely to smoke.

Continuing, Table 7-3 shows two factors underlying the conditional value domain. Factor 1 reflects reasons smokers might change their behavior to stop smoking (as examples, "concerned about my children's health," "personal health complications"); Factor 2 reveals situations that might influence a nonsmoker to start (e.g., "everyone else is smoking," "need of a stimulant"). Similarly, Table 7-4 shows two factors underlying emotional value. Factor 1 reflects positive feelings associated with not smoking (e.g., "confident," "safe," "intelligent"), while Factor 2 reflects positive feelings associated with smoking ("satisfied," "accepted," "sexy") and negative feelings associated with not smoking ("angry," "anxious"). Finally, as shown in Table 7-5, two factors are extracted relevant to the epistemic value domain.

Table 7-3   Rotated factor structure in use or not use cigarettes:
Conditional value

Conditions that might cause respondent to start or stop smoking	Factors	
	1	2
1. Personal health complications	.79	.19
2. Large sum of money	.28	.22
3. Need of a stimulant	.21	.83
4. Everyone else is smoking.	.17	.85
5. Pressure from loved ones	.70	.36
6. Lack of money	.50	.37
7. Excessive stress	.44	.66
8. Physically threatened	.75	.18
9. Concerned about my children's health	.84	.19
eigenvalue	4.22	1.02
% variance explained	46.9	11.3

Table 7-4   Rotated factor structure in use or not use cigarettes:
Emotional value

Feelings associated with the decision to smoke or not smoke cigarettes	Factors	
	1	2
1. I feel *satisfied* when I smoke.	-.44	.64
2. I feel *anxious* when I do not smoke.	-.30	.59
3. I feel *accepted* when I smoke.	-.02	.52
4. I feel *intelligent* when I do not smoke.	.71	-.03
5. I feel *sexy* when I smoke.	.05	.63
6. I feel *angry* when I do not smoke.	-.02	.77
7. I feel *confident* about not smoking.	.86	-.11
8. I feel *safe* when I do not smoke.	.80	-.07
eigenvalue	2.73	1.47
% variance explained	34.1	18.4

Table 7-5   Rotated factor structure in use or not use cigarettes:
Epistemic value

Reasons to smoke cigarettes or have thoughts of smoking	Factors	
	1	2
1. Need to eat less	.05	.64
2. Many friends started smoking	.04	.83
3. Because my parents smoke	.09	.63
4. Seeing advertisements	.77	.08
5. Rebellion against authority figures	.80	.17
6. Cost of cigarettes went down	.83	−.09
7. Simply curious about smoking	.57	.51
8. Want to learn more about smoking	.77	.12
eigenvalue	3.13	1.51
% variance explained	39.1	18.9

Table 7-6 presents the results of the stepwise discriminant analysis. Of the 13 extracted factors, only seven are retained by the stepwise procedure. Yet, as evidenced by the eigenvalue and chi-square statistics associated with both models, the reduced model is comparable to the full model in other respects. Thus, the stepwise procedure facilitates a more economical while equally powerful model.

As indicated by Table 7-6, *emotional value* dominates in discriminating the smokers and nonsmokers in this study. With coefficients of .73 and −.72, the two emotional value factors are by far the most influential. These factors reflect the positive and negative feelings associated with smoking and not smoking. Additionally, the conditional value factor reflecting reasons to stop smoking (coefficient = .37) is somewhat influential. Functional, social, and epistemic values have little influence in this application.

Table 7-7A (classification analysis using data also used in constructing the model) shows 91 percent of respondents correctly classified by the discriminant model. More specifically, 92 percent of smokers and 90 percent of nonsmokers are correctly classified on the basis of their values. Further, as shown in Table 7-7B, the more conservative split-half test reveals comparable results with 91 percent correctly classified. Thus, the theory demonstrates excellent predictive validity.

Table 7-6 Results of discriminant analysis of use or not use cigarettes factors

Variable description/Factor number	Coefficients: smoker/nonsmoker	Mean responses by group	
		Smoker (N=65)	Nonsmoker (N=80)
1. Emotional value (2) (angry/anxious when I do not smoke, satisfied, sexy)	.73	.60	−.43
2. Emotional value (1) (intelligent, confident, safe when I do not smoke)	−.72	−.60	.48
3. Conditional value (1) (personal health complications, pressure from loved ones, physically threatened, concern over children's health)	.37	.61	−.40
4. Social value (3) (insecure people, people with parents who smoke)	−.19	−.36	.23
5. Functional value (2) (causes heart and lung disease, annoys other people)	−.18	−.29	.17
6. Functional value (1) (stops nervousness, is relaxing, helps me fit into situations, keeps me busy)	.17	.43	−.39
7. Epistemic value (1) (seeing advertisements, cost went down, learn more, curious)	−.13	.01	−.02
	Group means:	1.38	−1.12

eigenvalue	Wilks' lambda	chi-squared	df	significance
1.56	.39	131.35	7	.0000

Comparative statistics for full model:

eigenvalue	Wilks' lambda	chi-squared	df	significance
1.60	.38	130.50	13	.0000

The demonstrated salience of emotional value in discriminating between smokers and nonsmokers suggests strategy implications for public policy makers, organizations such as the American Lung Association, and health care providers. The findings suggest that, rather than emphasizing the health problems (negative functional value) associated with smoking, efforts to discourage smoking might more appropriately

Table 7-7   Predictive validity: use or not use cigarettes

A. Classification analysis

Actual behavior	Predicted behavior		Subjects
	Smokers	Nonsmokers	
Smokers	60 (100%)	5 (7.7%)	65
Nonsmokers	8 (10%)	72 (90%)	80

Correctly classified: 91.03%

B. Classification analysis (holdout sample)

Actual behavior	Predicted behavior		Subjects
	Smokers	Nonsmokers	
Smokers	6 (100%)	0	6
Nonsmokers	2 (11.8%)	15 (88.2%)	17

Correctly classified: 91.3%

reinforce the *positive* feelings associated with *not smoking*. On the other hand, cigarette marketers also seem to be fully cognizant of salient emotional values and often emphasize satisfaction, sexiness, and other positive emotions in promoting their brands.

PRODUCT TYPE—FILTERED VERSUS NONFILTERED CIGARETTES

The survey instrument developed to measure the values driving the choice between filtered and nonfiltered cigarettes is presented in Exhibit 7-2. The questionnaire consists of items derived through focus group interviews with smokers of filtered and nonfiltered cigarettes, and it was administered to 124 respondents. After data cleaning, 104 usable questionnaires were retained—70 from the filtered cigarette smokers sample and 34 from the nonfiltered cigarette smokers sample. The smaller sample size associated with the nonfiltered smokers group reflects the lesser popularity of the nonfiltered product type. Data from 88 percent of the subjects (92 respondents) are used in constructing the discriminant model, while data from the other 12 percent (12 respondents) are retained as a holdout sample.

Exhibit 7-2   A survey of cigarette smoking—filtered versus nonfiltered

This is a survey to study cigarette smoking behavior. The results of this study will be used for academic research only, and your responses will be kept strictly confidential.

We are interested in your own personal feelings and opinions. *There are no right or wrong answers.*

On each page you will find several different kinds of statements about cigarette smoking. All you have to do is put an X in the spaces that reflect your own personal feelings and opinions.

PLEASE NOTE:

1. Check only one answer per statement.

2. When you are finished, please check to be sure you have not omitted any answers.

THANK YOU VERY MUCH!

- -

PART ONE

1. Which type of cigarette do you regularly smoke?
   Filtered   _____
   Nonfiltered   _____

2. How much do you smoke?
   Less than one pack a day   _____
   One pack a day   _____
   One and a half packs a day   _____
   Two or more packs a day   _____

3. Have you ever engaged in the following   YES   NO
   behaviors?
   a. Smoked filtered cigarettes and then   _____   _____
      change to nonfiltered cigarettes
   b. Smoked nonfiltered cigarettes and   _____   _____
      then changed to filtered cigarettes
   c. Always smoked filtered cigarettes   _____   _____
   d. Always smoked nonfiltered cigarettes   _____   _____

	YES	NO

4. Would you ever consider switching your behavior by smoking filtered cigarettes if you don't now, or vice versa? _____ _____

PART TWO

Please indicate whether you agree or disagree that the following benefits or problems are associated with smoking *your* type of cigarette:

Smoking filtered/nonfiltered cigarettes . . .   AGREE   DISAGREE

1. gives me a full tobacco taste. 1. _____ _____
2. is harsh on my throat. 2. _____ _____
3. prevents tobacco from getting in my mouth. 3. _____ _____
4. provides me with a mild tasting cigarette. 4. _____ _____
5. is hazardous to my health. 5. _____ _____
6. reduces the tar and nicotine intake. 6. _____ _____
7. turns my teeth yellow. 7. _____ _____
8. causes me to get yellow-looking fingers. 8. _____ _____
9. keeps me from coughing as badly. 9. _____ _____
10. prevents the cigarette from sticking to my lips. 10. _____ _____
11. makes it more difficult to draw in smoke. 11. _____ _____
12. helps me eat less. 12. _____ _____
13. gives me the most from each cigarette. 13. _____ _____

PART THREE

Not everyone smokes filtered or nonfiltered cigarettes. Which of the following groups of people do you believe are most and least likely to smoke *your type* of cigarette.

	MOST LIKELY	LEAST LIKELY
1. Young females	1. _____	_____
2. Older men	2. _____	_____
3. Athletes	3. _____	_____
4. Beginning smokers	4. _____	_____

		MOST LIKELY	LEAST LIKELY
5.	Truck drivers	5. _____	_____
6.	Working-class men	6. _____	_____
7.	Beer drinkers	7. _____	_____
8.	Older women	8. _____	_____
9.	Outdoorsmen	9. _____	_____
10.	Young people	10. _____	_____
11.	Health-conscious people	11. _____	_____

PART FOUR

Certain conditions motivate people to behave differently than their regular behavior or habit. Do you believe that the following conditions might cause you to switch from a filtered to a nonfiltered cigarette, or from a nonfiltered to a filtered cigarette (depending on the type of cigarette you presently smoke)?

	YES	NO
1. Price of my type of cigarette goes up sharply	1. _____	_____
2. Need to borrow a cigarette	2. _____	_____
3. Night out drinking with friends	3. _____	_____
4. New findings on hazards of smoking my type of cigarette	4. _____	_____
5. Nothing else available at the time	5. _____	_____
6. Doctor's orders	6. _____	_____
7. Increase in throat irritation	7. _____	_____
8. Family pressures	8. _____	_____
9. Bad health	9. _____	_____

PART FIVE

People sometimes smoke a particular type of cigarette for personal and emotional reasons. Please indicate whether you personally experience any of the following feelings associated with your decision to smoke filtered or nonfiltered cigarettes.

	YES	NO
1. I feel *guilty* when I smoke *my type* of cigarette.	1. _____	_____

	YES	NO
2. I feel *relaxed* when I smoke *my type* of cigarette.	2. _____	_____
3. I feel *anxious* when I smoke *my type* of cigarette.	3. _____	_____
4. I feel *content* when I smoke *my type* of cigarette.	4. _____	_____
5. I feel *worried* when I smoke *my type* of cigarette.	5. _____	_____
6. I feel *unhappy* when I smoke *my type* of cigarette.	6. _____	_____
7. I feel *calm* when I smoke *my type* of cigarette.	7. _____	_____
8. I feel *satisfied* when I smoke *my type* of cigarette.	8. _____	_____

PART SIX

Some people smoke their type of cigarettes because they are curious about them, or simply bored with whatever else they are smoking. Do you smoke *your type* of cigarette for any of the following reasons?

	YES	NO
1. Friend smoked them and I stuck with them	1. _____	_____
2. Saw an interesting commercial	2. _____	_____
3. Recommended by a friend	3. _____	_____
4. most popular type when I started smoking	4. _____	_____
5. As a change of pace	5. _____	_____
6. To reduce stress	6. _____	_____
7. Wanted to know what it was like to smoke them	7. _____	_____
8. Because of information I heard about them	8. _____	_____
9. Just curious to try them	9. _____	_____
10. Bored with what I used to smoke	10. _____	_____

Rotated factor structures for the five value domains (using varimax rotation to derive orthogonal dimensions) are presented in Tables 7-8 through 7-12. Again, only factors associated with eigenvalues of more than 1.0 are retained as potential independent variables. As shown, 15 factors are selected, and the large factor loadings (absolute value of .40 or more) that are used to interpret the factors are boxed.

Table 7-8 Rotated factor structure in filtered versus nonfiltered product type: Functional value

Smoking filtered/nonfiltered cigarettes . . .	Factors				
	1	2	3	4	5
1. gives me a full tobacco taste.	−.25	.05	.79	−.10	.13
2. is harsh on my throat.	−.37	.28	−.27	.56	−.05
3. prevents tobacco from getting in my mouth.	.82	.09	−.22	−.11	.07
4. provides me with a mild tasting cigarette.	.79	.04	−.15	−.03	−.01
5. is hazardous to my health.	.11	.73	−.14	−.13	−.09
6. reduces the tar and nicotine intake.	.79	.19	−.07	−.13	.04
7. turns my teeth yellow.	−.01	.78	.09	.23	.06
8. causes me to get yellow-looking fingers.	−.06	.34	.03	.67	.36
9. keeps me from coughing as badly.	.47	−.02	.19	.17	.36
10. prevents the cigarette from sticking to my lips.	.61	−.30	.09	.10	.11
11. makes it more difficult to draw in smoke.	.14	−.04	−.08	−.04	.88
12. helps me eat less.	.12	−.25	.20	.77	−.15
13. gives me the most from each cigarette.	.02	−.11	.82	.18	−.17
eigenvalue	2.96	1.81	1.68	1.11	1.00
% variance explained	22.8	13.9	12.9	8.5	7.7

As shown in Table 7-8, five functional value factors are extracted. Factors 1 and 5 reflect benefits associated with smoking filtered cigarettes (e.g., "prevents tobacco from getting in my mouth," "provides me

Table 7-9   Rotated factor structure in filtered versus nonfiltered product type: Social value

Groups most and least likely to smoke respondent's type of cigarette	Factors	
	1	2
1. Young females	.83	−.23
2. Older men	−.55	.46
3. Athletes	.71	−.09
4. Beginning smokers	.81	−.16
5. Truck drivers	−.46	.66
6. Working-class men	−.25	.74
7. Beer drinkers	.05	.74
8. Older women	.58	.16
9. Outdoorsmen	.04	.63
10. Young people	.83	−.15
11. Health-conscious people	.83	−.12
eigenvalue	4.74	1.70
% variance explained	43.1	15.4

with a mild tasting cigarette," "makes it more difficult to draw in smoke"), while Factor 3 reflects benefits associated with smoking nonfiltered cigarettes (e.g., "gives me the most from each cigarette," "gives me a full tobacco taste"). In contrast, Factors 2 and 4 reflect smoking-related problems and concerns (e.g., "turns my teeth yellow," "is hazardous to my health," "is harsh on my throat").

Table 7-9 shows two significant social value factors. Factor 1 loads high on groups believed most likely to smoke filtered cigarettes (e.g., "young females," "young people," "health-conscious people," "beginning smokers"), and Factor 2 loads high on groups believed most likely to smoke nonfiltered cigarettes (e.g., "working-class men," "beer drinkers," "truck drivers"). Continuing, Table 7-10 shows two conditional value factors. Factor 1 reflects a willingness to switch from nonfiltered to filtered cigarettes in the face of health concerns (e.g., "bad health," "increase in throat irritation," "doctor's orders"), and Factor 2 represents a willingness to smoke a different type of cigarette under certain social conditions ("I need to borrow a cigarette," "nothing else is available," "a night out drinking with friends").

Table 7-10 Rotated factor structure in filtered versus nonfiltered product type: Conditional value

Conditions that might cause respondents to switch product type	Factors	
	1	2
1. Price of my type of cigarette goes up sharply	.33	.26
2. Need to borrow a cigarette	–.04	.86
3. Night out drinking with friends	.02	.66
4. New findings on hazards of smoking my type of cigarette	.64	.17
5. Nothing else available at the time	.24	.79
6. Doctor's orders	.83	.11
7. Increase in throat irritation	.84	.18
8. Family pressures	.52	–.08
9. Bad health	.85	–.01
eigenvalue	3.20	1.70
% variance explained	35.6	18.9

Table 7-11 Rotated factor structure in filtered versus nonfiltered product type: Emotional value

Feelings associated with decision to smoke filtered or nonfiltered cigarettes	Factors	
	1	2
1. Guilty	–.13	.76
2. Relaxed	.82	.09
3. Anxious	–.17	.76
4. Content	.73	–.18
5. Worried	–.16	.81
6. Unhappy	.03	.70
7. Calm	.83	–.16
8. Satisfied	.78	–.17
eigenvalue	3.14	1.82
% variance explained	39.3	22.7

Table 7-12 Rotated factor structure in filtered versus nonfiltered product type: Epistemic value

Reasons for smoking type of cigarette	Factors			
	1	2	3	4
1. Friend smoked them and I stuck with them	.88	.07	.02	.03
2. Saw an interesting commercial	–.15	.02	–.13	.78
3. Recommended by a friend	.86	.20	–.08	.10
4. Most popular type when I started smoking	–.03	.42	–.65	.15
5. As a change of pace	.01	.17	.73	.19
6. To reduce stress	.11	.30	–.11	.40
7. Wanted to know what it was like to smoke them	.26	.75	.08	.05
8. Because of information I heard about them	.25	–.01	.15	.65
9. Just curious to try them	.04	.81	.15	.06
10. Bored with what I used to smoke	–.09	.25	.65	–.19
eigenvalue	2.27	1.55	1.23	1.06
% variance explained	22.7	15.5	12.3	10.6

Similarly, Table 7-11 shows two factors underlying the emotional value domain. Factor 1 reflects positive feelings associated with smoking ("calm," "relaxed," "satisfied," "content"), while Factor 2 reflects negative feelings ("worried," "guilty," "anxious," "unhappy"). Finally, as shown in Table 7-12, four factors are extracted from the epistemic value domain. Factor 1 reflects the influence of friends, Factor 2 reflects curiosity, Factor 3 reflects boredom and the desire for a change of pace, and Factor 4 reflects the influence of commercials and information.

Table 7-13 presents the results of the stepwise discriminant analysis. Of the 15 extracted factors, eight are retained by the stepwise procedure. As in the previous application, the stepwise procedure facilitates a more economical or parsimonious model, and the reduced model is comparable in other respects with the full model, as shown in the comparative statistics in Table 7-13.

As indicated by Table 7-13, *functional value* and *social value* are most important in discriminating filtered and nonfiltered cigarette smokers in

Table 7-13   Results of discriminant analysis of cigarette product type factors

Variable description/Factor number	Coefficients: filtered/nonfiltered	Mean responses by group	
		Filtered (N=63)	Nonfiltered (N=29)
1. Functional value (1) (prevents tobacco in mouth, mild tasting, prevents sticking to lips, reduces tar and nicotine intake)	.65	.50	−.99
2. Social value (1) (young females, athletes, beginning smokers, young people, health-conscious people)	.59	.47	−.95
3. Epistemic value (2) (wanted to know what it was like, curious)	−.28	−.12	.23
4. Epistemic value (1) (friend smoked them, recommended by friend)	.24	.17	−.11
5. Functional value (2) (hazardous to health, turns teeth yellow)	.24	.08	−.02
6. Functional value (3) (full tobacco taste, gives me most from each cigarette)	−.21	−.19	.24
7. Social value (2) (truck drivers, working class men, beer drinkers, outdoorsmen)	−.21	−.21	.28
8. Functional value (4) (harsh on throat, causes yellow fingers, helps me eat less)	−.19	−.16	.11
Group means:		.87	−1.88

eigenvalue	Wilks' lambda	chi-squared	df	significance
1.67	.37	84.37	8	.0000

Comparative statistics for full model:

eigenvalue	Wilks' lambda	chi-squared	df	significance
1.71	.37	82.10	15	.0000

this study. The most discriminating variable is Factor 1 from the functional value domain. This variable reflects the general functional benefits associated with smoking filtered versus nonfiltered cigarettes (coefficient = .65). Similarly, Factor 1 from the social value domain is quite discriminating (coefficient = .59). This variable reflects the groups of people believed most likely to smoke filtered versus nonfiltered cigarettes. Other factors extracted as independent variables have considerably less influence, and epistemic value is the only other value entering into the model.

Again, the theory demonstrates impressive predictive validity. The classification analysis presented in Table 7-14A, using data also used in constructing the model, shows 90 percent of respondents correctly classified. More specifically, 92 percent of filtered cigarette smokers and 86 percent of nonfiltered cigarette smokers are correctly classified on the basis of their values. The lower level of accuracy associated with the nonfiltered cigarette smokers sample is almost certainly a function of the smaller sample size. In turn, the smaller sample size reflects that product type's lesser popularity. While used to provide a more conservative estimate of predictive validity, the split-half test (Table 7-14B) shows perfect prediction.

Table 7-14 Predictive validity: filtered versus nonfiltered product type choice

A. Classification analysis

Actual choice	Predicted choice		Subjects
	Filtered	Nonfiltered	
Filtered	58 (92.1%)	5 (7.9%)	63
Nonfiltered	4 (13.8%)	25 (86.2%)	29

Correctly classified: 90.22%

B. Classification analysis (holdout sample)

Actual choice	Predicted choice		Subjects
	Filtered	Nonfiltered	
Filtered	7 (100%)	0	7
Nonfiltered	0	5 (100%)	5

Correctly classified: 100%

If it could be assumed that these preliminary findings are generalizable to the entire cigarette market, it would be suggested that parties hoping to influence choice between filtered and nonfiltered product types should emphasize salient functional concerns and social associations. Further, epistemic value might be emphasized as a secondary appeal. In contrast, appeals to emotional value and conditional value do not appear warranted.

BRAND CHOICE—MARLBORO VERSUS VIRGINIA SLIMS

The survey instrument developed for measuring the values influencing *Marlboro and Virginia Slims* smokers is presented in Exhibit 7-3. Items were derived through focus group interviews with smokers of both brands, and the questionnaire was administered to 165 respondents. After data cleaning, 138 usable questionnaires were retained, 85 from the Marlboro smokers sample and 53 from the Virginia Slims smokers sample. Data from 116 respondents (84 percent) are used in constructing the discriminant model, while data from the other 22 respondents (16 percent) are held out.

Exhibit 7-3   A survey of cigarette smoking—Marlboro versus Virginia Slims

This is a survey to study cigarette smoking behavior. The results of this study will be used for academic research only, and your responses will be kept strictly confidential.

We are interested in your own personal feelings and opinions. *There are no right or wrong answers.*

On each page you will find several different kinds of statements about cigarette smoking. All you have to do is put an X in the spaces that reflect your own personal feelings and opinions.

PLEASE NOTE:

1. Check only one answer per statement.

2. When you are finished, please check to be sure you have not omitted any answers.

THANK YOU VERY MUCH!

PART ONE

1. Do you consider yourself a brand-loyal smoker of
   Marlboro?   _____
   Virginia Slims?   _____

2. How much to you smoke?
   Less than 1 pack a week   _____
   1–2 packs a week   _____
   2–3 packs a week   _____
   More than 3 packs a week   _____

		YES	NO
3.	Have you ever engaged in any of the follow- ing behaviors?		
	a. Smoked your brand and then stopped	_____	_____
	b. Stopped smoking your brand and then started again	_____	_____
	c. Always smoked your brand	_____	_____
4.	Would you ever consider switching your behavior by smoking another brand of cigarettes?	_____	_____
5.	Do you think your past habits and experi- ences have determined your choice to smoke your brand?	_____	_____
6.	Are you very familiar with smoking cigarettes?	_____	_____
7.	Are you interested or involved in smoking cigarettes?	_____	_____
8.	Are you very committed to smoking cigarettes?	_____	_____
9.	Do you consider smoking cigarettes very important?	_____	_____

PART TWO

Please indicate whether you agree or disagree that the following benefits or
problems are associated with smoking your brand.

My brand of cigarette . . .	AGREE	DISAGREE
1. makes me feel lady-like.	1. _____	_____
2. is lower in tar and nicotine.	2. _____	_____
3. calms my nerves.	3. _____	_____
4. has a stronger taste than others.	4. _____	_____

	AGREE	DISAGREE
5. relieves tension.	5. _____	_____
6. is longer and thinner than others.	6. _____	_____

PART THREE

Not everybody smokes your brand. Which of the following groups of people do you believe are most and least likely to smoke your brand?

	MOST LIKELY	LEAST LIKELY
1. Women	1. _____	_____
2. Rich people	2. _____	_____
3. College students	3. _____	_____
4. Outdoorsmen	4. _____	_____
5. Older people	5. _____	_____
6. Blue-collar workers	6. _____	_____
7. Cowboys	7. _____	_____
8. Men	8. _____	_____
9. Sophisticated women	9. _____	_____
10. Beginner smokers	10. _____	_____

PART FOUR

Certain conditions motivate people to behave differently than their regular behavior or habit. Do you believe that the following conditions might cause you to *switch* from Marlboros to Virginia Slims or Virginia Slims to Marlboros (depending on the brand you presently smoke)?

	YES	NO
1. Price of my brand increased	1. _____	_____
2. Quality of my brand decreased	2. _____	_____
3. Moved into a higher social class	3. _____	_____
4. At a party	4. _____	_____
5. Needed a stronger tasting cigarette	5. _____	_____
6. Free sample	6. _____	_____
7. Only cigarette available at time	7. _____	_____
8. Friends stopped smoking my brand	8. _____	_____

PART FIVE

People sometimes smoke a particular brand for personal and emotional reasons. Please indicate whether you personally experience any of the following feelings associated with your decision to smoke your brand.

	YES	NO
1. I feel like I'm *in a higher class* when I smoke my brand.	1. _____	_____
2. I feel *calm* when I smoke my brand.	2. _____	_____
3. I feel *macho* when I smoke my brand.	3. _____	_____
4. I feel *tough* when I smoke my brand.	4. _____	_____
5. I feel *happy* when I smoke my brand.	5. _____	_____
6. I feel *feminine* when I smoke my brand.	6. _____	_____

PART SIX

Some people smoke a particular brand because they are curious about it, or simply bored with whatever else they are smoking. Do you smoke your brand for any of the following reasons?

	YES	NO
1. Just to see what it is like	1. _____	_____
2. For a change of pace	2. _____	_____
3. Ads were appealing	3. _____	_____
4. To get a smoother taste	4. _____	_____
5. To get more tar and nicotine	5. _____	_____
6. Friends smoke this brand	6. _____	_____
7. Liked the package design	7. _____	_____
8. Bought them on sale	8. _____	_____
9. Liked the image they convey	9. _____	_____

Tables 7-15 through 7-19 show varimax rotated factor structures. Thirteen factors with eigenvalues of more than 1.0 are retained as potential independent variables. Large factor loadings used in interpretation are boxed.

Table 7-15   Rotated factor structure in brand choice: Functional value

My brand of cigarette ...	Factors	
	1	2
1. makes me feel lady-like.	.65	−.08
2. is lower in tar and nicotine.	.79	.00
3. calms my nerves.	−.05	.80
4. has a stronger taste than others.	−.80	.03
5. relieves tension.	.05	.82
6. is longer and thinner than others.	.74	.12
eigenvalue	2.25	1.32
% variance explained	37.4	22.1

Table 7-16   Rotated factor structure in brand choice: Social value

Groups most and least likely to smoke respondent's brand	Factors	
	1	2
1. Women	−.89	−.04
2. Rich people	−.58	.01
3. College students	.38	.54
4. Outdoorsmen	.91	.02
5. Older people	.18	−.68
6. Blue-collar workers	.81	−.04
7. Cowboys	.93	.00
8. Men	.94	.05
9. Sophisticated women	−.89	−.02
10. Beginner smokers	−.01	.65
eigenvalue	5.34	1.18
% variance explained	53.4	11.8

As shown in Table 7-15, two functional value factors are extracted. Factor 1 reflects benefits associated with Virginia Slims, while Factor 2 less obviously reflects benefits associated with Marlboros. Similarly, Table 7-16 shows two significant social value factors. Positive coefficients in Factor 1 suggest groups believed most likely to smoke Marlboros ("men," "cowboys," "outdoorsmen," "blue collar workers"), while negative coefficients suggest those least likely to smoke the brand ("women," "sophisticated women," "rich people"). Factor 2 is also associated with Marlboros, loading high on "beginner smokers" and "college students."

Continuing, Table 7-17 shows three conditional value factors. Factors 1 and 3 reflect conditional functional value, while Factor 2 reflects conditional social value. Similarly, Table 7-18 shows three factors underlying emotional value. Factor 1 reflects feelings associated with smoking Marlboros ("tough," "macho"); Factor 2 reflects feelings associated with smoking Virginia Slims ("like I'm in a higher class," "feminine"); and Factor 3 reflects more general affective associations ("calm," "happy"). Finally, as shown in Table 7-19, three factors are also extracted from the epistemic value domain. Factors 1 and 3 reflect a desire for novelty and change, and Factor 2 reflects promotional influence.

Table 7-20 presents the results of the stepwise discriminant analysis. Of the 13 extracted factors, only two are retained by the stepwise procedure. Again, when compared with the full model, the stepwise model is much more economical or parsimonious and is comparable in other respects.

As indicated by Table 7-20, *social value* literally overwhelms the other values in this application. Specifically, Factor 1 from the social value

Table 7-17 Rotated factor structure in brand choice: Conditional value

Conditions that might cause respondents to switch from Marlboro to Virginia Slims or vice versa	Factors		
	1	2	3
1. Price of my brand increased	.21	−.12	.74
2. Quality of my brand decreased	.60	−.27	.15
3. Moved into a higher social class	−.04	.76	.09
4. At a party	.20	.63	.30
5. Needed a stronger tasting cigarette	.30	−.26	−.60
6. Free sample	.77	.14	−.01
7. Only cigarette available at time	.77	.11	−.05
8. Friends stopped smoking my brand	−.03	.65	−.25
eigenvalue	1.73	1.61	1.06
% variance explained	21.6	20.1	13.3

Table 7-18 Rotated factor structure in brand choice: Emotional value

Feelings associated with decision to smoke Marlboro or Virginia Slims	Factors		
	1	2	3
1. Like I'm in a higher class	.21	.87	−.01
2. Calm	.08	−.07	.85
3. Macho	.89	−.05	.06
4. Tough	.89	.04	.06
5. Happy	.03	.24	.78
6. Feminine	−.25	.82	.18
eigenvalue	1.80	1.65	1.13
% variance explained	30.0	27.5	18.8

Table 7-19 Rotated factor structure in brand choice: Epistemic value

Reasons for smoking particular brand	Factors		
	1	2	3
1. Just to see what it is like	.76	.13	.01
2. For a change of pace	.82	−.01	−.22
3. Ads were appealing	.19	.68	.29
4. To get a smoother taste	.05	.40	−.11
5. To get more tar and nicotine	−.04	.08	.79
6. Friends smoke this brand	.07	.32	−.58
7. Liked the package design	.13	.65	−.20
8. Bought them on sale	.72	.04	.04
9. Liked the image they convey	−.15	.76	.00
eigenvalue	2.11	1.53	1.10
% variance explained	23.5	17.0	12.3

domain (coefficient = .93) is dominant. The factor reflects the association of Marlboro with "men," "cowboys," "outdoorsmen," and "blue collar workers," and the brand's disassociation from "women," "sophisticated women,"

Table 7-20   Results of discriminant analysis of brand choice factors

Variable description/Factor number	Coefficients: Marlboro/Virginia Slims	Mean responses by group	
		Marlboro (N=70)	Virginia Slims (N=46)
1. Social value (1) (outdoorsmen, blue-collar workers, cow-boys, men)	.93	.75	−1.17
2. Emotional value (2) (in a higher class, feminine)	−.29	−.46	.81
	Group means:	1.67	−2.53

eigenvalue	Wilks' lambda	chi-squared	df	significance
4.30	.19	188.40	2	.0000

Comparative statistics for full model:

eigenvalue	Wilks' lambda	chi-squared	df	significance
4.46	.18	182.47	13	.0000

and "rich people." The only other variable entering the model is Factor 2 from the emotional value domain, having a coefficient of only .29. Further, this emotional value factor reflects *feelings relating to social imagery* ("I feel feminine when I smoke my brand," "I feel like I'm in a higher class when I smoke my brand").

As shown in Table 7-21A (using data also used in constructing the model), 96 percent of respondents are correctly classified. Specifically, 93 percent of Marlboro smokers and 100 percent of Virginia Slims smokers sampled are correctly classified. Further, as in the filtered versus nonfiltered cigarette application, the split-half test presented in Table 7-21B shows perfect prediction. Thus, as in the foregoing examples, the theory demonstrates excellent predictive validity.

The gender-based associations revealed in this application suggest that the social imagery communicated by Marlboro and Virginia Slims advertising has been internalized by consumers. Sex role identification is entrenched and appears as a primary driver of brand choice. Thus, the findings suggest that extraordinary marketing effort would be required for Marlboro to appeal to women or for Virginia Slims to appeal to men. Further, it might be almost as challenging for Marlboro to attract men identifying with a more urban and less rugged image or for Virginia Slims to attract women not identifying with a sophisticated image.

Table 7-21 Predictive validity: Marlboro versus Virginia Slims brand choice

A. Classification analysis

Actual choice	Predicted choice		Subjects
	Marlboro	Virginia Slims	
Marlboro	65 (92.9%)	5 (7.1%)	70
Virginia Slims	0	46 (100%)	46

Correctly classified: 95.69%

B. Classification analysis (holdout sample)

Actual choice	Predicted choice		Subjects
	Marlboro	Virginia Slims	
Marlboro	15 (100%)	0	15
Virginia Slims	0	7 (100%)	7

Correctly classified: 100%

SUMMARY

This chapter has demonstrated the theory's operationalization with three applications, thereby providing further guidance for readers intending to use the theory in their own research studies. All three applications involve market choices pertaining to cigarette smoking: the choice between smoking and not smoking (use versus do not use), the choice between filtered and nonfiltered cigarettes (product type), and the choice between Marlboro and Virginia Slims (brand choice). Thus, all three levels of choice are represented.

Data collection instruments are provided relevant to the three applications, and data are analyzed with discriminant analysis, using factor analysis to derive independent variables. Finally, the predictive validity of the theory is demonstrated through classification analysis.

Next, Chapter 8 evaluates the theory using metatheory criteria. As evidence of its descriptive, explanatory, and predictive validity, the theory performs well on organizational, relevance, and reality metatheory criteria. Further, Chapter 8 demonstrates the theory's applicability to a full range of choice situations involving both goods and services as well as profit and nonprofit sectors of the economy.

8

EVALUATION AND
IMPLICATIONS

Our purpose in advancing and operationalizing a theory of market choice behavior has been:

1. to contribute to the general understanding of consumer choice behavior.
2. to assist practitioners and academic researchers in determining which values drive specific choices.

In other words, we hope that the theory will be used for *predictive* purposes in specific choice settings, as well as for *descriptive* and *explanatory* purposes. This chapter evaluates our theory of consumer choice behavior, and it demonstrates its potential application to the wide range of choice situations within and outside the business sector.

EVALUATION OF THE THEORY

The validity and potential usefulness of a theory is necessarily of concern to those who would consider its application. Well-accepted criteria for evaluating theory are defined by the area of inquiry termed *metatheory* (Halbert 1964, Sheth 1967, Howard and Sheth 1969, Bartels 1970, Zaltman et al. 1973, Zaltman et al. 1982, Hunt 1983, Leong 1985, Sheth et al. 1988). As defined by Zaltman et al. (1973):

> Metatheory is the science of science or the investigation of investigation. Metatheory involves the careful appraisal of the methodology of science and the philosophical issues involved in the conduct of science. It is concerned with such topics as the operationalization of scientific concepts, the logic of testing theories, the use of theory, the nature of causality, and procedures for making predictions. Broadly defined, metatheory is the investigation, analysis, and the description of (1) technology of building theory, (2) the theory itself, and (3) the utilization of theory. (p. 4)

Based on a review of metatheory literature, Sheth et al. (1988) advanced three categories of metatheory criteria, each comprised of two specific tests. These six criteria are delineated as follows:

1. *Pragmatics (relevance) criteria*: relevance of the theory to its users.
   a. *Richness*: How comprehensive and generalizable is the theory?
   b. *Simplicity*: How readily can the theory be communicated to others and implemented in practice?

2. *Syntax (organization) criteria:* structural soundness and precise organizational pattern.
   a. *Structure*: Are the theoretical concepts properly defined and integrated to form a strong nomological (lawlike) network?
   b. *Specification*: Are the relationships between constructs specified in a manner to clearly delimit hypotheses?

3. *Semantics (reality) criteria*: relationship of the theory to reality.
   a. *Testability*: Are operational definitions provided to ensure testability and intersubjective consensus?
   b. *Empirical Support*: What is the degree of confirmation in terms of empirical support?

The following sections evaluate our theory in terms of these six meta-theory criteria.

Pragmatics (Relevance) Criteria

Richness. The conceptual development presented in Part One of this book demonstrates that the theory integrates a wide array of concepts, theories, and research traditions advanced across behavioral and social science disciplines. The five constructs central to the theory—functional value, social value, emotional value, epistemic value, and conditional value—represent a rich yet economical framework modeling the multiple values that work independently to drive market choice. These five concepts are pertinent to all individual, systematic, and voluntary choices involving a broad definition of "products." The theory is equally relevant to durable goods, nondurable goods, services, consumer products, industrial products, people, and ideas. Further, the theory has been demonstrated to be applicable to three distinct levels of choice: the decision to buy or not buy a product (or use or not use a product), the decision to use one type of product versus another (product type decision), and the decision to use one particular brand versus another (brand choice).

Simplicity. The constructs are easy to understand because, as consumers ourselves, all of us can relate to them. Additionally, because the theory's development has been influenced by a variety of research traditions, most potential users have been previously exposed to at least some of the theoretical and empirical work on which it is built. Further, the low level of abstraction used in operationalizing the theory makes research results very straightforward and easy to implement, and the theory is congruent with the familiar and well-accepted belief that marketing practice should be customer-oriented (e.g., "the marketing concept," "close to the customer"). The operationalization encourages researchers to learn about values driving market choice from the consumer's perspective.

Syntax (Organization) Criteria

Structure. Considerable attention is given in early chapters to the development of conceptual definitions. Further, each construct is related to pertinent interdisciplinary research and theoretical perspectives, with the domains of several social and behavioral science disciplines integrated to provide an explanation for market choice. By recognizing that consumer choice is driven by multiple and independent values, each making differential contributions, the concepts are also integrated to form a complete picture of the values driving choice.

Specification. The relationships among the five constructs are well specified in that the constructs are defined as being independent but as working additively to influence choice. Further, it is demonstrated that the constructs and their relationships can be utilized to develop and test specific hypotheses relevant to choice behavior. These hypotheses may be very situation-specific, as might be developed by a brand manager seeking to clarify the values differentiating users of his/her brand from those of the closest competitor; or they may be more generalized, as might be developed by an academic researcher seeking, for example, insight into the values that drive "excessive" or "deviant" consumer behavior.

Semantics (Reality) Criteria

Testability. The second and third sections of the book are devoted to operationalizing, applying, and testing the theory. A principal objective is to provide a tool that can be used by interested parties who want to learn more about consumers. As a result, the operationalization provided facilitates the translation from theory to either application or test. Because ease of operationalization is an important feature for the potential user, we have endeavored to develop standardized procedures for constructing measurement instruments and for analyzing data.

Also contributing to its strengths in terms of testability, the theory is a theory of *behavior* as opposed to, say, attitude or intention. Thus, the theory may be tested using data from respondents already *known* to engage in the consumption behavior of interest. Already, numerous studies have been conducted relevant to "buy versus no-buy" choices, product type choices, and brand choices; studies have been conducted with respect to products in the public sector (e.g., mass transit, food stamps), the private sector (e.g., automobile makes, aspirin brands), the nonprofit sector (e.g., churches, temples), and of interest to public policy makers (e.g., cocaine use, voter registration).

Empirical Support.   The applications presented in this book and other applications conducted by the authors demonstrate support for the fundamental axioms of the theory. As will be recalled, Chapter 1 delineated three fundamental axioms. The first asserts that consumer choice behavior is a function of multiple values; the second asserts that these values make differential contributions in given choice situations; and the third asserts that the values are independent.

The first axiom has found a great deal of empirical support. Our approximately 200 studies have confirmed that all five values are drivers of choice. Further, in any given choice situation, two or more values usually discriminate between groups. Thus, empirical support exists for the claim that multiple values drive choice. Additionally, the excellent predictive validity demonstrated by the theory suggests support for the claim that choice is driven specifically by the five values cited. Finally, research from a variety of disciplines suggests empirical support for those specific values emphasized by their research traditions—for example, social value in sociology and social psychology and epistemic value in experimental psychology).

The second axiom, pertaining to differential contributions, has found an equal degree of support. In applying the theory in various choice contexts, rarely have we found two values to be associated with even approximately the same sized coefficients. It is more common for one or two values to dominate, for one or two others to have a secondary influence, and for others to have either tertiary influence or no influence at all.

Finally, the third axiom asserts that the five values are independent. The validity of this claim is tested by checking for intercorrelation among the values. In all such tests conducted to date, independence has been confirmed. Thus, in practice as well as in theory, the five values are demonstrated to be independent.

IMPLICATIONS OF THE THEORY

A primary factor motivating the advancement of our theory is our fundamental belief in the importance of market choice behavior as a distinct area of study. Consumer choice behavior represents a significant subset of human behavior in general and of consumer behavior in particular. Consumer choice behavior is universal in that people in virtually all societies face consumption decisions. Further, consumption decisions impinge on nearly every aspect of life because goods and services, as well as allocations of scarce time, money, and effort resources, accompany most human endeavors. Finally, consumption decisions can be *very* important and involving to consumers. In a marketing environment characterized by increased domestic and global competition, changing demographics and lifestyles, advertising clutter, increased consumer sophistication, and the like, marketers are challenged more than ever to correctly segment markets and position their products to satisfy the specific needs and wants of target markets. An understanding of how consumers make choices and what motivates these choices can greatly facilitate marketing success.

Several specific applications have already been discussed in detail. In closing, the remaining pages are devoted to more clearly demonstrating the theory's potential application to a broad range of choices. The number of potential examples is limitless, and we will leave it to the reader to apply the theory to her or his own interests. However, we do briefly discuss just a few examples for illustrative purposes. As summarized in Table 8-1, two examples relevant to each of four sets of circumstances are discussed: goods in the profit sector, goods in the nonprofit sector, services in the profit sector, and services in the nonprofit sector.

Table 8-1   Application of the theory to profit/nonprofit and goods/services sectors

	Goods	Services
Profit sector	Microcomputers Videocassette recorders	Long-distance telephone service Health care
Nonprofit sector	Condoms Surplus farm products	Drug rehabilitation centers Charitable organizations

Goods in the Profit Sector

The applicability of the theory to the profit sector, especially as it involves goods, is quite obvious because this has been the traditional focus of marketing and consumer behavior. To illustrate the utility of our theory, we discuss potential applications to choices involving microcomputers and videocassette recorders. Both are innovations introduced to the mass market within the past decade, and both have been readily adopted by consumers. Further, both markets have experienced significant turbulence as competitors have fought for market dominance.

Microcomputers.   The microcomputer market has been one of the most competitive in recent history. Following Apple's lead, a great many companies entered the market during the late 1970s and early 1980s and were subsequently "shaken out," leaving only a few of the strongest. Those remaining faced fierce competition from one another and from lesser known companies with "lookalike" models. Further, competitive turbulence was increased by rapid technological change, resulting in an ongoing parade of design changes and new product introductions.

Although the initial storm of microcomputer competitive activity appears to have passed, we suggest that our theory is of value to surviving manufacturers as they regroup and prepare for future competitive challenges. Knowledge of what drives the decision to buy or not buy a computer, as well as what drives product type and brand choice, can greatly facilitate these firms' long-term planning.

It appears on the surface that a large number of computer buyers were initially motivated by epistemic value. Many consumers were curious about computers, intrigued by the novel technology and anxious to acquire some hands-on knowledge so as not to be "left behind in the computer age." However, once their computers were purchased, installed, and "played with," a large number of consumers found that they really had no practical need for them. Thus, these computers largely sat idle.

The consumers described above, however, differ markedly from "technophiles," students, home-based business owners, and others likely to be influenced primarily by functional value. These latter groups largely comprise the market for upgrading and updating computers, and they are likely to sustain an interest in functional superiority.

Determining just what values drive the decision to buy or not buy a computer, to buy a more sophisticated versus a less sophisticated model, to upgrade an existing home computer system, and so on can enable manufacturers to be more responsive to the market. This is increasingly important as the market becomes more "computer literate" and develops a clearer idea of its needs and wants.

Videocassette Recorders. The case of videocassette recorders is interesting in that it demonstrates a recent and clear-cut example of a product's relatively "instant" success. Consumers readily saw the functional value of the product and, with lowered prices and a plethora of movie rental outlets, the VCR quickly came to be regarded as almost "standard home equipment." Approximately 50 percent of households now own one or more videocassette recorders.

However, even in the beginning, consumers were faced with a difficult choice between two product types—the Beta format and the VHS format. Competitive battles raged between manufacturers of the two formats, with VHS taking a strong lead. From the consumer's perspective, it appears that the preference for VHS was largely driven by functional and social value. Since its introduction, the VHS format was slightly less expensive and, perhaps most importantly, capable of recording for a longer duration (originally two hours versus one hour for the Beta). Thus, functional value led early adopting groups to favor the VHS format. Later adopting groups, seeing the choice made by "opinion leaders," followed their lead, at least partially driven by social value. Finally, the choice of VHS was reinforced by the greater availability of rental tapes in VHS format, another functional value.

Despite the dominance of VHS, the Beta format—regarded by some as providing a higher quality recording and superior features (functional value)—has never lost its market presence. In fact, to appeal to consumers whose choices are driven by technical superiority (termed the "prosumer market"), Sony now has introduced an Extended Definition Beta format.

Determining just what values drive the choice between VHS and Beta could facilitate better directed target marketing among manufacturers of both formats. Further, knowledge of the values driving choice could contribute to more effective long-term planning in line with consumers' actual needs and wants.

Services in the Profit Sector

The services sectors of many advanced economies have recently experienced accelerated growth, generally exceeding growth in manufacturing. For example, in contrast to its traditional emphasis on agriculture and manufacturing, the United States is now sometimes referred to as a "services economy." Thus, the marketing of services as opposed to goods has enjoyed increased visibility. To illustrate the applicability of our theory to this growing sector, we discuss consumer decisions involving long distance telephone service and health care. Major structural changes have occurred in both industries, with one outcome being that consumers are now confronted with an unprecedented number and variety of service alternatives.

Long-Distance Telephone Service. During the 1980s, the telecommunications industry experienced massive structural change. One example of this change is in long-distance service. While only one source of long-distance service had traditionally been available (AT&T), the 1980s found consumers with a number of options.

In the beginning, the more successful new companies such as MCI and Sprint based their competitive strategies on the premise that choice is driven by functional value, primarily price. In turn, the response of AT&T reflected the premise that other functional attributes, primarily experience and quality of service, are of at least equal—if not greater—importance. AT&T also promoted emotional value, suggesting that consumers choosing AT&T could feel secure in that decision and emphasizing the positive feelings derived from maintaining long-distance telephone contact with loved ones.

During the latter part of the 1980s, the newer companies found it necessary to raise rates and were therefore less able to appeal to consumers solely on the basis of price. As a result, these companies began to emphasize other functional attributes. For example, similar to AT&T, the newer companies began to advertise quality of service.

We suggest that long-distance telephone companies may benefit from using our theory to determine just what values drive consumer choice. Even if it is confirmed that the functional and emotional values delineated above are most important, other secondary, but meaningful, values may be identified. Indeed, to the extent that consumers come to view the major competitors as equivalent in terms of price and service quality, they will no longer be able to base their patronage on those attributes alone. The company that emphasizes other salient, although possibly less obvious, values may therefore acquire a differential advantage.

Health Care. The health-care industry is another that has experienced intense competition concurrent with structural change. New forms of health care (for example, health maintenance organizations, walk-in clinics, alternative birthing centers, and substance abuse treatment programs) have claimed larger and larger shares of the market. Further, traditional health care providers have been forced to engage in marketing and promotional activities. For example, ambulatory care centers, specialized clinics, and private physicians now regularly advertise via billboard, radio, and local television. Even hospitals have found it necessary to be more responsive to patient needs by expanding and upgrading their customer-sensitive services. To illustrate, many hospitals now provide comfortably furnished rooms for their maternity patients and invite the father, as well as the baby, to "room in."

Clearly, a number of factors enter into health-care decisions, and the values driving choice are likely to vary from situation to situation (e.g., maternity, AIDS testing, emergency treatment, treatment of minor illness). We suggest that health-care providers use our theory to determine which values are most salient as consumers seeking specific types of health care choose among a growing array of services and facilities.

Goods in the Nonprofit Sector

The theory presented in this book is applicable to the nonprofit sector as well as to the profit sector. The same values driving choices among goods and services provided by business enterprises also drive choices regarding alternatives provided by nonprofit organizations. We demonstrate the applicability of the theory to goods in the nonprofit sector by discussing the free distribution of condoms and surplus farm products.

Condoms.   Concerned with the health threat posed by the AIDS virus, various public agencies and nonprofit organizations have undertaken programs to encourage condom use. In addition to programs to increase AIDS awareness and promote the use of condoms through public service announcements, educational brochures, and the like, various organizations have endeavored to encourage condom use by giving them away. Such efforts have primarily targeted young people (through, for example, schools and universities) and those in high-risk groups, particularly through health agencies.

Because the spread of AIDS is literally a matter of life and death, the agencies sponsoring these programs are highly concerned with their efficacy. If the targeted groups do not take the threat of AIDS seriously or continue to be negatively predisposed toward condom use, the public health threat accelerates.

Concerned agencies and organizations can utilize our theory to gain a better understanding of the groups they wish to reach. To illustrate, it is hoped that such groups *do* fear AIDS and see condoms as a necessary precaution (functional value). However, if they do not, or if they are put off by other functional concerns like cost or inconvenience, even more educational effort may be needed and specific measures may be required to counter the negative functional value. On the other hand, if it is found that such groups resist condom use because of negative social value (e.g., "It just isn't cool"), emotional value (e.g., "I don't want to plan to have sex"), or conditional value (e.g., "As long as I'm with my boyfriend, it isn't necessary"), then efforts will be needed to reverse such attitudes.

Surplus Farm Products.   Since the Great Depression, the United States government has periodically sponsored efforts to supply surplus farm products to low-income households. In addition to assisting disadvantaged consumers, these programs endeavor to maintain farm product prices at "more than the market can bear" so that farmers can continue to operate through periods of surplus. As a recent example, the government provided assistance to dairy farmers by buying surplus cheese to distribute free to consumers.

Although the role of consumers in such situations is to *receive* free goods rather than to purchase them, an understanding of choice values can facilitate government agencies' efforts to serve their various constituents. By examining the values of those who take advantage of such programs versus those who do not, areas for increased efficiency and efficacy may be identified. It may be found that a variety of factors inhibit qualified consumers from taking advantage of government programs. For example, various groups may have no means of travel to the dispersal site (functional value), may be too "proud" to receive free goods (social value), or may fail to take notice of the offer (epistemic value). Such information may be quite useful as government agencies endeavor to improve their programs.

Services in the Nonprofit Sector

Finally, many service alternatives are offered through the nonprofit sector. To illustrate, we discuss the potential application of our theory to nonprofit drug rehabilitation centers and charitable organizations.

Drug Rehabilitation Centers. Many drug rehabilitation programs are operated by nonprofit organizations, usually within rather tight budgetary constraints. Continued funding—from foundations, government sources, and private donations—is usually contingent on an organization's ability to attract clients.

We suggest that organizations involved in drug rehabilitation and similar programs may use the theory to conceptualize the value systems of their clients, their potential clients, and those who might refer clients to treatment centers, (for example, doctors, employee assistance counselors, school counselors, and therapists). By understanding the values motivating target groups, organizations can develop appropriate appeals. For example, various groups might base choice on specific functional values (e.g., recovery rates, credentials of the treatment staff), social values (e.g., assurances that other patients are people like themselves), or emotional values (e.g., testimonials from individuals who have been through the program and now "feel good about themselves").

Self-help organizations such as Alcoholics Anonymous and Narcotics Anonymous have been extremely successful in attracting people who seek recovery from addiction. The basis of these programs on anonymity, spiritual/emotional health and group support—as well as having good recovery rates—suggests that social and emotional value, as well as functional value, may be primary drivers of choice.

Charitable Organizations. Large numbers of charitable organizations exist who solicit contributions of both money and time for the support of various causes. With a growing number of "worthy" causes competing for donors' scarce resources, many such organizations find it difficult to attract adequate support for their programs. Thus, an understanding of the values differentiating active contributors, contributors to certain types of programs, and so on would be of benefit.

Given the wide range of charitable giving "opportunities," it is likely that choices are driven by any of the five values. Further, various segments of the population may be influenced by differing values. Charitable giving may be motivated by functional value associated with a genuine belief in the program being supported, by social value associated with the perception that members of various social classes are "expected" to give, by emotional value associated with the good feelings that come from helping, by epistemic value associated with an interest in a particular program, and by conditional value associated with emergency situations.

An understanding of the values that drive charitable behavior can facilitate a soliciting organization's appeals to salient motives. For example, a finding that a substantial number of contributors are driven by epistemic value would suggest that the charitable organization provide informative corollary materials with its solicitations. Individuals whose interests are provoked may then be more likely to give. On the other hand, a finding that contributors are driven by conditional value might suggest that the organization should emphasize the urgency associated with its cause.

SUMMARY

It is our purpose in advancing and operationalizing a theory of market choice behavior to (1) contribute to the general understanding of consumer choice behavior and (2) assist practitioners, policy makers, and academic researchers in determining what motivates specific choices. As such, we have endeavored to maximize the descriptive, explanatory, and predictive power of our theory.

The validity and potential usefulness of the theory is evidenced by its strong performance on metatheory criteria. First, the theory is demonstrated to be strong on *pragmatics*, or *relevance criteria*. It is both rich (comprehensive and generalizable) and simple (readily communicated to others and readily implemented in practice). Second, considerable attention has been given to the theory's *syntax*, or *organization*. The theory is strong in both structure—concepts are well defined and integrated—and specification—relationships are specified in a manner to delimit hypotheses. Finally, the theory is strong on *semantics*, or *reality criteria*. since operational definitions are provided, the theory is testable and substantial empirical support (confirmation) has been advanced.

In summary, we believe that our theory is applicable to the entire range of individual, systematic, and voluntary choices facing consumers. Thus, we encourage readers to apply it to their own areas of interest in both the profit and nonprofit sectors and with regard to both goods and services. Further, we encourage our academic colleagues to test the theory in a wide range of market choice situations.

REFERENCES

Aaker, David A., Douglas M. Stayman, and Michael R. Hagerty. "Warmth in Advertising: Measurement, Impact, and Sequence Effects." *Journal of Consumer Research* 12 (March 1986): 365–381.

Abelson, Robert P., and Milton J. Rosenberg. "Symbolic Psycho-Logic: A Model of Attitudinal Cognition." *Behavioral Science* 3 (January 1958): 1–13.

Acker, Mary, and Paul McReynolds. "The Obscure Figures Test: An Instrument for Measuring 'Cognitive Innovation'." *Perceptual and Motor Skills* 21 (December 1965): 815–821.

——— . "The 'Need for Novelty': A Comparison of Six Instruments." *Psychological Record* 17 (April 1967): 177–182.

Adams, Joe K. "Laboratory Studies of Behavior Without Awareness." *Psychological Bulletin* 54 (September 1957): 383–405.

Adler, Alfred. *Understanding Human Nature*, translated by Walter Beran Wolfe. London: George Allen & Unwin, 1928.

Adorno, T. W., Else Frenkel-Brunswik, Daniel J. Levinson, and R. Nevitt Sanford. *The Authoritarian Personality*. New York: Harper & Row, 1950.

Agarwal, Manoj K., and Brian T. Ratchford. "Estimating Demand Functions for Product Characteristics: The Case of Automobiles." *Journal of Consumer Research* 7 (December 1980): 249–262.

Akers, Fred C. "Negro and White Automobile-Buying Behavior: New Evidence." *Journal of Marketing Research* 5 (August 1968): 283–290.

Alchian, Armen A. "The Meaning of Utility Measurement." *American Economic Review* 43 (March 1953): 26–50.

Alderfer, Clayton P. "An Empirical Test of a New Theory of Human Needs." *Organizational Behavior and Human Performance* 4 (May 1969): 142–175.

——— . *Existence, Relatedness, and Growth: Human Needs in Organizational Settings*. New York: The Free Press, 1972.

Alexis, Marcus. "Some Negro-White Differences in Consumption." *American Journal of Economics and Sociology* 21 (January 1962): 11–28.

Allen, Vernon L. "Situational Factors in Conformity." In *Advances in Experimental Social Psychology*. Vol. 2, edited by Leonard Berkowitz, 133–175. New York: Academic Press, 1965.

Allport, Gordon W. "Attitudes." In *A Handbook of Social Psychology*. Vol. 2, edited by Carl Murchison, 798–844. Worcester, Mass.: Clark University Press, 1935.

Alpert, Mark L. "Personality and the Determinants of Product Choice." *Journal of Marketing Research* 9 (February 1972): 89–92.

Altman, Irwin, and Joachim F. Wohlwill. *Human Behavior and Environment: Advances in Theory and Research.* 6 vols. New York: Plenum Press, 1976.

Andreasen, Alan R. *The Disadvantaged Consumer.* New York: The Free Press, 1975.

————. "Disadvantaged Hispanic Consumers: A Research Perspectives and Agenda." *The Journal of Consumer Affairs* 16 (Summer 1982): 46–61.

————. "Life Status Changes and Changes in Consumer Preference and Satisfaction." *Journal of Consumer Research* 11 (December 1984): 784–794.

————, and Lloyd C. Hodges. "Clothing, Race and Consumer Decision Making." In *Minorities and Marketing: Research Challenges*, edited by Alan R. Andreasen and Frederick D. Sturdivant, 72–96. Chicago: American Marketing Association, 1977.

Apodaca, Anacleto. "Corn and Custom: The Introduction of Hybrid Corn to Spanish American Farmers in New Mexico." In *Human Problems in Technological Change*, edited by Edward H. Spicer, 35–39. New York: Russell Sage Foundation, 1952.

Archibald, Robert B., Clyde A. Haulman, and Carlisle E. Moody, Jr. "Quality, Price, Advertising, and Published Quality Ratings." *Journal of Consumer Research* 9 (March 1983): 347–356.

Armer, Michael, and Larry Isaac. "Determinants and Behavioral Consequences of Psychological Modernity: Empirical Evidence from Costa Rica." *American Sociological Review* 43 (June 1978): 316–334.

Arndt, Johan. *Word of Mouth Advertising: A Review of the Literature.* New York: Advertising Research Foundation, Inc., 1967.

————. "Selective Processes in Word of Mouth." *Journal of Advertising Research* 8 (September 1968): 19–22.

Arrow, Kenneth J. "Utility and Expectation in Economic Behavior." In *Psychology: A Study of Science*. Vol. 6, edited by Sigmund Koch, 724–752. New York: McGraw-Hill, 1963.

Asch, Solomon E. "Studies of Independence and Conformity: A Minority of One Against a Unanimous Majority." *Psychological Monographs* 70, no. 9 (No. 416, 1956): 1–70.

————. "Effects of Group Pressure Upon the Modification and Distortion of Judgments." In *Group Dynamics: Research and Theory*. 2d ed., edited by Dorwin Cartwright and Alvin Zander, 189–200. New York: Harper & Row, 1960.

Ashby, Harold J., Jr. "The Black Consumer." In *New Consumerism: Selected Readings*, edited by William T. Kelley, 149–176. Columbus, Ohio: Grid, 1973.

Auliciems, Andris. "Some Observed Relationships Between the Atmospheric Environment and Mental Work." *Environmental Research* 5 (June 1972): 217–240.

Bach, Sheldon, and George S. Klein. "Conscious Effects of Prolonged Subliminal Exposures of Words." *American Psychologist* 12 (July 1957): 397.

Barker, Roger G. *Ecological Psychology: Concepts and Methods for Studying the Environment of Human Behavior.* Stanford, Calif.: Stanford University Press, 1968.

Barnet, H. G. *Innovation: The Basis of Cultural Change.* New York: McGraw-Hill, 1953.

Barron, Frank. "Personality Style and Perceptual Choice." *Journal of Personality* 20 (1952): 385–401.

———. "Complexity-Simplicity as a Personality Dimension." *Journal of Abnormal and Social Psychology* 48 (April 1953): 163–172.

Bartels, Robert. *Marketing Theory and Metatheory.* Homewood, Ill.: Richard D. Irwin, 1970.

Barthol, Richard P., and Michael J. Goldstein. "Psychology and the Invisible Sell." *California Management Review* 1 (Winter 1959): 29–35.

Bass, Frank M., and W. Wayne Talarzyk. "An Attitude Model for the Study of Brand Preference." *Journal of Marketing Research* 9 (February 1972): 93–96.

Batra, Rajeev, and Michael L. Ray. "Affective Responses Mediating Acceptance of Advertising. *Journal of Consumer Research* 13 (September 1986): 234–249.

Bauer, Raymond A., and Scott M. Cunningham. *Studies in the Negro Market.* Cambridge, Mass.: Marketing Science Institute, 1970.

Baumgarten, Steven A. "The Innovative Communicator in the Diffusion Process." *Journal of Marketing Research* 12 (February 1975): 12–18.

Bearden, William O., and Michael J. Etzel. "Reference Group Influence on Product and Brand Purchase Decisions." *Journal of Consumer Research* 9 (September 1982): 183–194.

———, and Arch G. Woodside. "Situational Influence on Consumer Purchase Intentions." In *Consumer and Industrial Buying Behavior*, edited by Arch G. Woodside, Jagdish N. Sheth, and Peter D. Bennett, 167–177. New York: Elsevier North-Holland, 1977.

Becherer, Richard C., and Lawrence M. Richard. "Self-Monitoring as a Moderating Variable in Consumer Behavior." *Journal of Consumer Research* 5 (December 1978): 159–162.

Beckwith, Neil E., and Donald R. Lehmann. "The Importance of Halo Effects in Multi-Attribute Attitude Models." *Journal of Marketing Research* 12 (August 1975): 265–275.

Belch, George E. "The Effects of Television Commercial Repetition on Cognitive Response and Message Acceptance." *Journal of Consumer Research* 9 (June 1982): 56–65.

Belk, Russell W. "Application and Analysis of the Behavioral Differential Inventory for Assessing Situational Effects in Buyer Behavior." In *Advances in Consumer Research.* Vol. 1, edited by Scott Ward and Peter Wright, 370–380. Urbana, Ill.: Association for Consumer Research, 1973.

———. "An Exploratory Assessment of Situational Effects in Buyer Behavior." *Journal of Marketing* 11 (May 1974): 156–163.

———. "Situational Variables and Consumer Behavior." *Journal of Consumer Research* 2 (December 1975a): 157–164.

———. "The Objective Situation as a Determinant of Consumer Behavior." In *Advances in Consumer Research.* Vol. 2, edited by Mary Jane Schlinger, 427–437. Ann Arbor, Mich.: Association for Consumer Research, 1975b.

———. "It's the Thought That Counts: A Signed Digraph Analysis of Gift-Giving." *Journal of Consumer Research* 3 (December 1976): 155–162.

———. "Assessing the Effects of Visible Consumption on Impression Formation." In *Advances in Consumer Research.* Vol. 5, edited by H. Keith Hunt, 39–47. Ann Arbor, Mich.: Association for Consumer Research, 1978.

_____. "A Free Response Approach to Developing Product-Specific Consumption Situation Taxonomies." In *Analytic Approaches to Product and Marketing Planning*, edited by Allan D. Shocker, 177–196. Cambridge, Mass.: Marketing Science Institute, 1979.

_____. "Effects of Consistency of Visible Consumption Patterns on Impression Formation." In *Advances in Consumer Research*. Vol. 7, edited by Jerry C. Olson, 365–371. Ann Arbor, Mich.: Association for Consumer Research, 1980.

_____, Kenneth D. Bahn, and Robert N. Mayer. "Developmental Recognition of Consumption Symbolism." *Journal of Consumer Research* 9 (June 1982): 4–17.

_____, Robert Mayer, and Amy Driscoll. "Children's Recognition of Consumption Symbolism in Children's Products." *Journal of Consumer Research* 10 (March 1984): 386–397.

Bell, Gerald D. "Self-Confidence and Persuasion in Car Buying." *Journal of Marketing Research* 4 (February 1967): 46–52.

Bell, Paul A. "Physiological, Comfort, Performance, and Social Effects of Heat Stress." *Journal of Social Issues* 37 (Winter 1981): 71–94.

Bellows, Roger. "Toward a Taxonomy of Social Situations." In *Stimulus Determinants of Behavior*, edited by S. B. Sells, 197–212. New York: The Ronald Press, 1963.

Bendix, Reinhard. "Tradition and Modernity Reconsidered." *Comparative Studies in Society and History* 9 (April 1967): 292–346.

Benedict, Ruth. *Patterns of Culture*. Boston: Houghton Mifflin, 1934.

Berkowitz, Leonard, and Donald H. Cottingham. "The Interest Value and Relevance of Fear Arousing Communications." *Journal of Abnormal and Social Psychology* 60 (January 1960): 37–43.

Berlyne, D. E. *Conflict, Arousal, and Curiosity*. New York: McGraw-Hill, 1960.

_____. "Motivational Problems Raised by Exploratory and Epistemic Behavior." In *Psychology: A Study of Science*. Vol. 5, edited by Sigmund Koch, 284–364. New York: McGraw-Hill, 1963.

_____. "Curiosity and Exploration." *Science* 153 (July 1, 1966): 25–33.

_____. "Laughter, Humor, and Play." *The Handbook of Social Psychology*, 2d ed., vol. 3, edited by Gardner Lindzey and Elliot Aronson, 795–852. Reading Mass.: Addison-Wesley, 1969.

_____. "Novelty, Complexity, and Hedonic Value." *Perception and Psychophysics* 8 (November 1970): 279–286.

_____. *Aesthetics and Psychobiology*. New York: Meredith Corp., 1971.

Berry, Leonard L. "The Components of Department Store Image: A Theoretical and Empirical Analysis." *Journal of Retailing* 45 (Spring 1969): 3–20.

_____. "The Time-Buying Consumer." *Journal of Retailing* 55 (Winter 1979): 58–69.

Bettman, James R., Noel Capon, and Richard J. Lutz. "Multiattribute Measurement Models and Multiattribute Attitude Theory: A Test of Construct Validity." *Journal of Consumer Research* 1 (March 1975): 1–15.

Bevan, William. "Subliminal Stimulation: A Pervasive Problem for Psychology." *Psychological Bulletin* 61 (February 1964): 81–99.

Bexton, W. H., W. Heron, and T. H. Scott. "Effects of Decreased Variation in the Sensory Environment." *Canadian Journal of Psychology* 8 (June 1954): 70–76.

Bieri, James. "Complexity-Simplicity as a Personality Variable in Cognitive and Preferential Behavior." In *Functions of Varied Experience*, edited by Donald W. Fiske and Salvatore R. Maddi, 355–379. Homewood, Ill.: The Dorsey Press, 1961.

Birdwell, Al E. "A Study of the Influence of Image Congruence on Consumer Choice." *Journal of Business* 41 (January 1968): 76–88.

Bishop, Doyle W., and Ikeda Masaru. "Status and Role Factors in the Leisure Behavior of Different Occupations." *Sociology and Social Research* 54 (January 1970): 190–208.

————, and Peter A. Witt. "Sources of Behavioral Variance During Leisure Time." *Journal of Personality and Social Psychology* 16 (October 1970): 352–360.

Blake, Brian, Robert Perloff, and Richard Heslin. "Dogmatism and Acceptance of New Products." *Journal of Marketing Research* 7 (November 1970): 483–486.

Bliss, Wesley L. "In the Wake of the Wheel: Introduction of the Wagon to the Papago Indians in Southern Arizona." In *Human Problems in Technological Change*, edited by Edward H. Spicer, 23–27. New York: Russell Sage Foundation, 1952.

Blumberg, Paul. "The Decline and Fall of the Status Symbol: Some Thoughts on Status in a Post-Industrial Society." *Social Problems* 21 (April 1974): 480–498.

————. *Inequality in an Age of Decline*. New York: Oxford University Press, 1980.

Bogen, Joseph E. "Some Educational Implications of Hemispheric Specialization." In *The Human Brain*, edited by M. C. Wittrock et al., 133–152. Englewood Cliffs, N.J.: Prentice-Hall, 1977.

Bone, Ronald N., and Doil D. Montgomery. "Extraversion, Neuroticism, and Sensation Seeking." *Psychological Reports* 26 (June 1970): 971.

Boone, Louis E. "The Search for the Consumer Innovator." *Journal of Business* 43 (April 1970): 135–140.

Bourne, Francis S. "Group Influence in Marketing and Public Relations." In *Some Applications of Behavioral Research*, edited by Rensis Likert and Samuel P. Hayes, Jr., 207–257. Paris: United Nations Educational, Scientific and Cultural Organization, 1957.

Boyd, Harper W., Jr., Ralph Westfall, and Stanley F. Stasch. *Marketing Research: Text and Cases*. 5th ed. Homewood, Ill.: Richard D. Irwin, 1981.

Brady, Dorothy. "Family Savings in Relation to Changes in the Level and Distribution of Income." In *Studies in Income and Wealth*. Vol. 15, 103–130. New York: National Bureau of Economic Research, 1952.

Brean, Herbert "'Hidden Sell' Technique is Almost Here: New Subliminal Gimmicks Now Offer Blood, Skulls and Popcorn to Movie Fans." *Life* 44 (March 31, 1958): 102–114.

Breen-Lewis, Kristin, and John Wilding. "Noise, Time of Day and Test Expectations in Recall and Recognition." *British Journal of Psychology* 75 (February 1984): 51–63.

Bricker, Peter D., and A. Chapanis. "Do Incorrectly Perceived Tachiscopic Stimuli Convey Some Information? *Psychological Review* 60 (May 1953): 181–188.

Broadbent, Donald E. "The Hidden Preattentive Process." *American Psychologist* 32 (February 1977): 109–118.

Brooker, George. "The Self-Actualizing Socially Conscious Consumer." *Journal of Consumer Research* 3 (September 1976): 107–112.

———. "Representativeness of Shortened Personality Measures." *Journal of Consumer Research* 5 (September 1978): 143–145.

Brooks, John. *Showing Off in America: From Conspicuous Consumption to Parody Display*. Boston: Little, Brown, 1981.

Bruner, Jerome S., and Leo Postman. "Emotional Selectivity in Perception and Reaction." *Journal of Personality* 16 (September 1947): 69–77.

———, and ———. "Symbolic Value as an Organizing Factor in Perception." *Journal of Social Psychology*. 27 (May 1948): 203–208.

Bullock, Henry A. "Consumer Motivations in Black and White." *Harvard Business Review* 39 (May-June, July-August 1961): 89–104, 110–124.

Burk, Marguerite C. *Consumption Economics: A Multidisciplinary Approach*. New York: John Wiley and Sons, 1968.

Burnett, John J., and Richard Oliver. "Fear Appeal Effects in the Field: A Segmentation Approach." *Journal of Marketing Research* 16 (May 1979): 181–190.

Burnkrant, Robert E., and Alain Cousineau. "Informational and Normative Social Influence in Buyer Behavior." *Journal of Consumer Research* 2 (December 1975): 206–215.

Buss, Allan R., and Wayne Poley. *Individual Differences: Traits and Factors*. New York: The Gardner Press, 1976.

Butler, Robert A. "Incentive Conditions Which Influence Visual Exploration." *Journal of Experimental Psychology* 48 (July 1954): 19–23.

Byrne, Donn. "The Effect of a Subliminal Food Stimulus on Verbal Responses." *Journal of Applied Psychology* 43 (August 1959): 249–252.

Caccavale, John G., Thomas C. Wanty, III, and Julie A. Edell. "Subliminal Implants in Advertisements: An Experiment." In *Advances in Consumer Research*. Vol. 9, edited by Andrew Mitchell, 418–423. Ann Arbor, Mich.: Association for Consumer Research, 1982.

Cacioppo, John T., and Richard E. Petty. "The Effects of Message Repetition and Position on Cognitive Response, Recall, and Persuasion." *Journal of Personality and Social Psychology* 37 (January 1979): 97–109.

Calder, Bobby J., and Robert E. Burnkrant. "Interpersonal Influence on Consumer Behavior: An Attribution Theory Approach." *Journal of Consumer Research* 4 (June 1977): 29–38.

Caplovitz, David. *The Poor Pay More: Consumer Practices of Low-Income Families*. New York: The Free Press, 1963.

Carmines, Edward G., and Richard A. Zeller. *Reliability and Validity Assessment*. Newbury Park, Calif.: Sage Publications, 1979.

Cattell, Raymond B. *Personality and Motivation Structure and Measurement*. Yonkers-On-Hudson, N.Y.: World Book, 1957.

———. *The Scientific Analysis of Personality*. Baltimore, Penguin Books, 1965.

————— . "Anxiety and Motivation: Theory and Crucial Experiments." In *Anxiety and Behavior*, edited by Charles D. Spielberger, 23–62. New York: Academic Press, 1966.

Chapman, Randall G., and Kristian S. Palda. "Turnout in Rational Voting and Consumption Perspectives: A Politometric Study of Ten Canadian Elections." *Journal of Consumer Research* 9 (March 1983): 337–346.

Churchill, Gilbert A., Jr. *Marketing Research: Methodological Foundations*. 2d ed. Hinsdale, Ill.: The Dryden Press, 1979.

Claycamp, Henry J. "Characteristics of Owners of Thrift Deposits in Commercial Banks and Savings and Loan Associations." *Journal of Marketing Research* 2 (May 1965): 163–170.

Cocanougher, A. Benton, and Grady D. Bruce. "Socially Distant Reference Groups and Consumer Aspirations." *Journal of Marketing Research* 8 (August 1971): 379–381.

Cohen, Joel B. "An Interpersonal Orientation to the Study of Consumer Behavior." *Journal of Marketing Research* 4 (August 1967): 270–278.

————— . "Toward an Interpersonal Theory of Consumer Behavior." *California Management Review* 10 (Spring 1968): 73–80.

Coleman, James S., Elihu Katz, and Herbert Menzel. *Medical Innovation: A Diffusion Study*. Indianapolis: Bobbs Merrill, 1966.

Coleman, Richard P. "The Significance of Social Stratification in Selling." In *Marketing: A Maturing Discipline, Proceedings of the Winter Conference of the American Marketing Association*, edited by Martin L. Bell, 171–184. Chicago: American Marketing Association, 1961.

————— . "The Continuing Significance of Social Class to Marketing." *Journal of Consumer Research* 10 (December 1983): 265–280.

————— , Lee Rainwater, and Kent A. McClelland. *Social Standing in America: New Dimensions of Class*. New York: Basic Books, 1978.

Collier, R. M. "An Experimental Study of the Effects of Subliminal Stimuli." *Psychological Monographs* 52 (No. 5, 1940).

Converse, Jean M., and Stanley Presser. *Survey Questions: Handcrafting the Standardized Questionnaire*. Newbury Park, Calif.: Sage Publications, 1986.

Cook, Thomas D., and Donald T. Campbell. *Quasi-Experimentation: Design and Analysis Issues for Field Studies*. Boston: Houghton Mifflin, 1979.

Coombs, Clyde H. *A Theory of Psychological Scaling*. Ann Arbor: Engineering Research Institute, University of Michigan Press, 1952.

————— . *A Theory of Data*. New York: John Wiley & Sons, 1964.

————— , and George S. Avrunin. "Single-Peaked Functions and the Theory of Preference." *Psychological Review* 84 (March, 1977): 216–230.

Coover, John Edgar. *Psychical Research Monograph No. 1: Experiments in Psychical Research at Leland Stanford Junior University*. Stanford, Calif.: Stanford University Press, 1917.

Copley, T. P., and F. Callom. "Industrial Search Behavior and Perceived Risk." *Personal Communication*, 1971.

Cote, Joseph A., James McCullough, and Michael Reilly. "Effects of Unexpected Situations on Behavior-Intention Differences: A Garbology Analysis." *Journal of Consumer Research* 12 (September 1985): 188–194.

Cox, Dena S., and Anthony D. Cox. "What Does Familiarity Breed? Complexity as a Moderator of Repetition Effects in Advertisement Evaluation." *Journal of Consumer Research* 15 (June 1988): 111–116.

Cox, Donald F., ed. *Risk Taking and Information Handling in Consumer Behavior*. Boston: Division of Research, Graduate School of Business Administration, Harvard University, 1967.

————, and Raymond A. Bauer. "Self-Confidence and Persuasibility in Women." *Public Opinion Quarterly* 28 (Fall 1964): 453–466.

Craig, C. Samuel, and James L. Ginter. "An Empirical Test of a Scale for Innovativeness." In *Advances in Consumer Research*. Vol. 2, edited by Mary Jane Schlinger, 555–562. Ann Arbor, Mich.: Association for Consumer Research, 1975.

Danzig, Fred. "Relaxed Radio Soothes—But Subliminally." *Advertising Age* (September 15, 1980): 34.

Darlington, Richard B. "Multiple Regression in Psychological Research and Practice." *Psychological Bulletin* 69 (March 1968): 161–182.

Das, Jagannath Prasad, John R. Kirby, and Ronald F. Jarman. "Simultaneous and Successive Synthesis: An Alternative Model for Cognitive Abilities." *Psychological Bulletin* 82 (January 1975): 87–103.

————. *Simultaneous and Successive Cognitive Processes*. New York: Academic Press, 1979.

Davies, D. R., G. R. J. Hockey, and Ann Taylor. "Varied Auditory Stimulation, Temperament Differences and Vigilance Performance." *British Journal of Psychology* 60 (November 1969): 453–457.

Davis, Harry L. "Decision Making Within the Household." *Journal of Consumer Research* 2 (March 1976): 241–260.

DeFleur, Melvin L., and Robert M. Petranoff. "A Televised Test of Subliminal Persuasion." *Public Opinion Quarterly* 23 (Summer 1959): 168–180.

Deglin, Vadim L. "Our Split Brain." *U.N.E.S.C.O. Courier* 29 (January 1976): 4–19.

Dember, William N. *The Psychology of Perception*. New York: Holt, Rinehart & Winston, 1960.

————, and Robert W. Earl. "Analysis of Exploratory, Manipulatory, and Curiosity Behavior." *Psychological Review*. 64 (March 1957): 91–96.

————, ————, and Noel Paradise. "Response by Rats to Differential Stimulus Complexity." *Journal of Comparative and Physiological Psychology* 50 (1957): 514–518.

Dent, Oran B., and Edward C. Simmel. "Preference for Complex Stimuli as an Index of Diversive Exploration." *Perceptual and Motor Skills* 26 (June 1968): 896–898.

Deshpande, Rohit, Wayne D. Hoyer, and Naveen Donthu. "The Intensity of Ethnic Affiliation: A Study of the Sociology of Hispanic Consumption." *Journal of Consumer Research* 13 (September 1986): 214–220.

Desor, J. A. "Toward a Psychological Theory of Crowding." *Journal of Personality and Social Psychology*. 21 (January 1972): 79–83.

Deutsch, Morton, and Harold B. Gerard. "A Study of Normative and Informational Social Influences Upon Individual Judgment." In *Group Dynamics: Research and Theory*. 2d ed, edited by Dorwin Cartwright, and Alvin Zander, 201–213. Evanston, Ill.: Row, Peterson and Co., 1960.

Dichter, Ernest. "Psychology in Market Research." *Harvard Business Review* 25 (Summer 1947): 432–443.

———. "Toward an Understanding of Human Behavior." In *Motivation and Market Behavior*, edited by Robert Ferber, and Hugh G. Wales, 21–31. Homewood, Ill.: Richard D. Irwin, 1958.

———. *The Strategy of Desire*. New York: Doubleday, 1960.

———. *Handbook of Consumer Motivation: The Psychology of the World of Objects*. New York: McGraw-Hill, 1964.

———. *Motivating Human Behavior*. New York: McGraw-Hill, 1971.

———. *Packaging: the Sixth Sense? A Guide to Identifying Consumer Motivation*. Boston: Cahners Publishing Co., 1975.

———. *Getting Motivated: The Secret Behind Individual Motivations by the Man Who Was Not Afraid to Ask 'Why?'*. Elmsford, N.Y.: Pergamon Press, 1979.

Dickerson, Mary Dee, and James W. Gentry. "Characteristics of Adopters and Non-Adopters of Home Computers." *Journal of Consumer Research* 10 (September 1983): 225–235.

Dickson, Peter R. "Person–Situation: Segmentation's Missing Link." *Journal of Marketing* 46 (Fall 1982): 56–64.

Dixon, Norman F. *Subliminal Perception: The Nature of the Controversy*. New York: McGraw-Hill, 1971.

———. *Preconscious Processing*. New York: John Wiley & Sons, 1981.

Dobyns, Henry F. "Experiment in Conservation: Erosian Control and Forage Production on the Papago Indian Reservation in Arizona." In *Human Problems in Technological Change*, edited by Edward H. Spicer, 209–223. New York: Russell Sage Foundation, 1952.

Dolich, Ira J. "Congruence Relationships Between Self Images and Product Brands." *Journal of Marketing Research* 6 (February 1969): 80–84.

Donnelly, James H., Jr., "Social Character and Acceptance of New Products." *Journal of Marketing Research* 7 (February 1970): 111–113.

———, and Michael J. Etzel. "Degrees of Product Newness and Early Trial." *Journal of Marketing Research* 10 (August 1973): 295–300.

———, Michael J. Etzel, and Scott Roeth. "The Relationship Between Consumers' Category Width and Trial of New Products." *Journal of Applied Psychology*, 57 (June 1973): 335–338.

Douglas, Mary, and Baron Isherwood. *The World of Goods*. New York: Basic Books, 1979.

Downs, Anthony. *An Economic Theory of Democracy*. New York: Harper and Row, 1957.

Driver, M. J., and S. Streufert. "The 'General Incongruity Adaption Level' (GIAL) Hypothesis: An Analysis and Integration of Cognitive Approaches to Motivation." Paper No. 114. West Lafayette, Ind.: Purdue University, Graduate School of Industrial Administration, Institute for Research in the Behavioral, Economic and Management Sciences, 1965.

Duesenberry, James S. "Income–Consumption Relations and Their Implications." In *Income, Employment, and Public Policy: Essays in Honor of Alvin H. Hansen*, edited by Lloyd A. Metzler, 54–81. New York: W. W. Norton, 1948.

———. *Income, Saving and the Theory of Consumer Behavior*. Cambridge, Mass.: Harvard University Press, 1949.

Duncan, James A., and Burton W. Kreitlow. "Selected Cultural Characteristics and the Acceptance of Educational Programs and Practices." *Rural Sociology* 19 (December 1954): 349–357.

Durkheim, Emile. *Suicide: A Study in Sociology*, translated by John A. Spaulding and George Simpson. (Original French edition, 1897). New York: The Free Press, 1951.

Edell, Julie A., and Marian Chapman Burke. "The Power of Feelings in Understanding Advertising Effects." *Journal of Consumer Research* 14 (December 1987): 421–433.

Edwards, Allen L. *Manual for the Edwards Personal Preference Schedule*. New York: Psychological Corporation, 1957.

Ellenberger, Henri F. *The Discovery of the Unconscious: The History and Evolution of Dynamic Psychiatry*. New York: Basic Books, 1970.

Ellsberg, D. "Classic and Current Notions of 'MeasurableUtility'." *Economic Journal* 64 (September 1954): 528–556.

Engel, James F., Roger D. Blackwell, and Paul W. Miniard. *Consumer Behavior*. 5th ed. Chicago: The Dryden Press, 1986.

————, David T. Kollat, and Roger D. Blackwell. *Consumer Behavior*. New York: Holt, Rinehart and Winston, 1968.

Erasmus, Charles J. *Man Takes Control: Cultural Development and American Aid*. Minneapolis: University of Minnesota Press, 1961.

————, Solomon Miller, and Louis C. Faron. *Contemporary Change in Traditional Communities of Mexico and Peru*. Urbana: University of Illinois Press, 1978.

Erdelyi, M. H. "A New Look at the New Look: Perceptual Defense and Vigilance." *Psychological Review* 81 (January 1974): 1–25.

Erickson, Gary M., and Johny K. Johansson. "The Role of Price in Multi-Attribute Product Evaluations." *Journal of Consumer Research* 12 (September 1985): 195–199.

Erikson, Erik H. *Childhood and Society*. New York: W. W. Norton, 1950.

Esser, Aristide Henri. "A Biosocial Perspective on Crowding." In *Environment and the Social Sciences: Perspectives and Applications*, edited by Joachim F. Wohlwill and Daniel H. Carson, 15–28. Washington, D. C.: American Psychological Association, 1972.

Evans, Franklin B. "Psychological and Objective Factors in the Prediction of Brand Choice: Ford Versus Chevrolet." *Journal of Business* 32 (October 1959): 340–369.

————. "Ford Versus Chevrolet: Park Forest Revisited." *Journal of Business* 41 (October 1968): 445–459.

Eysenck, H. J. *The Structure of Human Personality*. London: Methuen and Co., 1953.

————. "Personality and the Law of Effect." In *Pleasure, Reward, Preference: Their Nature, Determinants, and Role in Behavior*, edited by D. E. Berlyne, and K. B. Madsen, 133–166. New York: Academic Press, 1973.

Faison, Edmond W. J. "The Neglected Variety Drive: A Useful Concept for Consumer Behavior." *Journal of Consumer Research* 4 (Dec. 1977): 172–175.

Farley, Frank, and Sonja V. Farley. "Extroversion and Stimulus-Seeking Motivation." *Journal of Consulting and Clinical Psychology* 31 (April 1967): 215–216.

Feick, Lawrence F., and Linda L. Price. "The Market Maven: A Diffuser of Marketplace Information." *Journal of Marketing* 51 (January 1987): 83–97.

Feldman, Laurence P., and Jacob Hornik. "The Use of Time: An Integrated Conceptual Model." *Journal of Consumer Research* 7 (March 1981): 407–419.

Fennell, Geraldine. "Motivation Research Revisited." *Journal of Advertising Research* 15 (June 1975): 23–28.

Ferber, Robert. "Consumer Economics, A Survey." *Journal of Economic Literature* 11 (December 1973): 1303–1342.

————— , and Lucy Chao Lee. "Husband-Wife Influence in Family Purchasing Behavior." *Journal of Consumer Research* 1 (June 1974): 43–50.

Festinger, Leon. "Informal Social Communication." In *Group Dynamics: Research and Theory*. 2d. ed., edited by Dorwin Cartwright, and Alvin Zander, 286–299. Evanston, Ill.: Row, Peterson and Co., 1960.

————— . "A Theory of Social Comparison Processes." In *Readings in Reference Group Theory and Research*, edited by Herbert H. Hyman and Eleanor Singer, 123–146. New York: The Free Press, 1968.

————— , Stanley Schachter, and Kurt Back. "The Operation of Group Standards." In *Group Dynamics: Research and Theory*. 2d ed., edited by Dorwin Cartwright and Alvin Zander, 241–259. New York: Harper & Row, 1960.

Filiatrault, Pierre, and J. R. Brent Ritchie. "Joint Purchasing Decisions: A Comparison of Influence Structure in Family and Couple Decision-Making Units." *Journal of Consumer Research* 7 (September 1980): 131–140.

Fischer, Claude S. "Urban-to-Rural Diffusion of Opinions in Contemporary America." *American Journal of Sociology* 84 (July 1978): 151–159.

Fishbein, Martin, ed. *Readings in Attitude Theory and Measurement*. New York: John Wiley and Sons, 1967.

————— , and Icek Ajzen. *Belief, Attitude, Intention, and Behavior: An Introduction to Theory and Research*. Reading, Mass.: Addison-Wesley, 1975.

Fiske, Donald W., and Salvatore R. Maddi, eds. *Functions of Varied Experience*. Homewood, Ill.: The Dorsey Press, 1961.

Folkard, Simon. "Time of Day and Level of Processing." *Memory and Cognition* 7 (July, 1979): 247–252.

Folkes, Valerie S. "Recent Attribution Research in Consumer Behavior: A Review and New Directions." *Journal of Consumer Research* 14 (March 1988): 548–565.

Form, William H., and Gregory P. Stone. "Urbanism, Anonymity, and Status Symbolism." *American Journal of Sociology* 62 (March 1957): 504–514.

Fowler, Carol A., George Wolford, Ronald Slade, and Louis Tassinary. "Lexical Access With and Without Awareness." *Journal of Experimental Psychology: General* 110 (September 1981): 341–362.

Foxall, Gordon R. "Social Factors in Consumer Choice: Replication and Extension." *Journal of Consumer Research* 2 (June 1975): 60–64.

Frederickson, Norman. "Towards a Taxonomy of Situation." *American Psychologist* 27 (February 1972): 114–123.

French, John R. P., Jr., and Bertram Raven. "The Bases of Social Power." In *Studies in Social Power*, edited by Dorwin Cartwright, 150–167. Ann Arbor: Research Center for Group Dynamics, Institute for Social Research, University of Michigan, 1959.

Frenkel-Brunswick, Else. "Intolerance of Ambiguity as an Emotional and Perceptual Personality Variable." *Journal of Personality* 18 (1949): 108–143.

Freud, Sigmund. *The Standard Edition of the Complete Psychological Works of Sigmund Freud*. 24 Volumes. Edited by James Strachey. London: The Hogarth Press, 1966.

Frohlich, Norman, Joe A. Oppenheimer, Jeffrey Smith, and Oran R. Young. "A Test of Downsian Voter Rationality: 1964 Presidential Voting." *American Political Science Review* 72 (March 1978): 178–197.

Fromkin, H. C. "Search for Uniqueness and Valuation of Scarcity: Neglected Dimensions of Value in Exchange Theory." Paper No. 558. West Lafayette, Ind.: Purdue University, Graduate School of Industrial Administration, Institute for Research in the Behavioral, Economic and Management Sciences, 1976.

Fromm, Erich. *The Sane Society*. New York: Holt, Rinehart & Winston, 1955.

Fry, Joseph N. "Personality Variables and Cigarette Brand Choice." *Journal of Marketing Research* 8 (August 1971): 298–304.

————, and Gordon H. McDougall. "Consumer Appraisal of Retail Price Advertisements." *Journal of Marketing* 38 (July 1974): 64–67.

Galbraith, John Kenneth. *The Affluent Society*. Boston: Houghton Mifflin Co., 1958.

Gardner, Burleigh B., and Sidney J. Levy. "The Product and the Brand." *Harvard Business Review* 33 (March-April 1955): 33–39.

Gardner, Meryl Paula. "Mood States and Consumer Behavior: A Critical Review." *Journal of Consumer Research* 12 (December 1985): 281–300.

Garlington, Warren K., and Helen E. Shimota. "The Change Seeker Index: A Measure of the Need for Variable Stimulus Input." *Psychological Reports* 14 (June 1964): 919–924.

Gatignon, Hubert, and Thomas S. Robertson. "A Propositional Inventory for New Diffusion Research." *Journal of Consumer Research* 11 (March 1985): 849–867.

Gazzaniga, Michael S. "Review of the Split Brain." In *The Human Brain*, edited by M. C. Wittrock et al., 89–96. Englewood Cliffs, N.J.: Prentice-Hall, 1977.

George, Stephen G., and Luther B. Jennings. "Effect of Subliminal Stimuli on Consumer Behavior: Negative Evidence." *Perceptual and Motor Skills* 41 (December 1975): 847–854.

Geschwind, Norman. "Specializations of the Brain." *Scientific American* 241 (September, 1979): 180–199.

Gilbert, Dennis, and Joseph A. Kahl. *The American Class Structure: A New Synthesis*. Homewood, Ill.: The Dorsey Press, 1982.

Goffman, Erving. "Symbols of Class Status." *British Journal of Sociology* 2 (December 1951): 294–304.

Goldberg, Marvin E., and Gerald J. Gorn. "Happy and Sad TV Programs: How

They Affect Reactions to Commercials." *Journal of Consumer Research* 14 (December 1987): 387–403.

Goldman, Alfred E., and Susan Schwartz McDonald. *The Group Depth Interview: Principles and Practice*. Englewood Cliffs, N.J.: Prentice-Hall, 1987.

Goldstein, Michael J. "The Relationship Between Coping and Avoiding Behavior and Response to Fear-Arousing Propaganda." *Journal of Abnormal and Social Psychology* 58 (March 1959): 247–252.

Gorn, Gerald J. "The Effects of Music in Advertising on Choice Behavior: A Classical Conditioning Approach." *Journal of Marketing* 46 (Winter 1982): 94–101.

Graham, Robert J. "The Role of Perception of Time in Consumer Research." *Journal of Consumer Research* 7 (March 1981): 335–342.

Green, Paul E., and Donald S. Tull. *Research for Marketing Decisions*. 4th ed. Englewood Cliffs, N.J.: Prentice-Hall, 1978.

_____ , J. Douglas Carroll, and Wayne S. DeSarbo. "Estimating Choice Probabilities in Multiattribute Decision Making." *Journal of Consumer Research* 8 (June 1981): 76–84.

Greenberg, Joseph H. "Social Variables in Acceptance or Rejection of Artificial Insemination." *American Sociological Review* 16 (February 1951): 86–91.

Greeno, Daniel W., Montrose S. Sommers, and Jerome B. Kernan. "Personality and Implicit Behavior Patterns." *Journal of Marketing Research* 10 (February 1973): 63–69.

Griffitt, William. "Environmental Effects on Interpersonal Affective Behavior: Ambient Effective Temperature and Attraction." *Journal of Personality and Social Psychology* 15 (July 1970): 240–244.

_____ , and Russell Veitch. "Hot and Crowded: Influence of Population Density and Temperature on Interpersonal Affective Behavior." *Journal of Personality and Social Psychology* 17 (January 1971): 92–98.

Gross, Barbara L. "Time Scarcity: Interdisciplinary Perspectives and Implications for Consumer Behavior." In *Research in Consumer Behavior*. Vol. 2, edited by Jagdish N. Sheth and Elizabeth C. Hirschman, 1–54. Greenwich, Conn.: JAI Press, 1987.

Grubb, Edward L., and Harrison L. Grathwohl. "Consumer Self-Concept, Symbolism and Market Behavior: A Theoretical Approach." *Journal of Marketing* 31 (October 1967): 22–27.

_____ , and Gregg Hupp. "Perception of Self, Generalized Stereotypes, and Brand Selection." *Journal of Marketing Research* 5 (February 1968): 58–63.

_____ , and Bruce L. Stern. "Self-Concept and Significant Others." *Journal of Marketing Research* 8 (August 1971): 382–385.

Guilford, J. P. *Personality*. New York: McGraw-Hill, 1959.

Gusfield, Joseph R. "Tradition and Modernity: Misplaced Polarities in the Study of Social Change." *American Journal of Sociology* 72 (Jan. 1967): 351–362.

Guttman, Louis. "The Quantification of a Class of Attributes: A Theory and Method of Scale Construction." In *The Prediction of Personal Adjustment: A Survey of Logical Problems and Research Techniques, with Illustrative Application to Problems of Vocational Selection, School Success, Marriage, and Crime*. Bulletin 48, edited by Paul Horst, 319–348. New York: Social Science Research Council, 1941.

_____ . "A Basis for Scaling Qualitative Data." *American Sociological Review* 9 (April 1944): 139–150.

Haines, George H., Jr. "A Study of Why People Purchase New Products." In *Science, Technology, and Marketing*, edited by Raymond M. Hass, 685–697. Chicago: American Marketing Association, 1966.

_____ . "Overview of Economic Models of Consumer Behavior." In *Consumer Behavior: Theoretical Sources*, edited by Scott Ward and Thomas S. Robertson, 276–300. Englewood Cliffs, N.J.: Prentice-Hall, 1973.

Hair, Joseph F., Jr., Rolph E. Anderson, Ronald L. Tatham, and Bernie J. Grablowsky. *Multivariate Data Analysis*. Tulsa, Okla.: Petroleum Publishing Co., 1979.

Haire, Mason. "Projective Techniques in Marketing Research." *Journal of Marketing* 14 (April 1950): 649–656.

Halbert, Michael. "The Requirements for Theory in Marketing." In *Theory in Marketing*, edited by Reavis Cox, Wroe Alderson, and Stanley J. Shapiro, 17–36. Homewood, Ill.: Richard D. Irwin, 1964.

Haley, Russell I., and Ronald Gatty. "The Trouble with Concept Testing." *Journal of Marketing Research* 8 (May 1971): 230–232.

Hall, Calvin S., and Gardner Lindzey. *Theories of Personality*. 2d ed. New York: John Wiley & Sons, 1970.

Hall, Edward T. *The Silent Language*. New York: Doubleday, 1959.

Hallowell, A. Irving. *Culture and Experience*. Philadelphia: University of Pennsylvania Press, 1955.

Hamid, Paul N. "Some Effects of Dress Cues on Observational Accuracy, a Perceptual Estimate, and Impression Formulation." *Journal of Social Psychology* 86 (April 1972): 279–289.

Hanna, Janice G. "A Typology of Consumer Needs." In *Research in Marketing*. Vol. 3, edited by Jagdish N. Sheth, 83–104. Greenwich, Conn.: JAI Press, 1980.

Hansen, Flemming. *Consumer Choice Behavior: A Cognitive Theory*. New York: The Free Press, 1972.

_____ . "Hemispheral Lateralization: Implications for Understanding Consumer Behavior." *Journal of Consumer Research* 8 (June 1981): 23–36.

_____ , and Niels Erik Lundsgaard. "Developing an Instrument to Identify Individual Differences in the Processing of Pictorial and Other Non-Verbal Information." In *Advances in Consumer Research*. Vol. 8, edited by Kent B. Monroe, 367–373. Ann Arbor, Mich.: Association for Consumer Research, 1981.

Harlow, Harry F., Margaret Kuenne Harlow, and Donald R. Meyer. "Learning Motivated by a Manipulation Drive." *Journal of Experimental Psychology* 40 (April 1950): 228–234.

Harrell, Gilbert D., Michael D. Hutt, and James C. Anderson. "Path Analysis of Buyer Behavior Under Conditions of Crowding." *Journal of Marketing Research* 17 (February 1980): 45–51.

Harrison, Albert A. "Response Competition, Frequency, Exploratory Behavior, and Liking." *Journal of Personality and Social Psychology* 9 (August 1968): 363–368.

Hart, Sandra H., and Stephen W. McDaniel. "Subliminal Stimulation—Marketing Applications." In *Consumer Behavior: Classical and Contemporary Dimensions*, edited by James U. McNeal and Stephen W. McDaniel, 165–175. Boston: Little, Brown and Co., 1982.

Hauser, John R., and Glen L. Urban. "Assessment of Attribute Importances and Consumer Utility Functions: von Neumann-Morgenstern Theory Applied to Consumer Behavior." Journal of Consumer Research 5 (March 1979): 251–262.

Havlena, William J., and Morris B. Holbrook. "The Varieties of Consumption Experience: Comparing Two Typologies of Emotion in Consumer Behavior." *Journal of Consumer Research* 13 (December 1986): 394–404.

Hawkins, Del. "The Effects of Subliminal Stimulation on Drive Level and Brand Preference." *Journal of Marketing Research* 7 (August 1970): 322–326.

Hawley, Florence. "The Role of Pueblo Social Organization in the Dissemination of Catholicism." *American Anthropologist* 48 (July-September 1946): 407–415.

Heath, Dwight B., Charles J. Erasmus, and Hans C. Buechler. *Land Reform and Social Revolution in Bolivia*. New York: Frederick A. Praeger, 1969.

Hechter, Michael. "Group Formation and the Cultural Division of Labor." *American Journal of Sociology* 84 (September 1978): 293–318.

Heider, Fritz. "Attitudes and Cognitive Organization." *Journalof Psychology* 21 (January 1946): 107–112.

―――― . *The Psychology of Interpersonal Relations*. New York: John Wiley and Sons, 1958.

Herzog, W. A. *Patterns of Diffusion in Rural Brazil*. East Lansing: Michigan State University, 1968.

Hirschman, Elizabeth C. "Innovativeness, Novelty Seeking, and Consumer Creativity." *Journal of Consumer Research* 7 (December 1980a): 283–295.

―――― . "Consumer Creativity: Nature, Measurement, and Application." In *Theoretical Developments in Marketing*, edited by Charles W. Lamb, Jr. and Patrick M. Dunne, 162–165. Chicago: American Marketing Association, 1980b.

―――― . "Comprehending Symbolic Consumption: The Theoretical Issues." In *Symbolic Consumer Behavior*, edited by Elizabeth C. Hirschman and Morris B. Holbrook, 4–6. Ann Arbor, Mich.: Association for Consumer Research, 1981.

―――― . "Primitive Aspects of Consumption in Modern American Society." *Journal of Consumer Research* 12 (September 1985): 142–154.

―――― . "Theoretical Perspectives of Time Use: Implications for Consumer Research." In *Research in Consumer Behavior*. Vol. 2, edited by Jagdish N. Sheth and Elizabeth C. Hirschman, 55–81. Greenwich, Conn.: JAI Press, 1987.

―――― , and Morris B. Holbrook, eds. *Symbolic Consumer Behavior*. Ann Arbor, Mich.: Association for Consumer Research, 1981.

―――― , and ―――― . "Hedonic Consumption: Emerging Concepts, Methods and Propositions." *Journal of Marketing* 46 (Summer 1982): 92–101.

Hoffer, Charles R., and Dale Strangland. "Farmer's Attitudes and Values in Relation to Adoption of Approved Practices of Corn Growing." *Rural Sociology* 23 (June 1958): 112–120.

Holahan, Charles J. *Environment and Behavior: A Dynamic Perspective*. New York: Plenum Press, 1978.

Holbrook, Morris B. "Comparing Multiattribute Models by Optimal Scaling." *Journal of Consumer Research* 4 (December 1977): 165–171.

———. "Using a Structural Model of Halo Effect to Assess Perceptual Distortion Due to Affective Overtones." *Journal of Consumer Research* 10 (September 1983): 247–252.

———. "Aims, Concepts, and Methods for the Representation of Individual Differences in Esthetic Responses to Design Features." *Journal of Consumer Research* 3 (December 1986): 337–347.

———, and Rajeev Batra. "Assessing the Role of Emotions as Mediators of Consumer Responses to Advertising." *Journal of Consumer Research* 14 (December 1987): 404–420.

———, Robert W. Chestnut, Terence A. Oliva, and Eric A. Greenleaf. "Play as a Consumption Experience: The Roles of Emotions, Performance, and Personality in the Enjoyment of Games." *Journal of Consumer Research* 11 (September 1984): 728–739.

———, and Mark W. Grayson. "The Semiology of Cinematic Consumption: Symbolic Consumer Behavior in *Out of Africa*." *Journal of Consumer Research* 13 (December 1986): 374–381.

———, and William J. Havlena. "Assessing the Real-to-Artificial Generalizability of Multiattribute Attitude Models in Tests of New Product Designs." *Journal of Marketing Research* 25 (February 1988): 25–35.

———, and Elizabeth C. Hirschman. "The Experiential Aspects of Consumption: Consumer Fantasies, Feelings, and Fun." *Journal of Consumer Research* 9 (September 1982): 132–140.

———, and Joel Huber. "Separating Perceptual Dimensions from Affective Overtones: An Application to Consumer Aesthetics." *Journal of Consumer Research* 5 (March 1979): 272–283.

———, and Donald R. Lehmann. "Allocating Discretionary Time: Complementarity Among Activities." *Journal of Consumer Research* 7 (March 1981): 395–406.

———, and William L. Moore. "Feature Interactions in Consumer Judgments of Verbal Versus Pictorial Presentations." *Journal of Consumer Research* 8 (June 1981): 103–113.

Holman, Rebecca H. "Product Use as Communication: A Fresh Appraisal of a Venerable Topic." In *Review in Marketing 1981*, edited by Ben M. Enis and Kenneth J. Roering, 106–119. Chicago: American Marketing Association, 1981.

———, and R. Dale Wilson. "The Availability of Discretionary Time: Influences on Interactive Patterns of Consumer Shopping Behavior." In *Advances in Consumer Research*. Vol. 7, edited by Jerry C. Olson, 431–436. Ann Arbor, Mich.: Association for Consumer Research, 1980.

———. "Temporal Equilibrium as a Basis for Retail Shopping Behavior." *Journal of Retailing* 58 (Spring 1982): 58–81.

Horney, Karen. *Our Inner Conflicts: A Constructive Theory of Neurosis*. New York: W. W. Norton, 1945.

Hornik, Jacob. "Situational Effects on the Consumption of Time." *Journal of Marketing* 46 (Fall 1982): 44–55.

———. "Diurnal Variation in Consumer Response." *Journal of Consumer Research* 14 (March 1988): 588–591.

Horton, Raymond L. "The Edwards Personal Preference Schedule and Consumer Personality Research." *Journal of Marketing Research* 11 (August 1974): 335–337.

Howard, John A. *Marketing Management: Analysis and Planning.* Rev. ed. Homewood, Ill.: Richard D. Irwin, 1963.

———, and Jagdish N. Sheth. *The Theory of Buyer Behavior.* New York: John Wiley and Sons, 1969.

Howard, Kenneth I. "A Test of Stimulus-Seeking Behavior." *Perceptual and Motor Skills* 13 (December 1961): 416.

Howarth, E., and M. S. Hoffman. "A Multidimensional Approach to the Relationship Between Mood and Weather." *British Journal of Psychology* 75 (February 1984): 15–23.

Hugstad, Paul S. "A Reexamination of the Concept of Privilege Groups." *Journal of the Academy of Marketing Science* 9 (Fall 1981): 399–408.

Huizinga, J. *Homo Ludens: A Study of the Play-Element in Culture.* Boston: Beacon Press, 1950.

Hull, Clark L. *Principles of Behavior: An Introduction to Behavior Theory.* New York: Appleton-Century-Crofts, 1943.

Hunt, J. McV. "Motivation Inherent in Information Processing and Action." In *Motivation and Social Interaction: Cognitive Determinants,* edited by O. J. Harvey, 35–94. New York: The Ronald Press Co., 1963.

Hunt, Shelby D. *Marketing Theory: The Philosophy of Marketing Science.* Homewood, Ill.: Richard D. Irwin, 1983.

Hyman, Herbert H. "The Psychology of Status." *Archives of Psychology* 38, No. 269 (June 1942).

Jackson, Barbara Bund. *Multivariate Data Analysis: An Introduction.* Homewood, Ill.: Richard D. Irwin, 1983.

Jacoby, Jacob. "Personality and Innovation Proneness." *Journal of Marketing Research* 8 (May 1971): 244–247.

———, and Jerry C. Olson. "Consumer Response to Price: An Attitudinal, Information Processing Perspective." In *Moving A Head With Attitude Research,* edited by Yoram Wind and Marshall G. Greenberg, 73–86. Chicago: American Marketing Association, 1977.

———, George J. Szybillo, and Carol Kohn Berning. "Time and Consumer Behavior: An Interdisciplinary Overview." *Journal of Consumer Research* 2 (March 1976): 320–339.

Jaher, Frederic Cople, ed. *The Rich, the Well Born, and the Powerful: Elites and Upper Classes in History.* Urbana: University of Illinois Press, 1973.

Jain, Arun K. "A Method for Investigating and Representing Implicit Social Class Theory." *Journal of Consumer Research* 2 (June 1975): 53–59.

Janis, Irving L., and Seymour Feshbach. "Effects of Fear-Arousing Communications." Journal of Abnormal and Social Psychology 48 (January 1953): 78–92.

Janiszewski, Chris. "Preconscious Processing Effects: The Independence of Attitude Formation and Conscious Thought." *Journal of Consumer Research* 15 (September 1988): 199–209.

Jeuland, Apel P. "Brand Preference Over Time: A Partially Deterministic Operationalization of the Notion of Variety Seeking." In *Research Frontiers in Marketing: Dialogues and Directions, 1978 Educators' Conference Proceedings, Series No. 43*, edited by Subhash C. Jain, 33–37. Chicago: American Marketing Association, 1978.

Joachimsthaler, Erich A., and John L. Lastovicka. "Optimal Stimulation Level— Exploratory Behavior Models." *Journal of Consumer Research* 11 (December 1984): 830–835.

Johnson, Richard A., and Dean W. Wichern. *Applied Multivariate Statistical Analysis*. Englewood Cliffs, N.J.: Prentice-Hall, 1982.

Johnston, Wesley J., and Thomas V. Bonoma. "The Buying Center: Structure and Interactions." *Journal of Marketing* 45 (Summer 1981): 143–156.

Jung, Carl G. *The Psychology of the Unconscious: A Study of the Transformations and Symbolisms of the Libido, A Contribution to the History of the Evolution of Thought*, translated by Beatrice M. Hinkle. New York: Dodd, Mead & Co., 1916.

Kahl, Joseph A. *The American Class Structure*. New York: Holt, Rinehart and Winston, 1953.

Kahn, Barbara E., Manohar U. Kalwani, and Donald G. Morrison. "Measuring Variety-Seeking and Reinforcement Behaviors Using Panel Data." *Journal of Marketing Research* 23 (May 1986): 89–100.

Kalton, Graham. *Introduction to Survey Sampling*. Newbury Park, Calif.: Sage Publications, 1983.

Kamen, Joseph M. "Personality and Food Preferences." *Journal of Advertising Research* 4 (September 1964): 29–32.

Kasmar, Joyce V. "The Development of a Usable Lexicon of Environmental Descriptors." *Environment and Behavior* 2 (September 1970): 153–169.

Kassarjian, Harold H. "Social Character and Differential Preference for Mass Communications." *Journal of Marketing Research* 2 (May 1965): 146–153.

———. "Personality and Consumer Behavior: A Review." *Journal of Marketing Research* 8 (November 1971): 409–418.

———. "Projective Methods." In *Handbook of Marketing Research*, edited by Robert Ferber, 3-85 through 3-100. New York: McGraw-Hill, 1974.

———. "Consumer Psychology." *Annual Review of Psychology* 33 (1982): 619–649.

———, and Mary Jane Sheffet. "Personality and Consumer Behavior: One More Time." In *1975 Combined Proceedings, Series No. 37, Marketing in Turbulent Times and Marketing: The Challenges and Opportunities*, edited by Edward M. Mazze, 197–201. Chicago: American Marketing Association, 1975.

Katona, George C. *Psychological Analysis of Economic Behavior*. New York: -McGraw-Hill, 1951.

———. "Rational Behavior and Economic Behavior." *Psychological Review* 60 (September 1953): 307–318.

————— . "The Relationship Between Psychology and Economics." In *Psychology: A Study of Science*. Vol. 6, edited by Sigmund Koch, 639–676. New York: McGraw-Hill, 1963.

————— . *Psychological Economics*. New York: Elsevier Scientific Publishing Co., 1975.

————— , and Eva Mueller. "A Study of Purchase Decisions." In *Consumer Behavior: The Dynamics of Consumer Reaction*, Vol. 1, edited by Lincoln H. Clark, 30–87. New York: New York University Press, 1954.

————— , Burkhard Strumpel, and Ernest Zahn. *Aspirations and Affluence: Comparative Studies in the United States and Western Europe*. New York: McGraw-Hill, 1971.

Katz, Daniel. "The Functional Approach to the Study of Attitudes." *Public Opinion Quarterly* 24 (Summer 1960): 163–204.

Katz, Elihu, and Paul F. Lazarsfeld. *Personal Influence: The Part Played by People in the Flow of Mass Communications*. New York: The Free Press, 1955.

Kelley, Harold H. "Two Functions of Reference Groups." In *Basic Studies in Social Psychology*, edited by Harold Proshansky, and Bernard Seidenberg, 210–214. New York: Holt, Rinehart and Winston, 1966.

————— . "Attribution Theory in Social Psychology." In *Nebraska Symposium on Motivation*, edited by David Levine, 192–238. Lincoln: University of Nebraska Press, 1967.

Kelly, J. Patrick, and Paul J. Solomon. "Humor in Television Advertising." *Journal of Advertising* 4 (Summer 1975): 31–35.

Kelly, J. Steven. "Subliminal Embeds in Print Advertising: A Challenge to Advertising Ethics." *Journal of Advertising* 8 (Summer 1979): 20–24.

Kerlinger, Fred N. *Foundations of Behavioral Research*. 3d ed. New York: CBS College Publishing, 1986.

Kernan, Jerome B. "Choice Criteria, Decision Behavior, and Personality." *Journal of Marketing Research* 5 (May 1968): 155–164.

Kerner Commission. *Report of the National Advisory Commission on Civil Disorders*. Washington, D. C.: U.S. Government Printing Office, 1968.

Key, Wilson Bryan. *Subliminal Seduction: Ad Media's Manipulation of Not So Innocent America*. Englewood Cliffs, N.J.: Prentice-Hall, 1973.

————— . *Media Sexploitation*. Englewood Cliffs, N.J.: Prentice-Hall, 1976.

————— . *The Clam-Plate Orgy: And Other Subliminal Techniques for Manipulating Your Behavior*. Englewood Cliffs, N.J.: Prentice-Hall, 1980.

Kiel, Geoffrey C., and Roger A. Layton. "Dimensions of Consumer Information Seeking Behavior." *Journal of Marketing Research* 18 (May 1981): 233–239.

Kim, Jae-On, and Charles W. Mueller. *Factor Analysis: Statistical Methods and Practical Issues*. Newbury Park, Calif.: Sage Publications, 1978a.

————— . *Introduction to Factor Analysis: What It Is and How to Do It*. Newbury Park, Calif.: Sage Publications, 1978b.

Kimura, Doreen. "The Asymmetry of the Human Brain—Recent Progress in Perception." *Scientific American* 228 (March 1973): 70–80.

King, Charles W., and John O. Summers. "Overlap of Opinion Leadership Across Consumer Product Categories." *Journal of Marketing Research* 7 (February 1970): 43–50.

Kish, George B., and William Busse. "Correlates of Stimulus-Seeking: Age, Education, Intelligence, and Aptitudes." *Journal of Consulting and Clinical Psychology* 32 (December 1968): 633–637.

_____ , and Gregory V. Donnenwerth. "Sex Differences in the Correlates of Stimulus Seeking." *Journal of Consulting and Clinical Psychology* 38 (February 1972): 42–49.

Klecka, William R. *Discriminant Analysis*. Newbury Park, Calif.: Sage Publications, 1980.

Kotler, Philip. "Atmospherics as a Marketing Tool." *Journal of Retailing* 49 (Winter 1974): 48–64.

Krishnamurthi, Lakshaman. "The Salience of Relevant Others and Its Effect on Individual and Joint Preferences: An Experimental Investigation." *Journal of Consumer Research* 10 (June 1983): 62–72.

Krueger, Richard A. *Focus Groups: A Practical Guide for Applied Research*. Newbury Park, Calif.: Sage Publications, 1988.

Krugman, Herbert E. "The Impact of Television Advertising: Learning Without Involvement." *Public Opinion Quarterly* 29 (Fall 1965): 349–356.

_____ . "Memory Without Recall, Exposure Without Perception." *Journal of Advertising Research* 17 (August 1977): 7–12.

_____ . "Low Involvement Theory in the Light of New Brain Research." In *Attitude Research Plays for High Stakes*, edited by John C. Maloney, and Bernard Silverman, 16–22. Chicago: American Marketing Association, 1979.

Kuehn, Alfred A. "Demonstration of a Relationship Between Psychological Factors and Brand Choice." *Journal of Business* 36 (April 1963): 237–241.

LaBay, Duncan G., and Thomas C. Kinnear. "Exploring the Consumer Decision Process in the Adoption of Solar Energy Systems." *Journal of Consumer Research* 8 (December 1981): 271–278.

Lancaster, Kelvin. *Consumer Demand: A New Approach*. New York: Columbia University Press, 1971.

Lancy, David F. "Play in Species Adaptation." *Annual Review of Anthropology* 9 (1980): 471–495.

Landon, E. Laird, Jr. "Self Concept, Ideal Self Concept, and Consumer Purchase Intentions." *Journal of Consumer Research* 1 (September 1974): 44–51.

Lasswell, Thomas E. *Class and Stratum: An Introduction to Concepts and Research*. Boston: Houghton Mifflin Co., 1965.

Lastovicka, John L., and Erich A. Joachimsthaler. "Improving the Detection of Personality–Behavior Relationships in Consumer Research." *Journal of Consumer Research* 14 (March 1988): 583–587.

Laurent, Gilles, and Jean-Noel Kapferer. "Measuring Consumer Involvement Profiles." *Journal of Marketing Research* 22 (February 1985): 41–53.

Lazarsfeld, Paul F., Bernard Berelson, and Hazel Gaudet. *The People's Choice: How the Voter Makes Up His Mind in a Presidential Campaign*. New York: Columbia University Press, 1944.

Lazarus, Richard S., and Robert A. McCleary. "Autonomic Discrimination Without Awareness: A Study of Subception." *Psychological Review* 58 (March 1951): 113–122.

Leavitt, Clark, and John Walton. "Development of a Scale of Innovativeness." In *Advances in Consumer Research*. Vol. 2, edited by Mary Jane Schlinger, 545–554. Ann Arbor, Mich.: Association for Consumer Research, 1975.

Leonard-Barton, Dorothy. "Experts as Negative Opinion Leaders in the Diffusion of a Technological Innovation." *Journal of Consumer Research* 11 (March 1985): 914–926.

Leong, Siew Meng. "Metatheory and Metamethodology in Marketing: A Lakatosian Reconstruction." *Journal of Marketing* 49 (Fall 1985): 23–40.

Leventhal, Howard, and Patricia Niles. "A Field Experiment on Fear Arousal with Data on the Validity of Questionnaire Measures." *Journal of Personality*. 32 (September 1964): 459–479.

————. "Persistence of Influence for Varying Durations of Exposure to Threat Stimuli." *Psychological Reports* 16 (February 1965): 223–233.

————, and Jean C. Watts. "Sources of Resistance to Fear-Arousing Communications on Smoking and Lung Cancer." *Journal of Personality* 34 (June 1966): 155–175.

————, Robert Singer, and Susan Jones. "Effects of Fear and Specificity of Recommendation Upon Attitudes and Behavior." *Journal of Personality and Social Psychology* 2 (July 1965): 20–29.

Levy, Sidney J. "Symbols by Which We Buy." In *Advancing Marketing Efficiency*, edited by Lynn H. Stockman, 409–416. Chicago: American Marketing Association, 1959a.

————. "Symbols for Sale." *Harvard Business Review* 37 (July-August 1959b): 117–124.

————. "Social Class and Consumer Behavior." In *On Knowing the Consumer*, edited by Joseph W. Newman, 146–160. New York: John Wiley and Sons, 1966.

————. "Interpreting Consumer Mythology: A Structural Approach to Consumer Behavior." *Journal of Marketing* 45 (Summer 1981): 49–61.

Lewin, Kurt. *A Dynamic Theory of Personality: Selected Papers*. New York: McGraw-Hill, 1935.

————. *Principles of Topological Psychology*. New York: McGraw-Hill, 1936.

Lindsay, Peter H., and Donald A. Norman. *Human Information Processing: An Introduction to Psychology*. New York: Academic Press, 1977.

Lionberger, Herbert F. *Adoption of New Ideas and Practices*. Ames, Iowa: The Iowa State University Press, 1960.

Lippitt, Ronald, Jeanne Watson, and Bruce Westley. *The Dynamics of Planned Change: A Comparative Study of Principles and Techniques*. New York: Harcourt Brace Jovanovich, 1953.

Looft, William R. "Conservatives, Liberals, Radicals, and Sensation-Seekers." *Perceptual and Motor Skills* 32 (February 1971): 98.

————, and Marc D. Baranowski. "An Analysis of Five Measures of Sensation Seeking and Preference for Complexity." *Journal of General Psychology* 85 (October 1971): 307–313.

Lussier, Denis A., and Richard W. Olshavsky. "Task Complexity and Contingent Processing in Brand Choice." *Journal of Consumer Research* 6 (September 1979): 154–165.

Lutz, Richard J. "Changing Brand Attitudes Through Modification of Cognitive Structure." *Journal of Consumer Research* 1 (March 1975): 49–59.

————. "An Experimental Investigation of Causal Relations Among Cognitions, Affect, and Behavioral Intention." *Journal of Consumer Research* 3 (March 1977): 197–208.

————, and James R. Bettman. "Multiattribute Models in Marketing: A Bicentennial Review." In *Consumer and Industrial Buying Behavior*, edited by Arch G. Woodside, Jagdish N. Sheth, and Peter D. Bennett, 137–149. New York: Elsevier North-Holland, 1977.

————, and Pradeep Kakkar. "Situational Influence in Interpersonal Persuasion." In *Advances in Consumer Research*. Vol. 2, edited by Mary Jane Schlinger, 439–453. Ann Arbor, Mich.: Association for Consumer Research, 1975.

Lynch, Mervin D., and Richard C. Hartman. "Dimensions of Humor in Advertising." *Journal of Advertising Research* 8 (December 1968): 39–45.

Maddi, Salvatore R. "Exploratory Behavior and Variation-Seeking in Man." In *Functions of Varied Experience*, edited by Donald W. Fiske, and Salvatore R. Maddi, 253–277. Homewood, Ill.: The Dorsey Press, 1961.

————. "The Pursuit of Consistency and Variety." In *Theories of Cognitive Consistency: A Sourcebook*, edited by Robert P. Abelson, Elliot Aronson, William J. McGuire, Theodore M. Newcomb, Milton J. Rosenberg, and Percy H. Tannenbaum, 267–274. Chicago: Rand McNally, 1968.

Marcus, Alan S. "Obtaining Group Measures from Personality Test Scores: Auto Brand Choice Predicted from the Edwards Personal Preference Schedule." *Psychological Reports* 17 (October 1965): 523–531.

Marshall, Alfred. *Principles of Economics: An Introductory Volume*. London: MacMillan and Co., 1890.

Martineau, Pierre. *Motivation in Advertising: Motives That Make People Buy*. New York: McGraw-Hill, 1957.

————. "A Case Study: What Automobiles Mean to Americans." In *Motivation and Market Behavior*, edited by Robert Ferber, and Hugh G. Wales, 36–49. Homewood, Ill.: Richard D. Irwin, 1958a.

————. "Social Classes and Spending Behavior." *Journal of Marketing* 23 (October 1958b): 121–130.

————. "The Personality of the Retail Store." *Harvard Business Review* 36 (January-February 1958c): 47–55.

Marx, Karl. "A Note on Classes." In *Class, Status, and Power: Social Stratification in Comparative Perspective*. 2d ed., edited by Reinhard Bendix, and Seymour Martin Lipset, 5–6. New York: The Free Press, 1966.

Maslow, Abraham H. "A Theory of Human Motivation." *Psychological Review* 50 (July 1943): 370–396.

————. *Motivation and Personality*. New York: Harper & Row, 1954.

————. *Motivation and Personality*. 2d ed. New York: Harper & Row, 1970.

Mason, Roger S. *Conspicuous Consumption: A Study of Exceptional Consumer Behavior*. New York: St. Martin's Press, 1981.

Massy, William F., Ronald E. Frank, and Thomas Lodahl. *Purchasing Behavior and Personal Attributes*. Philadelphia: University of Pennsylvania Press, 1968.

Mathews, H. Lee, and John W. Slocum, Jr. "Social Class and Commercial Bank Credit Card Usage." *Journal of Marketing* 33 (January 1969): 71–78.

Maxwell, Neil. "Words Whispered to Subconscious Supposedly Deter Thefts, Fainting." *Wall Street Journal* (November 25, 1980): 29.

Mazis, Michael B., and Timothy W. Sweeney. "Novelty and Personality with Risk as a Moderating Variable." *Combined Proceedings: Marketing Education in the Real World and Dynamic Marketing in a Changing World, Series No. 34*, edited by Boris W. Becker and Helmut Becker, 406–411. Chicago: American Marketing Association, 1973.

———, Olli T. Ahtola, and R. Eugene Klippel. "A Comparison of Four Multi-Attribute Models in the Prediction of Consumer Attitudes." *Journal of Consumer Research* 2 (June 1975): 38–52.

McAlister, Leigh, and Edgar Pessemier. "Variety Seeking Behavior: An Interdisciplinary Review." *Journal of Consumer Research* 9 (December 1982): 311–322.

McCallum, A. Steve, and Shawn M. Glynn. "Hemispheric Specialization and Creative Behavior." *Journal of Creative Behavior* 13 (Fourth Quarter 1979): 263–273.

McCleary, R., and R. Lazarus. "Autonomic Discrimination Without Awareness." *Journal of Personality* 28 (1949): 172–179.

McConnell, James V., Richard L. Cutler, and Elton M. McNeil. "Subliminal Stimulation: An Overview." *American Psychologist* 13 (May 1958): 229–242.

McCracken, Grant. "Culture and Consumption: A Theoretical Account of the Structure and Movement of the Cultural Meaning of Consumer Goods." *Journal of Consumer Research* 13 (June 1986): 71–84.

———. *Culture and Consumption: New Approaches to the Symbolic Character of Consumer Goods and Activities*. Bloomington: Indiana University Press, 1988.

McGee, Mark G. "Human Spatial Abilities: Psychometric Studies and Environmental, Genetic, Hormonal and Neurological Influences." *Psychological Bulletin* 86 (September 1979): 889–918.

McGinnies, Elliott. "Emotionality and Perceptual Defense." *Psychological Review*. 56 (September 1949): 244–251.

Mehrabian, Albert, and James A. Russell. "A Measure of Arousal Seeking Tendency." *Environment and Behavior* 5 (September 1973): 315–333.

———. *An Approach to Environmental Psychology*. Cambridge, Mass.: M. I. T. Press, 1974.

Mehrotra, Sunil, and William D. Wells. "Psychographics and Buyer Behavior: Theory and Recent Empirical Findings." In *Consumer and Industrial Buying Behavior*, edited by Arch G. Woodside, Jagdish N. Sheth, and Peter D. Bennett, 49–65. New York: Elsevier North-Holland, 1977.

Merton, Robert K. *Social Theory and Social Structure*. Rev. ed. New York: The Free Press, 1957.

Mick, David Glen. "Consumer Research and Semiotics: Exploring the Morphology of Signs, Symbols, and Significance." *Journal of Consumer Research* 13 (September 1986): 196–213.

Midgley, David F. "A Simple Mathematical Theory of Innovative Behavior." *Journal of Consumer Research* 3 (June 1976):31–41.

———, and Grahame R. Dowling. "Innovativeness: The Concept and Its Measurement." *Journal of Consumer Research* 4 (March 1978): 229–242.

Milgram, Stanley. "The Experience of Living in Cities." *Science* 167 (March 13, 1970): 1464–1468.

Miller, James Grier. "Discrimination Without Awareness." *American Journal of Psychology* 52 (October 1939): 562–578.

———. "The Role of Motivation in Learning Without Awareness." *American Journal of Psychology* 53 (April 1940): 229–239.

———. *Unconsciousness*. New York: John Wiley & Sons, 1942.

Miller, Kenneth E., and James L. Ginter. "An Investigation of Situational Variation in Brand Choice Behavior and Attitude." *Journal of Marketing Research* 16 (February 1979): 111–123.

Milliman, Ronald E. "Using Background Music to Affect the Behavior of Supermarket Shoppers." *Journal of Marketing* 46 (Summer 1982): 86–91.

———. "The Influence of Background Music on the Behavior of Restaurant Patrons." *Journal of Consumer Research* 13 (September 1986): 286–289.

Miniard, Paul W., and Joel B. Cohen. "Modeling Personal and Normative Influences on Behavior." *Journal of Consumer Research* 10 (September 1983): 169–180.

Mittelstaedt, R. A., S. L. Grossbart, W. W. Curtis, and S. P. DeVere. "Optimal Stimulation Level and the Adoption Decision Process." *Journal of Consumer Research* 3 (September 1976): 84–94.

Mizerski, Richard W., and Robert B. Settle. "The Influence of Social Character on Preference for Social Versus Objective Information in Advertising." *Journal of Marketing Research* 16 (November 1979): 552–558.

———, Linda L. Golden, and Jerome B. Kernan. "The Attribution Process in Consumer Decision Making." *Journal of Consumer Research* 6 (September 1979): 123–140.

Monroe, Kent B. "The Influence of Price Differences and Brand Familiarity on Brand Preferences." *Journal of Consumer Research* 3 (June 1976): 42–49.

Montgomery, David B., and Alvin J. Silk. "Clusters of Consumer Interests and Opinion Leaders' Spheres of Influence." *Journal of Marketing Research* 8 (August 1971): 317–321.

Moore, Timothy E. "Subliminal Advertising: What You See Is What You Get." *Journal of Marketing* 46 (Spring 1982): 38–47.

Moos, Rudolf H. "Conceptualizations of Human Environments." *American Psychologist* 28 (August 1973): 652–665.

———. *The Human Context: Environmental Determinants of Behavior*. New York: John Wiley and Sons, 1976.

Morgan, James N. "A Realistic Economics of the Consumer Requires Some Psychology." In *Essays on Behavioral Economics*, edited by George Katona, 27–36. Ann Arbor: Survey Research Center, Institute for Social Research, University of Michigan, 1980.

Moschis, George P. "Social Comparison and Informal Group Influence." *Journal of Marketing Research* 13 (August 1976): 237–244.

Murray, Henry A. *Explorations in Personality: A Clinical and Experimental Study of Fifty Men of College Age by the Workers of the Harvard Psychological Clinic*. New York: Oxford University Press, 1938.

Myers, James H., and John Mount. "More on Social Class vs. Income as Correlates of Buying Behavior." *Journal of Marketing* 37 (April 1973): 71–73.

———, and Thomas S. Robertson. "Dimensions of Opinion Leadership." *Journal of Marketing Research* 9 (February 1972): 41–46.

———, and Allan D. Shocker. "The Nature of Product-Related Attributes." In *Research in Marketing*. Vol. 5, edited by Jagdish N. Sheth, 211–236. Greenwich, Conn.: JAI Press, 1981.

———, Roger R. Stanton, and Arne Haug. "Correlates of Buying Behavior: Social Class vs. Income." *Journal of Marketing* 35 (October 1971): 8–15.

Nayler, J. C., and C. H. Lawshe. "An Analytical Review of the Experimental Basis of Subception." *Journal of Psychology* 46 (July 1958): 75–96.

Newcomb, Theodore M. "Attitude Development as a Function of Reference Groups: The Bennington Study." In *Basic Studies in Social Psychology*, edited by Harold Proshansky and Bernard Seidenberg, 215–225. New York: Holt, Reinhart and Winston, 1966.

Newman, Bruce I. "The Prediction and Explanation of Actual Voting Behavior in a Presidential Primary Election." Ph.D. diss., University of Illinois, Urbana-Champaign, 1981.

———, and Jagdish N. Sheth. "A Model of Primary Voter Behavior." *Journal of Consumer Research* 12 (September 1985): 178–187.

Newman, Joseph W. *Motivation Research and Marketing Management*. Boston: Harvard University, Graduate School of Business Administration, Division of Research, 1957.

———. "Consumer Behavior Potpourri." In *On Knowing the Consumer*, edited by Joseph W. Newman, 216–243. New York: John Wiley & Sons, 1966.

Nickols, Sharon Y., and Karen D. Fox. "Buying Time and Saving Time: Strategies for Managing Household Production." *Journal of Consumer Research* 10 (September 1983): 197–208.

Nicosia, Francesco M., and Robert N. Mayer. "Toward a Sociology of Consumption." *Journal of Consumer Research* 3 (September 1976): 65–75.

Noerager, Jon P. "An Assessment of CAD—A Personality Instrument Developed Specifically for Marketing Research." *Journal of Marketing Research* 16 (February 1979): 53–59.

Olshavsky, Richard W., and Donald H. Granbois. "Consumer Decision Making — Fact or Fiction?" *Journal of Consumer Research* 6 (September 1979): 93–100.

Olson, Jerry C. "Price as an Informational Cue: Effects on Product Evaluations." in *Consumer and Industrial Buying Behavior*, edited by Arch G. Woodside, Jagdish N. Sheth, and Peter D. Bennett, 267–286. New York: Elsevier North-Holland, 1977.

Orstein, Robert E. *The Psychology of Consciousness*. San Francisco: W. H. Freeman, 1972.

Ostlund, Lyman E. "Perceived Innovation Attributes as Predictors of Innovativeness." *Journal of Consumer Research* 1 (September 1974): 23–29.

Packard, Vance. *The Hidden Persuaders*. New York: David McKay Co., 1957.

Paivio, Allan. "Perceptual Comparisons Through the Mind's Eye." *Memory and Cognition* 3 (November 1975): 635–647.

———. *Imagery and Verbal Processes*. Hillsdale, N.J.: Lawrence Erlbaum Associates, 1979.

———, and Ian Begg. "Pictures and Words in Visual Search." *Memory and Cognition* 2 (July 1974): 515–521.

Park, C. Whan. "The Effect of Individual and Situation-Related Factors on Consumer Selection of Judgmental Models." *Journal of Marketing Research* 8 (May 1976): 144–151.

———, and V. Parker Lessig. "Students and Housewives: Differences in Susceptibility to Reference Group Influence." *Journal of Consumer Research* 4 (September 1977): 102–110.

———, and S. Mark Young. "Consumer Response to Television Commercials: The Impact of Involvement and Background Music on Brand Attitude Formation." *Journal of Marketing Research* 23 (February 1986): 11–24.

Peters, William H. "Relative Occupational Class Income: A Significant Variable in the Marketing of Automobiles." *Journal of Marketing* 34 (April 1970): 74–77.

Peterson, Kevin, and James P. Curran. "Trait Attribution as a Function of Hair Length and Correlates of Subjects' Preferences for Hair Style." *Journal of Psychology* 93 (July 1976): 331–339.

Peterson, Robert A., Wayne D. Hoyer, and William R. Wilson, eds., *The Role of Affect in Consumer Behavior: Emerging Theories and Applications*. Lexington, Mass.: D. C. Heath and Co., 1986.

Philipp, Rudolph L., and Gerald J. S. Wilde. "Stimulation Seeking Behaviour and Extraversion." *Acta Psychologica* 32 (June 1970): 269–280.

Pierce, C. S., and J. Jastrow. "On Small Differences of Sensation." *Memoirs of the National Academy of Sciences* 3 (1884): 73–84.

Politz, Alfred. "Motivation Research—Opportunity or Dilemma?" In *Motivation and Market Behavior*, edited by Robert Ferber, and Hugh G. Wales, 50–64. Homewood, Ill.: Richard D. Irwin, 1958.

Porter, James N., Jr. "Consumption Patterns of Professors and Businessmen: A Pilot Study of Conspicuous Consumption and Status." *Sociological Inquiry* 37 (Spring 1967): 255–265.

Punj, Girish N., and David W. Stewart. "An Interaction Framework of Consumer Decision Making." *Journal of Consumer Research* 10 (September 1983): 181–196.

Qualls, William J. "Household Decision Behavior: The Impact of Husbands' and Wives' Sex Role Orientation." *Journal of Consumer Research* 14 (September 1987): 264–279.

Quelch, John A., and Kristina Cannon-Bonventre. "Better Marketing at the Point of Purchase." *Harvard Business Review* 61 (Nov.-Dec. 1983): 162–169.

Raju, P. S. "Optimum Stimulation Level: Its Relationship to Personality, Demographics, and Exploratory Behavior." *Journal of Consumer Research* 7 (December 1980): 272–282.

———— . "Theories of Exploratory Behavior: Review and Consumer Research Implications." In *Research in Marketing*. Vol. 4, edited by Jagdish N. Sheth, 223–249. Greenwich, Conn.: JAI Press, 1981.

Rao, Vithala R. "Pricing Research in Marketing: The State of the Art." *Journal of Business* 57 (January, Part 2 1984): S39-S60.

———— , and David A. Gautschi. "The Role of Price in Individual Utility Judgments: Development and Empirical Validation of Alternative Models." In *Research in Marketing: Supplement 1, Choice Models for Buyer Behavior*, edited by Leigh McAlister, 57–80. Greenwich, Conn.: JAI Press, 1982.

Ratchford, Brian T. "The New Economic Theory of Consumer Behavior: An Interpretive Essay." *Journal of Consumer Research* 2 (September 1975): 65–75.

———— . "Operationalizing Economic Models of Demand for Product Characteristics." *Journal of Consumer Research* 6 (June 1979): 76–85.

Ray, Michael L., and William L. Wilkie. "Fear: The Potential of an Appeal Neglected by Marketing." *Journal of Marketing* 34 (January 1970): 54–62.

Reibstein, David J., Christopher H. Lovelock, and Ricardo de P. Dobson. "The Direction of Causality Between Perceptions, Affect, and Behavior: An Application to Travel Behavior." *Journal of Consumer Research* 6 (March 1980): 370–376.

Reingen, Peter H., and Jerome B. Kernan. "Analysis of Referral Networks in Marketing: Methods and Illustration." *Journal of Marketing Research* 23 (November 1986): 370–378.

Rethans, Arno J., John L. Swasy, and Lawrence J. Marks. "Effects of Television Commercial Repetition, Receiver Knowledge, and Commercial Length: A Test of the Two-Factor Model." *Journal of Marketing Research* 23 (February 1986): 50–61.

Rich, Stuart U., and Subhash C. Jain. "Social Class and Life Cycle as Predictors of Shopping Behavior." *Journal of Marketing Research* 5 (February 1968): 41–49.

Richins, Marsha L. "An Analysis of Consumer Interaction Styles in the Marketplace." *Journal of Consumer Research* 10 (June 1983): 73–82.

Richmond, David, and Timothy P. Hartman. "An Exploratory Study of Sex Appeal in Advertising." *Journal of Advertising Research* 22 (October-November 1982): 53–61.

Riesman, David. *The Lonely Crowd: A Study of the Changing American Character.* New Haven, Conn.: Yale University Press, 1950.

Roberto, Eduardo L. "Social Marketing Strategies for Diffusing the Adoption of Family Planning." *Social Science Quarterly* 53 (June 1972): 33–51.

Robertson, Thomas S. "The Process of Innovation and the Diffusion of Innovations." *Journal of Marketing* 31 (January 1967): 14–19.

———— , *Innovative Behavior and Communication*. New York: Holt, Rinehart & Winston, 1971.

———— , and James N. Kennedy. "Prediction of Consumer Innovators: Application of Multiple Discriminant Analysis." *Journal of Marketing Research* 5 (February 1968): 64–69.

———— , and James H. Myers. "Personality Correlates of Opinion Leadership and Innovative Buying Behavior." *Journal of Marketing Research* 6 (May 1969): 164–168.

Robinson, Dwight E. "The Economics of Fashion Demand." *Quarterly Journal of Economics* 75 (August 1961): 376–398.

Robinson, Patrick J., Charles W. Faris, and Yoram Wind. *Industrial Buying and Creative Marketing*. Boston: Allyn and Bacon, 1967.

Rogers, Everett M. *Characteristics of Agricultural Innovators and Other Adopter Categories*. Wooster, Ohio, Agricultural Experiment Station Bulletin 882, 1961.

————. *Diffusion of Innovations*. New York: The Free Press, 1962.

————. *Diffusion of Innovations*. 2d ed. New York: The Free Press, 1971.

————. "New Product Adoption and Diffusion." *Journal of Consumer Research* 2 (March 1976): 290–301.

————. *Diffusion of Innovations*. 3d ed. New York: The Free Press, 1983.

————, and Dilip K. Bhowmik. "Homophily-Heterophily: Relational Concepts for Communication Research." *Public Opinion Quarterly* 34 (Winter 1971): 523–538.

————, and F. Floyd Shoemaker. *Communication of Innovations: A Cross-Cultural Approach*. 2d ed. New York: The Free Press, 1971.

————, and Lynne Svenning. *Modernization Among Peasants: The Impact of Communication*. New York: Holt, Rinehart & Winston, 1969.

Rogers, Robert D. "Commentary on 'The Neglected Variety Drive'." *Journal of Consumer Research* 6 (June 1979): 88–91.

Rokeach, Milton. *Beliefs, Attitudes, and Values: A Theory of Organization and Change*. San Francisco: Jossey-Bass, 1968.

Rook, Dennis W. "The Ritual Dimension of Consumer Behavior." *Journal of Consumer Research* 12 (December 1985): 251–264.

————. "The Buying Impulse." *Journal of Consumer Research* 14 (September 1987): 189–199.

Roscoe, A. Marvin, Dorothy Lang, and Jagdish N. Sheth. "Follow-up Methods, Questionnaire Length, and Market Differences in Mail Surveys." *Journal of Marketing* 39 (April 1975): 20–27.

Rosen, Sherwin. "Hedonic Prices and Implicit Markets: Product Differentiation in Pure Competition." *Journal of Political Economy* 82 (January-February 1974): 34–55.

Rosenberg, Milton J. "Cognitive Structure and Attitudinal Affect." *Journal of Abnormal and Social Psychology* 53 (November 1956): 367–372.

Rothschild, Michael L., Yong J. Hyun, Byron Reeves, Esther Thorson, and Robert Goldstein. "Hemispherically Lateralized EEG as a Response to Television Commercials." *Journal of Consumer Research* 15 (September 1988): 185–198.

Rothwell, N. D. "Motivation Research Revisited." *Journal of Marketing* 20 (October 1955): 150–154.

Russell, James A., and Albert Mehrabian. "Environmental Variables in Consumer Research." *Journal of Consumer Research* 3 (June 1976): 62–63.

Ryan, Michael J. "Behavioral Intention Formation: The Interdependency of Attitudinal and Social Influence Variables." *Journal of Consumer Research* 9 (December 1982): 263–278.

————, and E. H. Bonfield. "The Fishbein Extended Model and Consumer Behavior." *Journal of Consumer Research* 2 (September 1975): 118–136.

Saegert, Joel. "Another Look at Subliminal Perception." *Journal of Advertising Research* 19 (February 1979): 55–58.

Saegert, Susan. "Crowding: Cognitive Overload and Behavioral Constraint." In *Environmental Design Research*. Vol. 2, edited by Wolfgang F. E. Preiser, 254–260. Stroudsburg, Penn.: Dowden, Hutchinson and Ross, 1973.

————, Elizabeth Mackintosh, and Sheree West. "Two Studies of Crowding in Urban Public Spaces." *Environment and Behavior* 7 (June 1975): 159–184.

Sampson, Peter. "Qualitative Research and Motivation Research." In *Consumer Market Research Handbook*, 3d rev. ed., edited by Robert M. Worcester and John Downham, 29–55. Amsterdam: Elsevier Science Publishers (North-Holland) on behalf of European Society for Opinion and Marketing Research, 1986.

Sandell, Rolf Gunnar. "Effects of Attitudinal and Situational Factors on Reported Choice Behavior." *Journal of Marketing Research* 5 (November 1968): 405–408.

Sargent, Helen D., Herbert C. Modlin, Mildred T. Faris, and Harold M. Voth. "The Research Strategy and Tactics of the Psychotherapy Research Project of the Menninger Foundation: Second Report. Situational Variables." *Bulletin of the Menninger Clinic* 22 (January 1958): 148–166.

Sawyer, Alan. "Repetition, Cognitive Responses, and Persuasion." In *Cognitive Responses in Persuasion*, edited by Richard E. Petty, Thomas M. Ostrum, and Timothy C. Brock, 237–261. Hillsdale, N.J.: Lawrence Erlbaum Associates, 1981.

Scheaffer, Richard L., William Mendenhall, and Lyman Ott. *Elementary Survey Sampling*. 3d ed. Boston: PWS Publishers, 1986.

Schaninger, Charles M. "Perceived Risk and Personality." *Journal of Consumer Research* 3 (September 1976): 95–100.

————. "Social Class Versus Income Revisited: An Empirical Investigation." *Journal of Marketing Research* 18 (May 1981): 192–208.

————, Jacques C. Bourgeois, and W. Christian Buss. "French-English Canadian Subcultural Consumption Differences." *Journal of Marketing*. 49 (Spring 1985): 82–92.

————, and Donald Sciglimpaglia. "The Influence of Cognitive Personality Traits and Demographics on Consumer Information Acquisition." *Journal of Consumer Research* 8 (September 1981): 208–216.

Schary, Philip B. "Consumption and the Problem of Time." *Journal of Marketing* 35 (April 1971): 50–55.

Schneider, Frank W., Wayne A. Lesko, and William A. Garrett. "Helping Behavior in Hot, Comfortable, Cold Temperatures: A Field Study." *Environment and Behavior* 12 (June 1980): 231–240.

Scitovsky, Tibor. *The Joyless Economy: An Inquiry into Human Satisfaction and Consumer Dissatisfaction*. New York: Oxford University Press, 1976.

Scriven, L. Edward. "Rationality and Irrationality in Motivation Research." In *Motivation and Market Behavior*, edited by Robert Ferber, and Hugh G. Wales, 64–72. Homewood, Ill.: Richard D. Irwin, 1958.

Secord, Paul F. "Consistency Theory and Self-Referrent Behavior." In *Theories of Cognitive Consistency: A Source Book*, edited by Robert P. Abelson, Elliot Aronson, William J. McGuire, Theodore M. Newcomb, Milton J. Rosenberg, and Percy H. Tannenbaum, 349–354. Chicago: Rand McNally, 1968.

"Secret Voices: Messages That Manipulate." *Time* 114 (September 10, 1979): 71.

Segal, Bernard. "Sensation Seeking and Anxiety: Assessment of Responses to Specific Stimulus Situations." *Journal of Consulting and Clinical Psychology* 41 (August 1973): 135–138.

Sells, S. B. "Dimensions of Stimulus Situations Which Account for Behavior Variance." In *Stimulus Determinants of Behavior*, edited by S. B. Sells, 3–15. New York: The Ronald Press, 1963.

Sexton, Donald E., Jr. "Comparing the Cost of Food to Blacks and to Whites—A Survey." *Journal of Marketing* 35 (July 1971): 40–46.

Sharp, Lauriston. "Steel Axes for Stone Age Australians." In *Human Problems in Technological Change*, edited by Edward H. Spicer, 69–90. New York: Russell Sage Foundation, 1952.

Sherif, Muzafer. "The Concept of Reference Groups in Human Relations." In *Group Relations at the Crossroads*, edited by Muzafer Sherif and M. O. Wilson, 203–231. New York: Harper & Row, 1953.

———, and Carolyn W. Sherif. *An Outline of Social Psychology*. Rev. ed. New York: Harper & Row, 1956.

Sherry, John F., Jr. "Gift Giving in Anthropological Perspective." *Journal of Consumer Research* 10 (September 1983): 157–168.

Sheth, Jagdish N. "A Review of Buyer Behavior." *Management Science* 13 (August 1967): B718-B756.

———. "A Model of Industrial Buyer Behavior." *Journal of Marketing* 37 (October 1973a): 50–56.

———. "The Role of Motivation Research in Consumer Psychology." In *Consumer Psychology and Motivation Research: ESOMAR Seminar on Developments in Consumer Psychology*, Maidenhead-Berkshire, England, 1973b.

———. "A Field Study of Attitude Structure and the Attitude-Behavior Relationship." In *Models of Buyer Behavior: Conceptual, Quantitative, and Empirical*, edited by Jagdish N. Sheth, 242–268. New York: Harper & Row, 1974a.

———. "A Theory of Family Buying Decisions." In *Models of Buyer Behavior: Conceptual, Quantitative, and Empirical*, edited by Jagdish N. Sheth, 17–33. New York: Harper & Row, 1974b.

———, David M. Gardner, and Dennis E. Garrett. *Marketing Theory: Evolution and Evaluation*. New York: John Wiley and Sons, 1988.

Shevrin, Howard, and Scott Dickman. "The Psychological Unconscious: A Necessary Assumption for All Psychological Theory?" *American Psychologist* 35 (May 1980): 421–434.

Shimp, Terence A., and Subhash Sharma. "Consumer Ethnocentrism: Construction and Validation of the CETSCALE." *Journal of Marketing Research* 24 (August 1987): 280–289.

Siegel, Alberta Engvall, and Sidney Siegel. "Reference Groups, Membership Groups, and Attitude Change." In *Group Dynamics: Research and Theory*.

2d. ed., edited by Dorwin Cartwright and Alvin Zander, 232–240. New York: Harper & Row, 1960.

Silberg, Eugene. "Economics as a Choice Theoretic Paradigm." In *Research in Marketing: Supplement 1, Choice Models for Buyer Behavior*, edited by Leigh McAlister, 1–12. Greenwich, Conn.: JAI Press, 1982.

Silk, Alvin J. "Overlap Among Self-Designated Opinion Leaders: A Study of Selected Dental Products and Services." *Journal of Marketing Research* 3 (August 1966): 255–259.

Silverman, Lloyd H. "Psychoanalytic Theory: The Reports of My Death Are Greatly Exaggerated." *American Psychologist* 31 (September 1976): 621–637.

Simon, Herbert. "Economics and Psychology." In *Psychology: A Study of Science*. Vol. 6, edited by Sigmund Koch, 685–723. New York: McGraw-Hill, 1963.

Slocum, John W., Jr., and H. Lee Mathews. "Social Class and Income as Indicators of Consumer Credit Behavior." *Journal of Marketing* 34 (April 1970): 69–74.

Smith, David Horton, and Alex Inkeles. "Individual Modernizing Experiences and Psycho-Social Modernity: Validation of the OM Scales in Six Developing Countries." *International Journal of Comparative Sociology* 16 (September-December 1975): 155–173.

Smith, George Horsley. *Motivation Research in Advertising and Marketing*. New York: McGraw-Hill, 1954.

Smith, M. Brewster. "The Personal Setting of Public Opinions: A Study of Attitudes Toward Russia." *Public Opinion Quarterly* 11 (Winter 1947): 507–523.

Solomon, Michael R. "The Role of Products as Social Stimuli: A Symbolic Interactionism Perspective." *Journal of Consumer Research* 10 (December 1983): 319–329.

Sommers, Montrose S. "Product Symbolism and the Perception of Social Strata." In *Toward Scientific Marketing: Proceedings of the Winter Conference of the American Marketing Association*, edited by Stephen A. Greyser, 200–216. Chicago: American Marketing Association, 1964.

Sparks, David L., and W. T. Tucker. "A Multivariate Analysis of Personality and Product Use." *Journal of Marketing* Research 8 (February 1971): 67–70.

Spence, Donald P. "Effects of a Continuously Flashing Subliminal Verbal Food Stimulus on Subjective Hunger Ratings." *Psychological Reports* 15 (December 1964): 993–994.

Spicer, Edward H. "Sheepmen and Technicians: A Program of Soil Conservation on the Navajo Reservation." In *Human Problems in Technological Change*, edited by Edward H. Spicer, 185–207. New York: Russell Sage Foundation, 1952.

Spiro, Rosann L. "Persuasion in Family Decision-Making." *Journal of Consumer Research* 9 (March 1983): 393–402.

Srinivasan, V. "Comments on the Role of Price in Individual Utility Judgments." In *Research in Marketing: Supplement 1, Choice Models for Buyer Behavior*, edited by Leigh McAlister, 81–90. Greenwich, Connecticut: JAI Press, 1982.

Srivastava, Rajendra K., Allan D. Shocker, and George S. Day. "An Exploratory Study of the Influences of Usage Situation on Perceptions of Product-Markets." In *Advances in Consumer Research*. Vol. 5, edited by H. Keith Hunt, 32–38. Ann Arbor, Mich.: Association for Consumer Research, 1978.

Stafford, James E. "Effects of Group Influences on Consumer Brand Preferences." *Journal of Marketing Research* 3 (February 1966): 68–75.

————, and A. Benton Cocanougher. "Reference Group Theory." In *Selected Aspects of Consumer Behavior: A Summary from the Perspective of Different Disciplines*, edited by Robert Ferber, 361–379. Washington, D. C.: National Science Foundation, Directorate for Research Applications, Research Applied to National Needs, 1977.

Steiner, Gary A. "Notes on Franklin B. Evans' 'Psychological and Objective Factors in the Prediction of Brand Choice'." *Journal of Business* 34 (January 1961): 57–60.

Stephenson, William. *The Play Theory of Mass Communication*. Chicago: University of Chicago Press, 1967.

Sternthal, Brian, and C. Samuel Craig. "Humor in Advertising." *Journal of Marketing* 37 (October 1973): 12–18.

————. "Fear Appeals: Revisited and Revised." *Journal of Consumer Research* 1 (December 1974): 22–34.

Stigler, George J. "The Development of Utility Theory." *Journal of Political Economy* 58 (August, October 1950): 307–327, 373–396.

Stokols, Daniel. "On the Distinction Between Density and Crowding: Some Implications for Future Research." *Psychological Review* 79 (May 1972): 275–277.

————. "The Experience of Crowding in Primary and Secondary Environments." *Environment and Behavior* 8 (March 1976): 49–86.

Strotz, Robert H. "Cardinal Utility." *American Economic Review* 43, part 2 (May 1953): 384–397.

Sturdivant, Frederick D. "Better Deal for Ghetto Shoppers." *Harvard Business Review* 46 (March-April 1968): 130–139.

————. "Subculture Theory: Poverty, Minorities, and Marketing." In *Consumer Behavior: Theoretical Sources*, edited by Scott Ward and Thomas S. Robertson, 469–520. Englewood Cliffs, N.J.: Prentice-Hall, 1973.

Sudman, Seymour. *Applied Sampling*. New York: Academic Press, 1976.

————, and Norman M. Bradburn. *Asking Questions: A Practical Guide to Questionnaire Design*. San Francisco: Jossey-Bass, 1982.

Sullivan, Harry Stack. *The Interpersonal Theory of Psychiatry*. New York: W. W. Norton, 1953.

Summers, John O. "The Identity of Women's Clothing Fashion Opinion Leaders." *Journal of Marketing Research* 7 (May 1970): 178–185.

————. "Generalized Change Agents and Innovativeness." *Journal of Marketing Research* 8 (August 1971): 313–316.

Suttles, Wayne. "The Early Diffusion of the Potato Among the Coast Salish." *The Southwestern Journal of Anthropology* 7 (Autumn 1951): 272–288.

Suzman, Richard M. "The Modernization of Personality." In *We the People: American Character and Social Change*, edited by Gordon J. DiRenzo, 40–77. Westport, Conn.: Greenwood Press, 1977.

Szybillo, George J. "The Effects of Price and Scarcity on the Valuation of Fashions by Fashion Opinion Leaders and Non-Opinion Leaders." PhD. diss. West Lafayette, Ind.: Purdue University, 1973.

————, Arlene K. Sosanie, and Aaron Tenenbein. "Family Member Influence in Household Decision Making." *Journal of Consumer Research* 6 (December 1979): 312–316.

Tan, Chin Tiong, and John U. Farley. "The Impact of Cultural Patterns on Cognition and Intention in Singapore." *Journal of Consumer Research* 13 (March 1987): 540–544.

Taylor, Janet A., "A Personality Scale of Manifest Anxiety." *Journal of Abnormal and Social Psychology* 48 (April 1953): 285–290.

Thibaut, John W., and Harold H. Kelley. *The Social Psychology of Groups*. New York: John Wiley and Sons, 1959.

Thomas, Robert J. "Correlates of Interpersonal Purchase Influence in Organizations." *Journal of Consumer Research* 9 (September 1982): 171–182.

Thorelli, Hans B., Helmut Becker, and Jack Engledow. *The Information Seekers: An International Study of Consumer Information and Advertising Image.* Cambridge, Mass.: Ballinger, 1975.

Thurstone, L. L. *The Measurement of Values*. Chicago: University of Chicago Press, 1959.

————, and E. J. Clave. *The Measurement of Attitude: A Psychophysical Method and Some Experiments with a Scale for Measuring Attitude Toward the Church*. Chicago: University of Chicago Press, 1929.

Triandis, Harry C. *Attitude and Attitude Change*. New York: John Wiley and Sons, 1971.

Tsal, Yehoshua. "On the Relationship Between Cognitive and Affective Processes: A Critique of Zajonc and Markus." *Journal of Consumer Research* 12 (December 1985): 358–362.

Tucker, W. T., and John J. Painter. "Personality and Product Use." *Journal of Applied Psychology* 45 (October 1961): 325–329.

Veblen, Thorstein. *The Theory of the Leisure Class*. New York: The Macmillan Co., 1899.

————. *The Theory of the Leisure Class*. New York: Mentor, 1953.

Venkatesan, M. "Experimental Study of Consumer Behavior Conformity and Independence." *Journal of Marketing Research* 3 (November 1966): 384–387.

————. "Cognitive Consistency and Novelty Seeking." In *Consumer Behavior: Theoretical Sources*, edited by Scott Ward and Thomas S. Robertson, 354–384. Englewood Cliffs, N.J.: Prentice-Hall, 1973.

Vicary, James M. "How Psychiatric Methods Can Be Applied to Market Research." In *Motivation and Market Behavior,* edited by Robert Ferber, and Hugh G. Wales, 31–36. Homewood, Ill.: Richard D. Irwin, 1958.

Villani, Kathryn E. A., and Yoram Wind. "On the Usage of 'Modified' Personality Trait Measures in Consumer Research." *Journal of Consumer Research* 2 (December 1975): 223–228.

Vincent, Mark, and William G. Zikmund. "An Experimental Investigation of Situational Effects on Risk Perception." In *Advances in Consumer Research*. Vol. 3, edited by Beverlee B. Anderson, 125–129. Ann Arbor, Mich.: Association for Consumer Research, 1976.

Vitz, Paul C., and Donald Johnston. "Masculinity of Smokers and the Masculinity of Cigarette Images." *Journal of Applied Psychology* 49 (June 1965): 155–159.

Voor, Joseph H. "Subliminal Perception and Subception." *Journal of Psychology* 41 (April 1956): 437–458.

Voss, Justin, and Roger D. Blackwell. "The Role of Time Resources in Consumer Behavior." In *Conceptual and Theoretical Developments in Marketing*, edited by O. C. Ferrell, Stephen W. Brown, and Charles W. Lamb, Jr., 296–311. Chicago: American Marketing Association, 1979.

Wallace, Anthony F. C. *Culture and Personality*. New York: Random House, 1961.

Wallendorf, Melanie, and Michael D. Reilly. "Ethnic Migration, Assimilation, and Consumption." *Journal of Consumer Research* 10 (December 1983): 292–302.

———, and George Zinkhan. "Individual Modernity and Cognitive Complexity as Conceptual Bases for Marketing." In *Theoretical Developments in Marketing*, edited by Charles W. Lamb, Jr. and Patrick M. Dunne, 59–63. Chicago: American Marketing Association, 1980.

———, ———, and Lydia Zinkhan. "Cognitive Complexity and Aesthetic Preference." In *Symbolic Consumer Behavior*, edited by Elizabeth C. Hirshman, and Morris B. Holbrook, 52–59. Ann Arbor, Mich.: Association for Consumer Research, 1981.

Warner, W. Lloyd, and Paul S. Lunt. *The Social Life of a Modern Community*. New Haven, Conn.: Yale University Press, 1941.

Waters, Carrie Wherry. "Multi-Dimensional Measures of Novelty Experiencing, Sensation Seeking, and Ability: Correlational Analysis for Male and Female College Sample." *Psychological Reports* 34 (February 1974): 43–46.

Weber, Max. "Class Status and Party." In *Class, Status, and Power: Social Stratification in Comparative Perspective*. 2d ed., edited by Reinhard Bendix and Seymour Martin Lipset, 21–28. New York: The Free Press, 1966.

Webster, Frederick E., Jr., "Determining the Characteristics of the Socially -Conscious Consumer." *Journal of Consumer Research* 2 (December 1975): 188–196.

———, and Yoram Wind. "A General Model for Understanding Organizational Buying Behavior." *Journal of Marketing* 36 (April 1972): 12–19.

Weinberg, Peter, and Wolfgang Gottwald. "Impulsive Consumer Buying as a Result of Emotions." *Journal of Business Research* 10 (March 1982): 43–57.

Weiner, Bernard. *An Attributional Theory of Motivation and Emotion*. New York: Springer-Verlag, 1986.

Wells, William D. "General Personality Tests and Consumer Behavior." In *On Knowing the Consumer,* edited by Joseph W. Newman, 187–189. New York: John Wiley & Sons, 1966.

———, "Psychographics: A Critical Review." *Journal of Marketing Research* 12 (May 1975): 196–213.

———, and Arthur D. Beard. "Personality and Consumer Behavior." In *Consumer Behavior: Theoretical Sources*, edited by Scott Ward, and Thomas S. Robertson, 141–199. Englewood Cliffs, N.J.: Prentice-Hall, 1973.

———, and Douglas J. Tigert. "Activities, Interests and Opinions." *Journal of Advertising Research* 11 (August 1971): 27–35.

Westbrook, Robert A. "Product/Consumption-Based Affective Responses and Postpurchase Processes." *Journal of Marketing Research* 24 (August 1987): 258–270.

Westfall, Ralph. "Psychological Factors in Predicting Product Choice." *Journal of Marketing* 26 (April 1962): 34–40.

Wexler, Bruce E. "Cerebral Laterality and Psychiatry: A Review of the Literature." *The American Journal of Psychiatry*. 137 (March 1980): 279–291.

White, Leslie A. *The Science of Culture: A Study of Man and Civilization*. New York: Farrar, Straus & Giroux, 1949.

Whyte, William H., Jr. "The Web of Word of Mouth." In *Consumer Behavior (Vol. 2): The Life Cycle and Consumer Behavior*, edited by Lincoln H. Clark, 113–122. New York: New York University Press, 1955.

Wiener, Morton, and Peter H. Schiller. "Subliminal Perception or Perception of Partial Cues." *Journal of Abnormal and Social Psychology* 61 (July 1960): 124–137.

Wilkes, Robert E., and Humberto Valencia. "A Note on Generic Purchaser Generalizations and Subcultural Variations." *Journal of Marketing* 49 (Summer 1985): 114–120.

Wilkie, William L., and Edgar A. Pessemier. "Issues in Marketing's Use of Multi-Attribute Attitude Models." *Journal of Marketing Research* 10 (November 1973): 428–441.

Williams, Margaret Aasterud. "Reference Groups: A Review and Commentary." *Sociological Quarterly* 11 (Fall 1970): 545–554.

Wilton, Peter C., and John G. Myers. "Task, Expectancy, and Information Assessment Effects in Information Utilization Processes." *Journal of Consumer Research* 12 (March 1986): 469–486.

Wind, Yoram. "Preference of Relevant Others and Individual Choice Models." *Journal of Consumer Research* 3 (June 1976): 50–57.

Winick, Charles. "The Relationship Among Personality Needs, Objective Factors, and Brand Choice: A Re-examination." *Journal of Business* 34 (January 1961): 61–66.

Wiseman, Frederick. "A Segmentation Analysis on Automobile Buyers During the New Model Year Transition Period." *Journal of Marketing* 35 (April 1971): 42–49.

Witt, Robert E. "Informal Social Group Influence on Consumer Brand Choice." *Journal of Marketing Research* 6 (November 1969): 473–476.

————, and Grady D. Bruce. "Purchase Decisions and Group Influence." *Journal of Marketing Research* 7 (November 1970): 533–535.

Wittrock, M. C. et al., eds. *The Human Brain*. Englewood Cliffs, N.J.: Prentice-Hall, 1977.

Wolf, Richard. "The Measurement of Environments." In *Testing Problems in Perspective*, edited by Anne Anastasi, 491–503. Washington, D. C.: American Council on Education, 1966.

Woods, Walter A. "Psychological Dimensions of Consumer Decision." *Journal of Marketing* 24 (January 1960): 15–19.

Woodside, Arch G., and Ruth Andress. "CAD Eight Years Later." *Journal of the Academy of Marketing Science* 3 (Summer 1975): 309–313.

———— , and William H. Motes. "Image Versus Direct-Response Advertising." *Journal of Advertising Research* 20 (August 1980): 31–37.

Wright, Peter. "Factors Affecting Cognitive Resistance to Advertising." *Journal of Consumer Research* 2 (June 1975): 1–9.

Zaichkowsky, Judith Lynne. "Measuring the Involvement Construct." *Journal of Consumer Research* 12 (December 1985): 341–352.

Zajonc, Robert B. "Attitudinal Effects of Mere Exposure." *Journal of Personality and Social Psychology Monograph Supplement* 9 (June 1968): 1–28.

———— . "Feeling and Thinking: Preferences Need No Inferences." *American Psychologist* 35 (February 1980): 151–175.

———— , and Hazel Markus. "Affective and Cognitive Factors in Preferences." *Journal of Consumer Research* 9 (September 1982): 123–131.

Zaltman, Gerald, and Ronald Stiff. "Theories of Diffusion." In *Consumer Behavior: Theoretical Sources*, edited by Scott Ward and Thomas S. Robertson, 416–468. Englewood Cliffs, N.J.: Prentice-Hall, 1973.

———— , Karen LeMasters, and Michael Heffring. *Theory Construction in Marketing*. New York: John Wiley and Sons, 1982.

———— , Christian R. A. Pinson, and Reinhard Angelmar. *Metatheory in Consumer Research*. New York: Holt, Rinehart & Winston, 1973.

Zanot, Eric J., J. David Pincus, and E. Joseph Lamp. "Public Perceptions of Subliminal Advertising." *Journal of Advertising* 12 (No. 1, 1983): 39–45.

Zeithaml, Valarie A. "Consumer Response to In-Store Price Information Environments." *Journal of Consumer Research* 8 (March 1982): 357–369.

Zielinski, Joan, and Thomas S. Robertson. "Consumer Behavior Theory: Excesses and Limitations." In *Advances in Consumer Research*. Vol. 9, edited by Andrew A. Mitchell, 8–12. Ann Arbor, Mich.: Association for Consumer Research, 1982.

Zielske, Hubert A. "Does Day-After Recall Penalize 'Feeling' Ads?" *Journal of Advertising Research* 22 (February-March 1982): 19–22.

Zuckerman, Marvin. "Dimensions of Sensation Seeking." *Journal of Consulting and Clinical Psychology* 36 (February 1971): 45–52.

———— . *Sensation Seeking: Beyond the Optimal Level of Arousal*. Hillsdale, N.J.: Lawrence Erlbaum Associates, 1979.

———— , Elizabeth A. Kolin, Leah Price, and Ina Zoob. "Development of a Sensation-Seeking Scale." *Journal of Consulting Psychology* 28 (December 1964): 477–482.

———— , and Kathryn Link. "Construct Validity for the Sensation-Seeking Scale." *Journal of Consulting and Clinical Psychology* 32 (August 1968): 420–426.

NAME INDEX

Aaker, David A., 53, 57
Abelson, Robert P., 41, 46
Acker, Mary, 64, 67
Adams, Joe K., 53, 60
Adler, Alfred, 25, 52, 55
Adorno, T. W., 52, 55
Agarwal, Manoj K., 33, 35
Ajzen, Icek, 25, 33, 35, 41, 46, 71
Akers, Fred C., 41, 45, 46
Alchian, Armen A., 33, 34
Alderfer, Clayton P., 33, 36
Alexis, Marcus, 40, 45
Allen, Vernon L., 72, 74
Allport, Gordon W., 41, 46
Alpert, Mark L., 52, 56
Altman, Irwin, 72, 76, 77
Andreasen, Alan R., 41, 46, 72, 76
Andress, Ruth, 52, 55
Apodaca, Anacleto, 41, 48
Archibald, Robert B., 33, 34
Armer, Michael, 65, 69
Arndt, Johan, 40, 41, 44, 47
Arrow, Kenneth J., 33, 34
Asch, Solomon E., 27, 40, 44
Ashby, Harold J., Jr., 41, 46
Aulicieums, Andris, 72, 76
Avrunin, George S., 64, 67

Bach, Sheldon, 53, 60
Baranowski, Marc D., 64, 67
Barker, Roger G., 72, 78
Barnet, H. G., 41, 48, 65, 68
Barron, Frank, 64, 67
Bartels, Robert, 164
Barthol, Richard P., 53, 61
Bass, Frank M., 33, 36
Batra, Rajeev, 72, 76
Bauer, Raymond A., 40, 41, 45, 46, 52, 56
Baumgarten, Steven A., 41, 47
Beard, Arthur D., 52, 54, 56
Bearden, William O., 40, 44, 70–72
Becherer, Richard C., 52, 57
Beckwith, Neil E., 53, 57
Begg, Ian, 53, 59
Belch, George E., 64, 67
Belk, Russell W., 40, 43, 70–75, 78
Bell, Gerald D., 52, 56
Bell, Paul A., 72, 81

Bellows, Roger, 72, 74
Bendix, Reinhard, 65, 69
Benedict, Ruth, 40, 42
Berkowitz, Leonard, 53, 57
Berlyne, D. E., 63, 64, 66, 67
Berry, Leonard L., 53, 58, 73, 79
Bettman, James R., 33, 36
Bevan, William, 53, 60
Bexton, W. H., 64, 66
Bhowmik, Dilip K., 41, 47
Bieri, James, 64, 67
Birdwell, Al E., 40, 43
Bishop, Doyle W., 40, 42, 71, 72
Blackwell, Roger D., 28, 73, 79
Blake, Brian, 52, 56
Bliss, Wesley L., 41, 48
Blumberg, Paul, 40, 42
Bogen, Joseph E., 53, 59
Bone, Ronald N., 64, 67
Bonfield, E. H., 33, 36
Bonoma, Thomas V., 73, 78
Boone, Louis E., 52, 56
Bourne, Francis S., 40, 44
Boyd, Harper W., Jr., 102
Bradburn, Norman M., 30
Brady, Dorothy, 40, 43
Brean, Herbert, 53, 61
Breen-Lewis, Kristin, 72, 76, 78
Bricker, Peter D., 53, 61
Broadbent, Donald E., 53, 59
Brooker, George, 52, 56
Brooks, John, 41, 45
Bruce, Grady D., 40, 44, 45
Bruner, Jerome S., 53, 60
Bullock, Henry A., 41, 46
Burk, Marguerite C., 33, 34
Burke, Marian Chapman, 72, 76
Burnett, John J., 53, 57
Burnkrant, Robert E., 40, 43, 44, 73, 77
Buss, Allan R., 52, 55
Busse, William, 64, 67
Butler, Robert A., 63, 64
Byrne, Donn, 53, 60, 61

Caccavale, John G., 53, 61
Cacioppo, John T., 64, 67
Calder, Bobby J., 40, 43, 73, 77
Callom, F., 63, 64
Campbell, Donald T., 30

Cannon-Bonventre, Kristina, 53, 58
Caplovitz, David, 40–42, 46
Carmines, Edward G., 30
Cattell, Raymond B., 52, 56, 63, 64, 67
Chapanis, A., 53, 61
Chapman, Randall G., 33, 34
Churchill, Gilbert A., Jr., 103
Clave, E. J., 93
Claycamp, Henry J., 52, 56
Cocanougher, A. Benton, 40, 44, 45
Cohen, Joel B., 41, 46, 52, 55
Coleman, James S., 41, 47
Coleman, Richard P., 39, 40, 42
Collier, R. M., 53, 60
Converse, Jean M., 30
Cook, Thomas D., 30
Coombs, Clyde H., 64, 67, 93
Coover, John Edgar, 53, 60
Copley, T. P., 63, 64
Cote, Joseph A., 70, 72, 74
Cottingham, Donald H., 53, 57
Cousineau, Alain, 40, 44
Cox, Anthony D., 64, 67
Cox, Dena S., 64, 67
Cox, Donald F., 52, 56, 63, 64
Craig, C. Samuel, 53, 57, 65, 69
Cunningham, Scott M., 40, 41, 45, 46
Curran, James P., 40, 43

Danzig, Fred, 61
Darlington, Richard B., 111
Das, Jagannath Prasad, 53, 59
Davies, D. R., 64, 67
Davis, Harry L., 73, 77
DeFleur, Melvin L., 53, 61
Deglin, Vadim L., 53, 59
Dember, William N., 53, 60, 64, 66
Dent, Oran B., 64, 67
Deshpande, Rohit, 40, 45
Desor, J. A., 53, 58
Deutsch, Morton, 40, 44
Dichter, Ernest, 25, 33, 36, 51–55, 58
Dickerson, Mary Dee, 41, 48
Dickman, Scott, 53, 61
Dickson, Peter R., 72, 74

211

SUBJECT INDEX

Adler, Alfred, psychoanalytic theory of, 25, 52
Advertising. *See also* Marketing; Promotional mix
brain encoding and, 59–60; emotional arousal and, 57
Antecedent states, 74, 75–76
Arousal. *See also* Stimulation; Stimulus
advertising and, 57; as a predictor of exploratory behavior, 63; Berlyne's theory of, 64, 66–67; epistemic behavior and, 66–68; external situation and, 75; need, 37; propensity toward, 67
Atmospherics, 58. *See also* Surroundings
Attitude
balance theory and, 46; choice making and, 23; Fishbein model and, 25, 46; multi-attribute models and, 36; Rosenberg model, 24–25; Katz's theory of, 46; social components of, 23, 46; regarding product attributes, 35–36; theories of, 41
Attributes
demand and supply functions of, 35; functional value and, 18, 35; models including, 33; of American social classes, 39; product referent, 35; task (outcome attributes), 35; utility and, 35

Balance theory, 46
Behavior. *See also* Consumer choice behavior
American social classes and, 39; curiosity-driven, 9, 63, 64, 66; knowledge-seeking, 9, 63, 64, 66; novelty-seeking, 9, 63, 64, 66; satisficing, 27
Behavioral intention, 25
Beliefs
choice-making behavior and, 23; normative, 46
Berlyne's theory

of arousal potential, 66–67; of optimal stimulation, 64, 66, 67
Bias, 30. *See also* "Goodness-of-fit"
Brain, hemispheres of, 53, 58–60

Charitable organizations, consumption values and, 173
Chi-square test, 131, 142, 143, 153, 162
Choice. *See also* Consumer choice behavior
activity, 19, 21; aesthetic, 9; brand, 3, 13, 16, 17–18, 20, 21; domains, 29–30; dyadic, 13; group, 13; individual, 13; influencing, 5–6. *See also* Marketing, Promotion; involuntary (by mandate), 13, 14; limited, 14; location, 19; product type, 3, 16, 17, 19, 20, 21, 22; random (stochastic), 13, 14; systematic, 13; to buy or not to buy, 3, 16–17, 19, 20, 21, 22; voluntary, 14
Classification analysis, 112, 114, 131, 132, 144, 154, 163
Coding, 103, 104–10
Coefficient, 131, 142, 154, 160, 161, 167
Cognitive consistency, 46
Computers
consumption values and, 168–69; reasons for buying, 6
Conditional value
as an extrinsic value, 69; definition of, 7, 10, 22–23; Durkheim's suicide theory and, 76; economic situations and, 10; emergencies and, 10, 22; factor rotation and, 127–28, 140–41; functional utility and, 86; Katona's theory of situational influences, 77–78; learning theory and, 26; measurement of, 86–87, 89, 92, 96; physical situations and, 10; situational characteristics and, 74–79; situational contingencies and, 70–71, 74, 86; social

situations and, 10; social utility and, 86; sociological theory and, 28; theory and research regarding, 70, 72–73; Triandis model and, 24, 25, 71; Triandis's situational focus and, 77
Condoms, consumption values and, 172
Conformity, 44–45, 46
Consumer choice behavior (market choice behavior). *See also* Choice; Consumption values; Consumption value theory of consumer choice behavior
differential contributions to, 10–12; irrationality of, 77–78; models of, 23–29, 33, 40–41, 52–53, 64–65, 72–73; multiple values and, 7–10; predictability of, 30, 42. *See also* Discriminant analysis, predictive validity of; reference groups and, 44, 45; situational contingencies and, 70–71, 74; trade-offs and, 4–5, 12; universality of, 4–5; values affecting, 7–10, 24, 165–67
Consumer goods
decisions regarding, 84; durable, 3, 19, 20, 21, 22, 84; needs and, 37–38; nondurable, 3, 19, 20, 21, 22, 84; nonprofit sector and, 171–73; profit sector and, 168–70; services. *See* Services
Consumption
compensatory, 41, 45–46; conspicuous, 41, 45–46; demand, 35; economics, 24, 27, 33; hedonic, 54
Consumption values. *See also* Conditional value; Emotional value; Epistemic value; Functional value; Social value
as affecting purchase of specific products and services, 168–74; differential contributions of, 10–12